SCIENTISTS: Their Lives and Works

SCIENTISTS: Their Lives and Works

Marie C. Ellavich, Editor

VOLUME 5

U·X·L®
AN IMPRINT OF GALE

DETROIT · NEW YORK · LONDON

Scientists: Their Lives and Works

Edited by Marie C. Ellavich

Staff

Elizabeth Des Chenes, *U·X·L Senior Editor*
Carol DeKane Nagel, *U·X·L Managing Editor*
Thomas L. Romig, *U·X·L Publisher*

Margaret Chamberlain, *Permissions Specialist*
Shalice Shah, *Permission Associate*

Shanna P. Heilveil, *Production Assistant*
Evi Seoud, *Assistant Production Manager*
Mary Beth Trimper, *Production Director*

Pamela A. E. Galbreath, *Senior Art Director*
Cynthia Baldwin, *Product Design Manager*

Linda Mahoney, *Typesetting*

Library of Congress Cataloging-in-Publication Data

Scientists : Their lives and works
    edited by Marie C. Ellavich.
        p. cm.
    Includes bibliographical references and index.

    Contents: v. 5. A-Z

    ISBN 0-7876-2797-6

    1. Physical Scientists–Biography. 2. Social Scientists–Biography.
    Q141.S3717 1998
    509'.2'2–dc20
    [B]   96-25579
                                                                      CIP

Printed in the United States of America
10 9 8 7 6 5 4 3 2 1

Contents

Sophie Germain

Scientists by Field of Specialization

Includes *Scientists*, volumes 1-5.
Italic type indicates volume numbers.

Hippocrates of Cos

Anthropology

Archaeology

Astronomy and Space

Astrophysics

Atmospheric Chemistry

Atomic/Nuclear Physics

Bacteriology

Biochemistry

Biology

Biomedical Engineering

Biophysics

Botany

Cardiology

Chemical Engineering

Chemistry

Climatology

Computer Science

Social Science

Surgery

Theoretical Physics

Virology

Wildlife Conservation

Zoology

Reader's Guide

Fang Lizhi

Budding scientists and those entering the fascinating world of science for fun or study will find inspiration in this fifth volume of *Scientists.* The series presents detailed biographies of the women and men whose theories, discoveries, and inventions have revolutionized science and society. From Nicolaus Copernicus to Bill Gates and Elijah McCoy to Margaret Mead, *Scientists* explores the pioneers and their innovations that students most want to learn about.

Scientists from around the world and from all times are featured, in fields such as astronomy, ecology, oceanography, physics, and more.

In *Scientists,* volume 5, students will find:

- Thirty-four scientist biographies, each focusing on the scientist's early life, formative experiences, and inspirations—details that keep students reading

- "Impact" boxes that draw out important information and sum up why each scientist's work is indeed revolutionary

- Sixteen boxes that highlight individuals who influenced the work of the featured scientist or who conducted similar research, as well as related information of special interest to students

- Sources for further reading so students know where to delve even deeper

- More than thirty black-and-white portraits and additional photographs that give students a better understanding of the people and inventions discussed

Scientists, volume 5, begins with a list of the scientists in all five volumes, categorized by fields ranging from aeronautical engineering to zoology; a timeline of major scientific breakthroughs; and a glossary of scientific terms used in the text. Cross references, appearing in bold in the text, direct the student to related entries throughout the five-volume set. The volume concludes with a cumulative subject index for the series so students can easily find the people, inventions, and theories discussed throughout *Scientists.*

Suggestions

We welcome any comments on this work and suggestions for individuals to feature in future editions of *Scientists.* Please write: Editors, *Scientists,* U• X• L, Gale Research, 835 Penobscot Bldg., Detroit, Michigan 48226-4094; call toll-free: 800-877-4253; or fax to: 313-961-6347.

Timeline of Scientific Breakthroughs

Maria Agnesi

431 B.C.   **Hippocrates of Cos** establishes the basis of modern medicine by stressing the diagnosis of physical symptoms over a reliance on magic.

1748   **Maria Agnesi** publishes *Analytical Institutions,* a summary of the mathematical knowledge of her day. The work becomes a popular text for European scholars and teachers.

1800   **Alessandro Volta** invents the voltaic pile, the first electric battery.

1809   **Jean Baptiste Lamarck** introduces the law of inheritance of acquired characteristics, which is considered the basis of the theory of evolution.

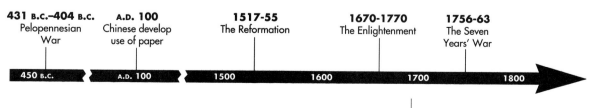

431 B.C.–404 B.C.
Pelopennesian War

A.D. 100
Chinese develop use of paper

1517-55
The Reformation

1670-1770
The Enlightenment

1756-63
The Seven Years' War

450 B.C.   A.D. 100   1500   1600   1700   1800

1815   **Sophie Germain** explains the formation of Chladni figures. Germain is eventually credited with founding the field of modern physics.

1831   **Mary Somerville** publishes *The Mechanics of Heaven,* the first of her popular books on science.

1883   **Jan Ernst Matzeliger** invents the shoe-lasting machine, a device that revolutionizes the shoemaking industry.

1894   **Anna W. Williams** discovers the *Corynebacterium diphtheria* bacillus, the first step in the development of a diphtheria antitoxin.

1898   **Annie Russell Maunder** takes a photograph of the largest solar prominence ever captured on film.

1913   **Henrietta Leavitt**'s star classification system is adopted by the International Committee on Photographic Magnitudes.

1914   **Lillian Gilbreth** publishes *The Psychology of Management,* a work which introduces the theory of industrial management.

1915   **Aldo Leopold** begins developing his conservation concepts.

1916   **Gilbert Newton Lewis** proposes the theory of covalent bonding.

1920   **Emmy Noether** lays the foundation for modern abstract algebra, making possible the use of mathematics in chemistry and physics.

1928   **Philo T. Farnsworth** introduces the world's first television system. Farnsworth later becomes known as the "Father of Television."

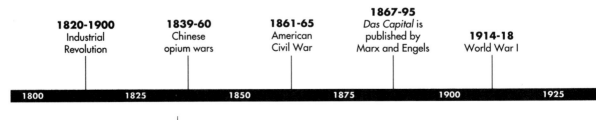

1820-1900
Industrial
Revolution

1839-60
Chinese
opium wars

1861-65
American
Civil War

1867-95
Das Capital is
published by
Marx and Engels

1914-18
World War I

1800   1825   1850   1875   1900   1925

1932	**Miriam Rothschild** begins her career as a zoologist. She eventually becomes a famous authority on fleas and parasites.
1935	**Dorothy Andersen** discovers cystic fibrosis. Her discovery paves the way for further study and treatment of this leading fatal genetic disease.
1939	**Franz Weidenreich** introduces his theory of the evolution of human racial groups.
1942	**Ernst Mayr** publishes *Systemics and the Origin of the Species.* Mayr's work is credited with giving new life to the study of evolution.
1950	**Fred Hoyle** is the first person to use the term "big bang" to describe the theory of the central event that created the universe.
1950-1953	**Thomas Dale Stewart** pioneers forensic anthropology while studying of the remains of soldiers killed in the Korean War.
1954	**Mary G. Ross** joins the first Lockheed Missiles Systems Division and is the only female engineer on the 40-member team.
1954	**David Blackwell** is coauthor of *Theory of Games and Statistical Decisions,* a book which perfects game theory and leads to improved military strategies.
1957	**Yoichiri Nambu** predicts the existence of the omega particle. The particle is discovered the following year.

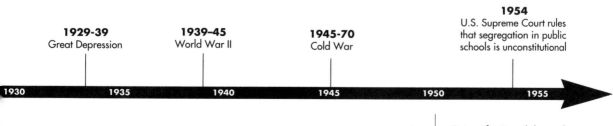

1954
U.S. Supreme Court rules that segregation in public schools is unconstitutional

1929-39
Great Depression

1939–45
World War II

1945-70
Cold War

1930   1935   1940   1945   1950   1955

1960   **Min-Chueh Chang** codevelops the birth control pill, initiating a revolution in family planning and human reproduction.

1960   **Grace Hopper** codevelops COBOL, the first computer language designed for use by businesses and a major advancement in making the computer available to general users.

1975   **Masakasu Konishi** begins his influential research on the brains of birds.

1984   **George T. Tsao** produces usable fuel from garbage and farm waste products.

1985   **Susan Solomon** discovers that chlorofluorocarbons are causing the hole in the ozone layer. Her research leads to worldwide restrictions on aerosol cans and refrigerator fluids.

1989   **Christine Darden** is named head of the Sonic Boom Group, a NASA research team working on methods of reducing the impact of sonic booms caused by supersonic aircraft.

1990   Astrophysicist and Chinese activist **Fang Lizhi** receives political asylum in the United States.

1991   **Walter Munk** is a leader of the Acoustic Thermometry of Ocean Climate Project to detect global warming. The project is later suspended because of environmental concerns.

1993   **Marc Andreessen** cofounds Netscape Communications, which soon becomes the leading designer of Internet software technology.

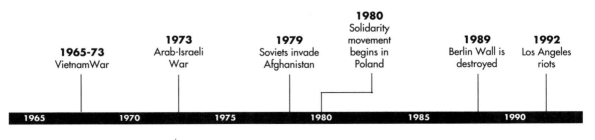

1965-73 VietnamWar

1973 Arab-Israeli War

1979 Soviets invade Afghanistan

1980 Solidarity movement begins in Poland

1989 Berlin Wall is destroyed

1992 Los Angeles riots

1965   1970   1975   1980   1985   1990

Words to Know

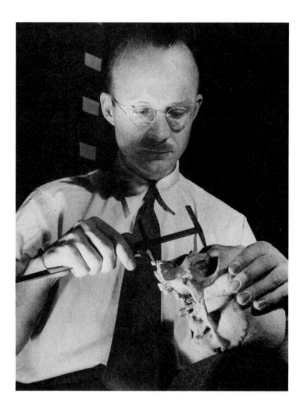

A

Absolute zero: the theoretical point at which a substance has no heat and motion ceases; equivalent to -276°C or -459.67°F.

Algae: a diverse group of plant or plantlike organisms that grow mainly in water.

Alpha particle: a positively charged nuclear particle that consists of two protons and two electrons; it is ejected at a high speed from disintegrating radioactive materials.

Alternating current: the flow of electrons first in one direction and then in the other at regular intervals.

Amino acids: organic acids that are the chief components of proteins.

Anatomy: the study of the structure and form of biological organisms.

Anthropology: the science that deals with the study of human beings, especially their origin, development, divisions, and customs.

Aorta: the main artery of the human body that starts out at the left ventricle of the heart and carries blood to all organs except the heart.

Archaeology: the scientific study of material remains, such as fossils and relics, of past societies.

Artificial intelligence: the branch of science concerned with the development of machines having the ability to perform tasks normally thought to require human intelligence, such as problem solving, discriminating among single objects, and response to spoken commands.

Asteroid: one of thousands of small planets located in a belt between the orbits of Mars and Jupiter.

Astronomy: the study of the physical and chemical properties of objects and matter outside Earth's atmosphere.

Astrophysics: the branch of physics involving the study of the physical and chemical nature of celestial objects and events.

Atomic bomb: a weapon of mass destruction that derives its explosive energy from nuclear fission.

Atomic weight: the mass of one atom of an element.

B

Bacteria: a large, diverse group of mostly single-celled organisms that play a key role in the decay of organic matter and the cycling of nutrients.

Bacteriology: the scientific study of bacteria, their characteristics, and their activities as related to medicine, industry, and agriculture.

Bacteriophage: a virus that infects bacteria.

Ballistic missile: a self-propelled object (like a rocket) that is guided as it ascends into the air and usually falls freely.

Behaviorism: the school of psychology that holds that human and animal behavior is based not on independent will nor motivation but rather on response to reward and punishment.

Beta decay: process by which a neutron in an atomic nucleus breaks apart into a proton and an electron.

Big bang: in astronomy, the theory that the universe resulted from a cosmic explosion that occurred billions of years ago and then expanded over time.

Binary stars: a system of two stars revolving around each other under a mutual gravitation system.

Binary system: a system that uses the numbers 1 and 0 to correspond to the on or off states of electric current.

Biochemistry: the study of chemical compounds and processes occurring in living organisms.

Biodiversity: the number of different species of plants and animals in a specified region.

Biofeedback: a method of learning to gain some voluntary control over involuntary bodily functions like heartbeat or blood pressure.

Biology: the scientific study of living organisms.

Biophysics: the branch of biology in which the methods and principles of physics are applied to the study of living things.

Biosynthesis: the creation of a chemical compound in the body.

Biotechnology: use of biological organisms, systems, or processes to make or modify products.

Black holes: regions in space that exert an extremely intense gravitational force from which nothing, including light, can escape.

Botany: the branch of biology involving the study of plant life.

Byte: a group of binary digits (0 and 1) that a computer processes as a unit.

C

Carbon filament: a threadlike object in a lamp that glows when electricity passes through it.

Carburetor: the device that supplies an internal-combustion engine with a mixture of vaporized fuel and air that, when ignited, produces the engine's energy.

Carcinogen: a cancer-causing agent, such as a chemical or a virus.

Catalyst: a substance that enables a chemical reaction to take place either more quickly or under otherwise difficult conditions.

Cathode: a negatively charged electrode.

Cathode rays: electrons emitted by a cathode when heated.

Cerebrum: the uppermost part of the brain that, in higher mammals, covers the rest of the brain and is considered to be the seat of conscious mental processes.

Chemistry: the science of the nature, composition, and properties of material substances and their transformations.

Chromosome: threadlike structure in the nucleus of a cell that carries thousands of genes.

Circuit: the complete path of an electric current including the source of electric energy; an assemblage of electronic elements.

Classification: a system of naming and categorizing plants and animals in which they are grouped by the number of physical traits they have in common. The ranking system goes from general to specific: kingdom, phylum, class, order, family, genus, and species.

Climatology: the scientific study of climates and their phenomena.

Combustion: a rapid chemical process that produces heat and light.

Conductor: a substance able to carry an electrical current.

Conservation biology: the branch of biology that involves conserving rapidly vanishing wild animals, plants, and places.

Conservation laws: laws of physics that state that a particular property, mass, energy, momentum, or electrical charge is not lost during any change.

Cosmic rays: charged particles, mainly the nuclei of hydrogen and other atoms, that bombard Earth's upper atmosphere at velocities close to that of light.

Cosmology: the study of the structure and evolution of the universe.

Cross-fertilization: a method of fertilization in which the gametes (mature male or female cells) are produced by separate individuals or sometimes by individuals of different kinds.

Cryogenics: the branch of physics that involves the production and effects of very low temperatures.

Crystallography: the science that deals with the forms and structures of crystals.

Cytology: the branch of biology concerned with the study of cells.

D

Deforestation: the process of cutting down all the trees in a forest.

Desertification: the changing of productive land to desert, often by clearing the land of trees and other plant life.

Diffraction: the spreading and bending of light waves as they pass through a hole or slit.

Direct current: a regular flow of electrons, always in the same direction.

DNA (deoxyribonucleic acid): a long molecule composed of two chains of nucleotides (organic chemicals) that contain the genetic information carried from one generation to another.

E

Earthquake: an unpredictable event in which masses of rock shift below Earth's surface, releasing enormous amounts of energy and sending out shockwaves that sometimes cause the ground to shake dramatically.

Ecology: the branch of science dealing with the interrelationship of organisms and their environments.

Ecosystem: community of plants and animals and the physical environment with which they interact.

Electrocardiograph: an instrument that makes a graphic record of the heart's movements.

Electrochemistry: the branch of physical chemistry involving the relation of electricity to chemical changes.

Electrodes: conductors used to establish electrical contact with a nonmetallic part of a circuit.

Electromagnetism: the study of electric and magnetic fields and their interaction with electric charges and currents.

Electron: a negatively charged particle that orbits the nucleus of an atom.

Embryo: an animal in the early stages of development before birth.

Embryology: the study of embryos and their development.

Entomology: the branch of zoology dealing with the study of insects.

Environmentalism: the movement to preserve and improve the natural environment, and particularly to control pollution.

Enzyme: any of numerous complex proteins that are produced by living cells and spark specific biochemical reactions.

Epidemiology: the study of the causes, distribution, and control of disease in populations.

Equinox: the two times each year when the Sun crosses the plane of Earth's equator; at these times, day and night are of equal length everywhere on Earth.

Ethnobotany: the plant lore of a race of people.

Ethnology: science that deals with the division of human beings into races and their origin, distribution, relations, and characteristics.

Ethology: the scientific and objective study of the behavior of animals in the wild rather than in captivity.

Evolution: in the struggle for survival, the process by which successive generations of a species pass on to their offspring the characteristics that enable the species to survive.

Extinction: the total disappearance of a species or the disappearance of a species from a given area.

F

Flora: the plants of a particular region or environment.

Foramen magnum: the opening at the base of the skull through which the spinal cord enters the cranial cavity.

Fossils: the remains, traces, or impressions of living organisms that inhabited Earth more than ten thousand years ago.

Frontal systems: a weather term denoting the boundaries between air masses of different temperatures and humidities.

G

Gamma rays: short electromagnetic wavelengths that come from the nuclei of atoms during radioactive decay.

Game theory: the mathematics involved in determining the effect of a particular strategy in a competition, as in a game of chess, a military battle, or in selling products.

Gene: in classical genetics, a unit of hereditary information that is carried on chromosomes and determines observable characteristics; in molecular genetics, a special sequence of DNA or RNA located on the chromosome.

Genetic code: the means by which genetic information is translated into the chromosomes that make up living organisms.

Genetics: the study of inheritance in living organisms.

Genome: genetic material of a human being; the complete genetic structure of a species.

Geochemistry: the study of the chemistry of Earth (and other planets).

Geology: the study of the origin, history, and structure of Earth.

Geophysics: the physics of Earth, including studies of the atmosphere, earthquakes, volcanism, and oceans.

Global warming: the rise in Earth's temperature that is attributed to the buildup of carbon dioxide and other pollutants in the atmosphere.

Gravity: the force of attraction (causing free objects to accelerate toward each other) that exists between the surface of Earth (as well as other planets) and bodies at or near its surface.

Greenhouse effect: warming of Earth's atmosphere due to the absorption of heat by molecules of water vapor, carbon dioxide, methane, ozone, nitrous oxide, and chlorofluorocarbons.

H

Heliocentric: having the Sun as the center.

Herpetology: the branch of zoology that deals with reptiles and amphibians.

Histology: the study of microscopic plant and animal tissues.

Hominids: humanlike creatures.

Hormones: chemical messengers produced in living organisms that play significant roles in the body, such as affecting growth, metabolism, and digestion.

Horticulture: the science of growing fruits, vegetables, and ornamental plants.

Hybridization: cross-pollination of plants of different varieties to produce seed.

Hydraulics: the study of the forces of fluids as they apply to accomplishing mechanical or practical tasks.

Hydrodynamics: the study of the forces exerted by fluids in motion.

Hydrostatics: a branch of physics that studies fluids at rest and the forces they exert, particularly on submerged objects.

Hypothesis: an assumption made on the basis of scientific data that is an attempt to explain a principle in nature but remains tentative because of lack of solid evidence.

I

Immunology: the branch of medicine concerned with the body's ability to protect itself from disease.

Imprinting: the rapid learning process that takes place early in the life of a social animal and establishes a behavioral pattern, such as a recognition of and attraction to its own kind or a substitute.

In vitro fertilization: fertilization of eggs outside of the body.

Infrared radiation: electromagnetic rays released by hot objects; also known as a heat radiation.

Infertility: the inability to produce offspring for any reason.

Internal-combustion engine: an engine in which the combustion (burning) that generates the heat that powers it goes on inside the engine itself, rather than in a furnace.

Invertebrates: animals lacking a spinal column.

Ion: an atom or groups of atoms that carries an electrical charge—-either positive or negative—-as a result of losing or gaining one or more electrons.

Isomers: compound that have the same number of atoms of the same elements, but different properties because their atoms are arranged differently.

Isotope: one of two or more atoms of a chemical element that have the same structure but different physical properties.

L

Laser: acronym for light amplification by stimulated emission of radiation; a device that produces intense light with a precisely defined wavelength.

Light-year: in astronomy, the distance light travels in one year, about six trillion miles.

Limnology: the branch of biology concerning freshwater plants.

Logic: the science of the formal principles of reasoning.

Lunar eclipse: the passing of the Moon either wholly or partially into the shadow created by Earth's position in front of the Sun; that is, when the three bodies align thus: Moon—Earth—Sun.

M

Magnetic field: the space around an electric current or a magnet in which a magnetic force can be observed.

Maser: acronym for microwave amplification of stimulated emission of radiation; a device that produces radiation in short wavelengths.

Metabolism: the process by which living cells break down organic compounds to produce energy.

Metallurgy: the science and technology of metals.

Meteorology: the science that deals with the atmosphere and its phenomena and with weather and weather forecasting.

Microbiology: branch of biology dealing with microscopic forms of life.

Microwaves: electromagnetic radiation waves between one millimeter and one centimeter in length.

Molecular biology: the study of the structure and function of molecules that make up living organisms.

Molecule: the smallest particle of a substance that retains all the properties of the substance and is composed of one or more atoms.

Moving assembly line: a system in a plant or factory in which an item that is being made is carried past a series of workers who remain in their places. Each worker assembles a particular portion of the finished product and then repeats the same process with the next item.

Mutation: any permanent change in hereditary material, involving either a physical change in chromosome relations or a biochemical change in genes.

N

Natural selection: the natural process by which groups best adjusted to their environment survive and reproduce, thereby passing on to their offspring genetic qualities best suited to that environment.

Nebulae: large, cloudy bodies of dust in space.

Nerve Growth Factor (NGF): the nutrients that determine how nerve cells take on their specific roles in the nervous system.

Nervous system: the bodily system that in vertebrates is made up of the brain and spinal cord, nerves, ganglia, and other organs and that receives and interprets stimuli and transmits impulses to targeted organs.

Neurology: the scientific study of the nervous system, especially its structure, functions, and abnormalities.

Neurosecretion: the process of producing a secretion by nerve cells.

Neurosurgery: surgery on the nerves, brain, or spinal cord.

Neurosis: any emotional or mental disorder that affects only part of the personality, such as anxiety or mild depression, as a result of stress.

Neutron: an uncharged particle found in atomic nuclei.

Neutron star: a hypothetical dense celestial object that consists primarily of closely packed neutrons that results from the collapse of a much larger celestial body.

Nova: a star that suddenly increases in light output and then fades away to its former obscure state within a few months or years.

Nuclear fallout: the drifting of radioactive particles into the atmosphere as the result of nuclear explosions.

Nuclear fission: the process in which an atomic nucleus is split, resulting in the release of large amounts of energy.

Nuclear physics: physics that deals with the atomic nucleus, atomic energy, the atom bomb, or atomic power.

Nucleotides: compounds that form the basic stuctural units—the stairs on the spiral staircase—of DNA, and are arranged on the staircase in a pattern of heredity-carrying code "words."

Nutritionist: someone who studies the ways in which living organisms take in and make use of food.

O

Oceanography: the science that deals with the study of oceans and seas.

Optics: the study of light and vision.

Organic: of, relating to, or arising in a bodily organ

Ozone layer: the atmospheric layer of approximately twenty to thirty miles above Earth's surface that protects the lower atmosphere from harmful solar radiation.

P

Paleoanthropology: the branch of anthropology dealing with the study of mammal fossils.

Paleontology: the study of the life of past geological periods as known from fossil remains.

Particle physics: the branch of physics concerned with the study of the constitution, properties, and interactions of elementary particles.

Particles: the smallest building blocks of energy and matter.

Patent: a government grant giving an inventor the right to be the only person to sell an invention for a set length of time.

Pathology: the study of the essential nature of diseases, especially the structural and functional changes produced by them.

Pediatrics: a branch of medicine involving the development, care, and diseases of children.

Pendulum: an object that hangs freely from a fixed point and swings back and forth under the action of gravity; often used to regulate movement, as the pendulum in a clock.

Periodic table: a table of the elements in order of atomic number, arranged in rows and columns to show periodic similarities and trends in physical and chemical properties.

Pharmacology: the science dealing with the properties, reactions, and therapeutic values of drugs.

Phylum: the first division of the animal kingdom in the Linnaeus classification system. The ranking of the system is in order from the general to the specific—kingdom, phylum, class, order, family, genus, and species.

Physics: the science that explores the physical properties and composition of objects and the forces that affect them.

Physiology: the branch of biology that deals with the functions and actions of life or of living matter, such as organs, tissues, and cells.

Planetologist: a person who studies the physical bodies in the solar system, including planets and their satellites, comets, and meteorites.

Plankton: floating animal and plant life.

Plasma physics: the branch of physics involving the study of electrically charged, extremely hot gases.

Primate: any order of mammals composed of humans, apes, or monkeys.

Projectile motion: the movement of an object thrust forward by an external force—for example, a cannonball shot out of a cannon.

Protein: large molecules found in all living organisms that are essential to the structure and functioning of all living cells.

Proton: a positively charged particle found in atomic nuclei.

Psychiatry: the branch of medicine that deals with mental, emotional, and behavioral disorders.

Psychoanalysis: the method of analyzing psychic phenomenon and treating emotional disorders that involves treatment sessions during which the patient is encouraged to talk freely about personal experiences, especially about early childhood and dreams.

Psychophysiology: a branch of psychology that focuses on combined mental and bodily processes.

Psychology: the study of human and animal behavior.

Psychotic: a person with severe emotional or mental disorders that cause a loss of contact with reality.

Q

Quantum: any of the very small increments or parcels into which many forms of energy are subdivided.

Quasar: celestial object more distant than stars that emits excessive amounts of radiation.

R

Radar: acronym for radio detection and ranging; the process of using radio waves to detect objects.

Radiation: energy emitted in the form of waves or particles.

Radio waves: electromagnetic radiation.

Radioactive fallout: the radioactive particles resulting from a nuclear explosion.

Radioactivity: the property possessed by some elements (as uranium) or isotopes (as carbon 14) of spontaneously emitting energetic particles (as electrons or alpha particles) by disintegration of their atomic nuclei.

Radiology: the branch of medicine that uses X rays and radium (an intensely radioactive metallic element) to diagnose and treat disease.

Redshift: the increase in the wavelength of all light received from a celestial object (or wave source), usually because the object is moving away from the observer.

RNA (ribonucleic acid): any of various nucleic acids that are associated with the control of cellular chemical activities.

S

Scientific method: collecting evidence meticulously and theorizing from it.

Seismograph: a device that records vibrations of the ground and within Earth.

Seismology: the study and measurement of earthquakes.

Semiconductor: substances whose ability to carry electrical current is lower than that of a conductor (like metal) and higher than that of insulators (like rubber).

Shortwave: a radio wave having a wavelength between ten and one hundred meters.

Slide rule: a calculating device that, in its simplest form, consists of a ruler and a sliding attachment that are graduated with logarithm tables.

Social science: the study of human society and individual relationships within it, including the fields of sociology, anthropology, economics, political sicence, and history.

Sociobiology: the systematic study of the biological basis for all social behavior.

Soil erosion: the loss of usable topsoil, often due to clearing trees and other plant life from the land.

Solid state: using semiconductor devices rather than electron tubes.

Spectrum: the range of colors produced by individual elements within a light source.

Statics: a branch of physics that explores the forces of equilibrium, or balance.

Steady-state theory: a theory that proposes that the universe has neither a beginning nor an end.

Stellar spectra: the distinctive mix of radiation emitted by every star.

Stellar spectroscopy: the process that breaks a star's light into component colors so that the various elements of the star can be observed.

Sterilization: boiling or heating of instruments and food to prevent proliferation of microorganisms.

Supernova: a catastrophic explosion in which a large portion of a star's mass is blown out into space, or the star is entirely destroyed.

T

Theorem: in mathematics, a formula, proposition, or statement.

Theory: an assumption drawn from scientific evidence that provides a plausible explanation for the principle or principles behind a natural phenomenon. (A *theory* generally has more evidence behind it and finds more acceptance in the scientific community than a *hypothesis.*)

Thermodynamics: the branch of physics that deals with the mechanical action or relations of heat.

Trace element: a chemical element present in minute quantities.

Transistor: a solid-state electronic device that is used to control the flow of electricity in electronic equipment and consists of a small block of semiconductor with at least three electrodes.

V

Vaccine: a preparation administered to increase immunity to polio.

Vacuum tube: an electric tube from which all matter has been removed.

Variable stars: stars whose light output varies because of internal fluctuations or because they are eclipsed by another star.

Variation: in genetics, differences in traits of a particular species.

Vertebrate: an animal that has a spinal column.

Virology: the study of viruses.

Virtual reality: an artificial computer-created environment that seeks to mimic reality.

Virus: a microscopic agent of infection.

Voltaic pile: a basic form of battery that was the first source of continuous and controllable electric current.

W

Wavelength: the distance between one peak of a wave of light, heat, or energy and the next corresponding peak.

X

X ray: a form of electromagnetic radiation with an extremely short wavelength that is produced by bombarding a metallic target with electrons in a vacuum.

Z

Zoology: the branch of biology concerned with the study of animal life.

Zooplankton: small drifting animal life in the ocean.

SCIENTISTS: Their Lives and Works

Maria Agnesi

Born May 16, 1718
Milan, Italy
Died January 9, 1799
Milan, Italy

Maria Agnesi was an intellectual and mathematician known throughout Europe during the eighteenth century. Although few women received an education at that time, and even fewer became scholars, Agnesi independently pursued the study of mathematics and developed her own theories. In 1748 she published *Analytical Institutions* (*Instituzioni analitiche ad uso della gioventù italiana*), a summary of the mathematical knowledge of her day. When the book became a popular text for European scholars and teachers, Agnesi received recognition and awards from such leaders as the pope and the Empress of Austria. She was also admitted into all-male professional academic circles. Agnesi's achievement has earned her a place in scientific history as perhaps the first female mathematician in the Western world.

Maria Agnesi was a well–known female mathematician of the eighteenth century.

Father supports gifted student

Maria Gaetana Agnesi was born on May 16, 1718, in Milan, Italy. She was the oldest daughter of Ann Fortunato

Mathematician Maria Agnesi became a respected scholar during the eighteenth century—a time when women were considered incapable of undertaking academic work. After receiving extensive education at home, Agnesi independently pursued the newest and most difficult concepts in mathematics. In 1748 she published *Analytical Institutions,* the first comprehensive text to cover mathematics from the basics of algebra and geometry to the relatively new fields of calculus (mathematical calculation or computation using special symbols) and analysis. Her explanations were so thorough and clear that the book was used throughout Europe. For her accomplishments, Agnesi received praise from other scholars, professional organizations, the pope, and the Empress of Austria.

Brivio and Pietro Agnesi, a professor of mathematics at the University of Milan. A wealthy and educated couple, the Agnesis encouraged all their children—boys and girls—to develop their intellectual talents. Pietro was married three times and ultimately had twenty-one children, yet he was so attentive to his sons and daughters that he was able to recognize the young Maria's special gift for learning. To encourage her talents he hired professors from the university to tutor her in academic subjects as well as a number of foreign languages. By the age of eleven, Maria was known as "the Seven–Tongued Orator" for her ability to communicate fluently in Italian, Spanish, French, German, Latin, Greek, and Hebrew.

Debates scholars as a young woman

Agnesi also became known for her intellectual brilliance. As was customary among scholars at the time, her father hosted gatherings of noted European thinkers in the Agnesi family home. When Maria was in her early teens, he featured her at "debates" in which she presented a series of "theses" (ideas) on a variety of topics, including gravity (the physical force that unites bodies in the universe), mechanics, logic, zoology, chemistry, and the education of women. She would then discuss her ideas with the visiting scholars. They were impressed not only with her insightful and wide–ranging knowledge but also by the fact that she could speak with each person in his own language. In 1738, at the age of twenty, Agnesi published a collection of essays, *Philosophical Propositions (Propositiones philosophicae).* The book contained about 190 of the theses she had defended at the debates.

Begins study of mathematics

As Agnesi approached adulthood, however, her achievements took a toll on her health and she frequently became ill. Her doctors blamed the problem on her intense study habits, so they advised more physical exercise such as dancing and horseback riding. Yet Agnesi attacked these new ventures with equal vigor, to the extent that she suffered even more serious symptoms, including severe convulsions (violent muscle spasms). When the doctors suggested that she cut back on physical activities as well, she turned her energies to religion. Predictably, Agnesi wholeheartedly embraced the spiritual life. Shortly after writing *Philosophical Propositions,* she asked her father's permission to become a nun. Since she was shy by nature, she had decided she no longer wanted to be the center of attention at the scholarly meetings. Instead, she preferred to enter a convent where she could quietly pursue her studies and help the poor. Her father strongly opposed her plan, however, so they reached a compromise: Agnesi would stay at home but she would no longer be required to appear in public. Content with this arrangement, she turned to the study of mathematics, which had engaged her since she was a child.

Plans a guide to mathematics

By the this time Agnesi had already mastered difficult problems in the fields of geometry and ballistics (the motion of projectile objects). When she was seventeen, for instance, she had prepared a commentary about a prominent mathematician's work on conic sections (segments of cones). Her father's university colleagues had praised the high quality of her analysis, but she never published the study. Once relieved of her social obligations, Agnesi was able to undertake an ambitious project—a summary of all mathematical knowledge to date.

During Agnesi's lifetime many new ideas were taking hold in mathematics, among them calculus (mathematical calculation or computation using special symbols), which had been developed by English mathematician and physicist Isaac

Newton (1642–1727) and German mathematician Gottfried Leibniz (1646–1716). But it was difficult to keep up with the latest knowledge because information about recent developments was scattered among diverse sources. Agnesi's goal was to collect all this information into a single book as a study aid for her younger brothers, whom she tutored.

Publishes *Analytical Institutions*

Agnesi worked for ten years before finally publishing *Analytical Institutions* in 1748. She had chosen not to write the two-volume, thousand-page work in Latin, which was the traditional language of scholars. Instead she used her native Italian so that it would be easy for students to understand. The work contained a complete overview of current mathematical knowledge, beginning with basic algebra and leading to more difficult subjects like integral calculus (a branch of calculus dealing with integers, or natural numbers) and differential equations (a branch of calculus dealing with the rate of change in mathematical functions). While Agnesi was careful to note that many of the ideas presented in her text were originated by other people, she also identified her own methods and interpretations.

Praised by European scholars

After *Analytical Institutions* was translated into French and English, the magnitude of Agnesi's achievement was recognized throughout Europe. The text was widely used both by scholars and teachers of mathematics. In fact, according to the *Dictionary of Scientific Biography,* the French Academy of Sciences proclaimed: "There is no other book, in any language, which would enable a reader to penetrate as deeply, or as rapidly, into the fundamental concepts of analysis. We consider this treatise the most complete and best written work of its kind." Despite this praise, however, Agnesi was not admitted to the French Academy, which prohibited women from joining the organization. Nevertheless, her work was rewarded by male scholars in Italy, who elected her to the Bologna Academy of Sciences.

Receives honors from empress and pope

Agnesi also received recognition from political and religious leaders. Empress Maria Theresa of Austria, to whom Agnesi had dedicated *Analytical Institutions,* honored the mathematician with a diamond ring and a letter enclosed in a jeweled box. In 1749 Pope Benedict XIV acknowledged Agnesi's accomplishment with a letter accompanied by a gold medal and a wreath of fine jewels set in gold. The following year the pope also appointed Agnesi chair of the department of mathematics and natural philosophy at the University of Bologna. It is unclear if she ever accepted this position. Some historians suggest it was only an honorary title and she never actually lectured at the university, while others have found evidence that she appeared at the university for a short time.

The "Witch of Agnesi"

The "witch of Agnesi" is a mathematical concept mistakenly attributed to Maria Agnesi. In her monumental summary of mathematical knowledge, *Analytical Institutions* (1748), Agnesi presented a formula for a cubic curve known as a *versiera*. The *versiera* had been first discovered by Pierre de Fermat (1601–1665) in 1665. Since *versiera* is also an Italian term for "witch," one translator of Agnesi's book used this meaning when describing the equation. The "witch of Agnesi" thus became a popular name for the curve formula, even though Fermat had actually originated the idea.

Devotes later years to charity

After the death of her father in 1752, Agnesi began to turn away from mathematics. Increasingly she devoted her energies to religion and charity. Using her own money to support these activities, she worked with the sick at a nearby hospital and assisted the poor in her church parish. In addition, she began to care for the old, sick, and poor in her home. To raise additional funding for her projects, she eventually sold the gifts and jewels she had received from the empress and the pope.

Remembered by people of Milan

In 1771 Agnesi became the director of Pio Instituto Trivulzio, a home for the poor and sick in Milan, while continuing to operate the hospital in her home. By 1783 she could no longer sustain this strenuous schedule, so she went to live and work at Pio Instituto Trivulzio. Agnesi remained there until her death at the age of eighty-one on January 9, 1799. She was buried in a common grave for poor people in a cemetery outside the walls of the city. In 1899, on the one-hundredth anniversary of Agnesi's death, the citizens of Milan honored her intellectual and charitable contributions by naming streets and a school in her memory.

Further Reading

Dictionary of Scientific Biography, Volume I, Scribner's, 1970, pp. 75–77.

Ogilvie, Marilyn Bailey, *Women in Science: Antiquity through the Nineteenth Century,* MIT Press, 1986, pp. 26–28.

Osen, Lynn M., *Women in Mathematics,* MIT Press, 1974, pp. 33–48.

Dorothy Andersen

Born May 15, 1901
Asheville, North Carolina
Died March 3, 1963
New York, New York

Dorothy Andersen was a pathologist and medical researcher who recognized the disorder that she named cystic fibrosis (CF). A colorful and unconventional figure who refused to give in to sexism, Andersen devoted much of her life to the investigation of cystic fibrosis. She also did extensive work on congenital (present at birth) defects of the heart. During World War II (1939–1945) she developed a training program in cardiac embryology (development of the heart before birth) and anatomy (study of the structure of the body) for surgeons learning how to perform open-heart surgery.

Dorothy Andersen discovered and named the disease cystic fibrosis.

Becomes independent at an early age

Dorothy Hansine Andersen was born on May 15, 1901, in Asheville, North Carolina, the only child of Hans Peter and Mary Louise (Mason) Andersen. Her father, a native of Den-

Pathologist and medical researcher Dorothy Andersen is credited with identifying and naming the disease known as cystic fibrosis. She devoted her career to finding ways to diagnose and treat this frequently fatal condition which affects children. Andersen developed a method of accurately detecting cystic fibrosis, thus allowing patients to receive treatments that can lengthen and improve the quality of their lives. While no cure for the disease has yet been found, research based on Andersen's early work has resulted in improved medication and treatment.

mark, was employed by the Young Men's Christian Association (YMCA) in Asheville. Her mother was a descendent of Benning Wentworth, for whom the town of Bennington, Vermont, was named. Andersen was forced to take responsibility for her own upbringing and education at an early age. When she was thirteen her father died, leaving her to care for her ailing mother. Dorothy moved with Mary to Saint Johnsbury, Vermont, where Mary died in 1920. Barely nineteen years old, Andersen was left on her own without any close relatives.

Career as doctor is thwarted

Andersen was nevertheless able to continue her education. After graduating from Saint Johnsbury Academy and then Mount Holyoke College, she decided to become a doctor. She enrolled at the prestigious Johns Hopkins School of Medicine in Baltimore, Maryland. While at Johns Hopkins, Andersen published two scientific papers about the reproductive system of the female pig in the journal *Contributions to Embryology*—an unusual accomplishment for a student. After earning a medical degree in 1926, she accepted a one-year teaching appointment in anatomy at the Rochester School of Medicine in Rochester, New York.

Andersen's progress toward becoming a doctor continued the following year, when she served an internship (a period of medical practice under the supervision of more experienced doctors) in surgery at the Strong Memorial Hospital in Rochester. Normally, an internship is followed by a more advanced period of supervised practice known as a residency, which ultimately leads to certification as a physician. Upon completing her own internship, however, Andersen found that because she was a woman hospitals would not allow her to serve a residency in surgery. She was also not allowed to work in pathology, her other area of expertise.(Pathology is the study of the effects of disease on the body).

Turns to medical research

Although Andersen had been denied the opportunity to practice medicine, she was determined to remain in the medical field. She therefore turned to research and teaching. Taking a job as a research assistant in pathology, she began a doctoral program in endocrinology (the study of glands) at the Columbia University College of Physicians and Surgeons. Simultaneously she served as an instructor in pathology at the Columbia Medical School. After earning a doctor of medical science degree in 1935, Andersen was appointed a pathologist at Babies Hospital of the Columbia-Presbyterian Medical Center in New York City. She stayed in that position for more than twenty years, becoming chief of pathology in 1952. By 1958 Andersen had been appointed a full professor at the College of Physicians and Surgeons.

Becomes expert on heart defects

As a pathologist, Andersen conducted research in two major areas. The first involved a long and careful study of congenital heart problems based on the examination of infants who had died of cardiac (heart) conditions. Beginning this work in her first year at Babies Hospital, she continued to publish her findings on the subject into the late 1950s. Andersen's experience with cardiac problems was put to use during World War II, when she was asked to teach courses for physicians learning how to perform open-heart surgery. (Open-heart surgery involves tying off the arteries to the heart and opening the heart for inspection and treatment.)

Identifies cystic fibrosis

Andersen's second area of research, for which she is probably best known, evolved out of her discovery of cystic fibrosis in 1935. That year she had conducted a postmortem (after death) examination of a child who had supposedly died of celiac disease (a nutritional disorder). But after noticing damage to the child's pancreas(the gland that secretes digestive enzymes and the hormones insulin and glucagon), Andersen began searching medical records and literature for a similar case. Eventually she realized she had found a disease that had never been described in medical literature. Andersen reported her discovery, which she named cystic fibrosis, at a meeting of the American Pediatric Society and the Society for Pediatric Research on May 5, 1938.

Cystic fibrosis: a fatal genetic disease

Andersen's contribution to medical science is important because she opened the way for further study and treatment of the leading fatal genetic disease in the United States. Children born to parents who each carry one recessive (non-dominant) gene for cystic fibrosis have a twenty-five percent chance of inheriting both copies of the defective gene—and with them the disease. The seriousness of cystic fibrosis can be best understood by comparing it with the common cold. Almost everyone has experienced the congestion that accompanies a bad cold, when thick mucus that forms in the nose and throat makes breathing difficult. Luckily, the congestion decreases in a few days as the body fights off the cold. People who suffer from cystic fibrosis, however, must constantly cope with mucus that accumulates in the lungs, large intestine, and pancreas.

Cystic fibrosis patients may suffer from pneumonia caused by bacterial infections, and the disease can be fatal if the mucus blocks the lungs. Other serious complications include respiratory failure, diabetes, enlarged heart, liver cirrhosis (hardening), intestinal blockage, pancreatic dysfunction, sodium deficiency, and sterility (inability to have children). Abdominal cramps, malnutrition, growth retardation, and coughing are all symptoms associated with cystic fibrosis. This disorder mainly affects about one out of every two thousand Caucasians of European descent. The disease is less common in African Americans and rare among Asians and Native Americans.

Advances in Identifying and Treating CF

Cystic fibrosis was classified as a disease in 1938 as a result of discoveries made by medical researcher and pathologist Dorothy Andersen. Since that time many strides have been made in treating the disorder, although there is still no known cure and it remains the leading fatal genetic disease in the United States. In 1989 scientists at the University of Michigan and the Hospital for Sick Children in Toronto, Canada, announced that they had identified the defective gene that causes cystic fibrosis. In 1990 researchers used laboratory cell cultures to correct the genetic defect that causes cystic fibrosis. Two years later scientists at the Cystic Fibrosis Center at the University of North Carolina were able to breed mice that showed human symptoms of cystic fibrosis. Researchers are currently developing an aerosol spray to introduce the genetically altered virus into the lungs of the patient. This technology holds new hope of a cure for cystic fibrosis.

Searches for answers about disease

Not satisfied with simply describing the effects of cystic fibrosis, Andersen searched for a way to identify and treat the disease. For the next twenty years, she taught herself about chemistry and pediatrics (children's medicine) so she could obtain and analyze body fluids from children suffering from the disease. While these techniques eventually allowed Andersen to diagnose cystic fibrosis accurately, some of her colleagues in the medical field criticized her for venturing into areas in which she had no formal training.

An unconventional life

Andersen's unconventional style in her professional practice and her personal life generated both respect and disapproval. In the hospital, she was loved by many of her students and coworkers for her excellent teaching style and her willingness to spend time assisting others with their research projects. Some people, however, were bothered what they considered to be her strange and unprofessional behavior. For example,

Andersen did not pay much attention to her physical appearance: her hair was usually a mess and her constant cigarette smoking left her clothes covered with ashes. Her laboratory was equally untidy. And while Andersen's hobbies—canoeing, hiking, skiing, and carpentry—do not seem especially unusual today, during her lifetime these pursuits were not considered proper pastimes for a woman. Refusing to conform to others' ideas of appropriate behavior, she fought for the rights of other women as well, speaking out against sexual discrimination in the medical profession.

Develops tests and treatments

While Andersen succeeded in developing methods for treating cystic fibrosis, such as the use of chemotherapy (treatment with chemicals) for certain related infections, she was not able to find a cure for the disease. Her research team, however, eventually found that the sweat of people with the disease contains higher than normal levels of salt. This allowed the team to develop a simple test for easier detection of cystic fibrosis. Andersen also conducted pioneering work on identifying the genes that pass on this hereditary disease from parents to children.

Medical career is honored

Andersen died of lung cancer in New York City on March 3, 1963. For her discovery of cystic fibrosis, she had received the Mead Johnson Award for Pediatric Research in 1938. During her career she was also honored with the Borden Award for Research in Nutrition from the American Academy of Pediatrics in 1948, the Elizabeth Blackwell Citation for Women in Medicine from the New York Infirmary in 1954, and a citation for outstanding performance from Mount Holyoke College in 1952. After Andersen's death, her exceptional medical achievements were recognized with the distinguished service medal of the Columbia-Presbyterian Medical Center.

Further Reading

Sicherman, Barbara, and Carol Hurd Green, editors, *Notable American Women, the Modern Period: A Biographical Dictionary,* Belknap Press, 1980, pp. 18-20.

Dorothy Andersen

Marc Andreessen

Born 1972
Iowa

*Marc Andreessen
is a cofounder
of Netscape
Communications,
a leading designer
of World Wide
Web browser
software.*

M arc Andreessen became one of the best-known designers in the computer software industry when he cofounded the Netscape Communications company in 1994. (Software is a set of programs, procedures, and documentation used on a computer.) Netscape's most popular product is the Netscape Navigator, an Internet browser. (The Internet is a system of linked computer networks. A browser is a software program that enables the computer user to find text, graphics, and other items on the Internet.) It is based on the Mosaic software Andreessen helped to create while he was still a student at the University of Illinois, Champaign-Urbana. The advantage of Netscape Navigator is that it allows average computer users to simply point and click their way to text, graphics, and other media available on the World Wide Web. (The World Wide Web is a program that links documents on the Internet.) Ease of use has made Netscape Navigator not only the most commonly preferred Web browser but also a crucial factor in introducing the Internet to the general public. Despite his youth and relative newness to the business world, Andreessen continues to be a major force in the direction of both the company and the Internet community. He currently holds the title of senior vice president of technology at Netscape. According to *Fortune* magazine, computer industry experts believe "Andreessen is the main man behind the most dramatic shift in computing since the advent of the PC [personal computer]: the rise of the Internet."

Teaches himself programming

Andreessen was born in Iowa in 1972 to Lowell and Patricia Andreessen. He spent his childhood, however, in the town of New Lisbon, Wisconsin, where his father was a seed salesman and his mother worked for the Lands' End mail-order catalog company. At that time most people in New Lisbon engaged in athletic activities for recreation and entertainment, but Andreessen was not particularly interested in sports. Therefore he decided to find something else to do in his spare time. While he was still in grade school he became interested in computers and borrowed books on the subject from the library. Before he even had access to a computer he had taught himself how to write computer programs using BASIC (a simplified language for programming a computer).

Parents give him first computer

During the sixth grade Andreessen finally had a chance to work on a computer at the school library. He designed his first program to do his mathematics homework. When he was in the seventh grade, his parents bought him a computer—an early model that cost only a few hundred dollars. Computer programming continued to be Andreessen's past time in high school. For one of his projects he designed a dating program for his classmates. One of Andreessen's high school friends told a *Fortune* interviewer that the date Andreessen's program selected for him did not work out, yet even then the young programmer seemed determined to make a career out of his hobby.

Marc Andreessen is one of the foremost designers of Internet software. He began his career as an innovative computer software programmer and entrepreneur while he was a student intern at the University of Illinois. Since 1992 he has helped design the World Wide Web browser Mosaic and cofounded Netscape Communications, the company that produced Netscape Navigator. Mosaic and Netscape Navigator have both contributed to an increase in Internet use by individuals and businesses throughout the world during the 1990s.

Interns at national computer center

After Andreessen entered the University of Illinois, Champaign-Urbana, he secured a position as an intern at the university's prestigious National Center for Supercomputing Applications (NCSA). The institute was devoted to developing software that could be used by scientists and researchers. Andreessen was initially assigned to write computer code (sets of instructions) for a graphics application called Polyview. Then he had his first experience with the relatively new world of the Internet and the World Wide Web.

Problems with Internet

The Internet is a system of linked networks that was first created by the U.S. government in 1969 as a way for people working on defense projects at universities and other sites to share information. Since then, many smaller, commercial networks have connected to the original structure. Through this network of computers, millions of people are now able to access information on the Internet at the same time. For many years, however, the Internet was confusing and difficult to use, preventing users who were not computer specialists from getting "online" (entering the computer network). The first major innovation that revolutionized use of the Internet was the World Wide Web, which was designed by British physicist Tim Berners-Lee in 1990.

While the World Wide Web marked a major advance in increasing the potential for the Internet, it was still too complicated for most people to use. Different software programs had to be used for individual tasks: for example, File Transfer Protocol (FTP) was needed to download (transfer) files from another computer. Then, Gopher (known as a search engine) was used to find specific documents. Finally, logging on (gaining access) to another computer through the Internet involved yet another program called Telnet.

Designs Mosaic

Easier use of the World Wide Web required browser software that would simplify the steps a user needed to connect to the Internet and then find and share information. Several browsers were created in the early 1990s, but they could not display graphics alongside text. In addition, early browsers could access only parts of the Web, and they were fairly difficult to install and run. In 1992 Dave Thompson, one of Andreessen's colleagues at NCSA, began looking into the new World Wide Web and browser software. When Thompson showed Andreessen the programs he had found, Andreessen was so intrigued that one weekend he decided to try to create a better Web browser.

By the end of that weekend, Andreessen had written a rough set of codes for a new browser. He then received permission from his supervisor at NCSA to continue working on the project with Eric Bina, one of the center's best programmers. Over the next six weeks, the two men completed the programming for a browser they called Mosaic. This first program, designed to run on Unix computers, was mainly used by scientists. Later, other programmers at the research center became involved in creating versions of Mosaic for PCs and Macintosh computers. A relatively simple program—it contained only 9000 lines of code—Mosaic was a major step forward in browser technology. Through the use of graphics and a point-and-click interface (connector), it provided a less complicated way of searching the full scope of information on the Web. In addition, Mosaic was easy to get running, and it smoothly integrated text, graphics, and sound technology on the same screen.

Leaves Midwest for Silicon Valley

When NCSA made Mosaic available free of charge on the Internet in 1993, the program was an immediate hit. By the

Tim Berners-Lee, British Software Designer

The first major innovation that revolutionized use of the Internet was the World Wide Web. The Web was designed in 1990 by Tim Berners-Lee, a British physicist at the Center for European Particle Research (CERN) in Switzerland. Berners-Lee's idea was to link documents stored on computer servers around the world in the form of a computer language known as HTML. By means of embedded (built into the document via software) links, which are marked by underlined or colored text in a document, a user could simply click on the "hyperlink" and instantly jump to another related document on the Internet.

Berners-Lee installed his program for the World Wide Web on the Internet in 1991. Three years later he joined the Laboratory for Computer Science at the Massachusetts Institute of Technology (MIT) in Cambridge. As director of a consortium (group of cooperating organizations) based at MIT, he coordinates the World Wide Web with a team in France. The goal of the consortium is to maintain international stability of the Web during technological change and growth.

end of the year, millions of copies of the software had been downloaded by people around the world. When Andreessen graduated with his bachelor of science degree in late 1993, he was known as the "idea man" behind Mosaic. His reputation drew the attention of Enterprise Integration Technologies, a California software company that recruited him to work on security software for Internet business transactions. Soon after graduation Andreessen left the Midwest for Silicon Valley. (Silicon Valley is an area in California that is the heart of the United States computer industry. It has been given this name because silicon is the semiconductor material used to make computer chips, which form the base for the integrated system that runs a computer.)

Becomes cofounder of Netscape

Shortly after arriving in California, Andreessen was approached by Jim Clark, founder of Silicon Graphics, who had recently departed from the company. Clark wanted to start a business with Andreessen, and he suggested they try creating technology for interactive television. But Andreessen convinced Clark that the World Wide Web would be the center of the next big technological trend for consumers and businesses. Andreessen proposed creating a new and improved version of Mosaic software. In 1994 they founded Mosaic Communications. After legal issues arose with the University of Illinois over use of the Mosaic name, Andreessen and Clark renamed their company Netscape Communications.

Netscape Navigator leads the industry

As senior vice president of technology at Netscape, Andreessen recruited a number of programmers from NCSA. Together they fine-tuned Mosaic into a faster and more dynamic Web browser. The updated version was then distributed free to universities and government agencies. After gaining consumer loyalty to their product, Andreessen and Clark planned to make a profit later by selling updated versions of the software and related products. Because the program was released to anyone who wanted it, estimates of the number of computers running the Netscape browser quickly ran into the millions. Reportedly almost 75 percent of Web surfers used Netscape, making it the undisputed leader in the industry. Netscape released the first consumer version of its browser software in 1995 under the name Netscape Navigator Personal Edition. Navigator software has since been followed by a number of updates and new products, including Netscape Internet Applications, a set of software tools allowing businesses to conduct sales online.

Captures media attention

Andreessen's quick rise to success made him the subject of numerous media profiles, particularly after Netscape Communications offered public stock in the company in 1995. On the first day of stock sales, the value skyrocketed. As a primary stockholder, Andreessen became a multi-millionaire at the age of 24. For his achievements in developing Internet technology, he has won a number of awards. In 1994 *Time* magazine selected him as one of the top 50 people under the age of 40, and *MicroTimes* named him Man of the Year. Andreessen was also honored with the Computerworld Smithsonian Award for Leadership in 1995.

Further Reading

Deutschman, Alan, "Imposter Boy," *GQ,* January 1997, pp. 120–27.

Kaplan, David A., "Nothing but Net," *Newsweek,* December 25, 1995, pp. 32–36.

Sandberg, Jared, "Netscape Has Technical Whiz in Andreessen," *Wall Street Journal,* August 11, 1995, pp. B1–B2.

Tetzeli, Rick, "What It's Really Like to Be Marc Andreessen," *Fortune,* December 9, 1996, pp. 136–56.

David Blackwell

Born April 24, 1919
Centralia, Illinois

avid Blackwell is a theoretical statistician (a mathematician specializing in theories about statistics) who has done important work in set theory and probability theory. (Set theory deals with the nature and relations of a collection of numbers or points. Probability theory is the analysis of the ratio between likely outcomes and possible outcomes.) Known primarily for his contributions to game theory (the analysis of decision-making in situations of conflict or competition), he has also made advances in Bayesian statistical analysis, dynamic programming, and information theory. (Bayesian statistical analysis is a method of using observed data to predict probability. Dynamic programming theory involves making decisions on several interrelated levels. Information theory uses probability in determining ways to maintain and send information). In 1979 Blackwell was awarded the von Neumann Prize by the Operations Research Society of America and the Institute of Management Science. In 1986 he received the R. A. Fisher Award from the Committee of Presidents of

David Blackwell has made important contributions to the mathematical field of game theory.

Mathematician David Blackwell has made significant advances in statistical theory, especially game theory. Blackwell's work in game theory has been used in military combat strategies, as well as in economics and accounting. Although Blackwell gained early prominence in the field of mathematics, he was initially prevented from teaching at major universities because he is African American. He later went on to hold important positions at the University of California, Berkeley, and the RAND Corporation. Blackwell was the first black mathematician elected to the National Academy of Sciences.

Statistical Societies, the most prestigious honor in the field of statistics.

Displays talent in mathematics

David Harold Blackwell was born in Centralia, Illinois, on April 24, 1919, to Grover and Mabel (Johnson) Blackwell. His father operated an inn for the Illinois Central Railroad. As an African American, David Blackwell could have attended either of two racially segregated elementary schools in Centralia. However, his parents sent him to a school that enrolled both black and white students. Showing a high level of curiosity at an early age, he became intrigued with games like checkers and enjoyed thinking about such questions as whether the first player in a checkers match could always win. During high school, as he became increasingly interested in mathematics, he joined the mathematics club. As part of the group's activities, the advisor would challenge members with problems from the *School Science and Mathematics* journal. He then sent their solutions to the publication. Blackwell was identified three times in the magazine as having solved a problem, and one of his solutions was even published.

Chooses to pursue math

After graduating from high school at the age of 16, Blackwell entered the University of Illinois. A family friend had assured him of a job teaching elementary school after graduation. Blackwell was so intrigued with his mathematics courses, however, that he never enrolled in the education courses required for teacher certification. After his freshman year he became concerned at his father's having to borrow money to send him to college. At that point Blackwell began supporting himself with jobs such as washing dishes, waiting tables, and cleaning lab equipment. In spite of his busy work schedule, he completed his studies within three years by taking summer courses and proficiency exams.

Blackwell remained at the University of Illinois to earn a master's degree, tentatively planning to become a high school or college teacher if he could not make his mark as a theoretical mathematician (one whose work is not applied to real situations). As he noted in an interview with Donald J. Albers in *Mathematical People,* "During my first year of graduate work I knew that I could understand mathematics.... But whether I could do anything original I didn't know." When Blackwell completed the degree a year later, he received a fellowship to continue toward a doctorate at the university. Under the direction of American mathematician Joe Doob, he wrote his dissertation on Markov chains. Named after the Russian mathematician Andrei Markov (1856–1922), the theory holds that the probability of each "state" in a sequence of events (chain) depends only on what happens in the preceding state. This research led to Blackwell's first publications, in 1942 and 1945. After receiving his Ph.D. in 1941, he was appointed a Rosenwald Fellow for a year at the Institute for Advanced Study in Princeton, New Jersey. While working at the Institute, he became acquainted with the Hungarian-born American mathematician **John von Neumann** (1903–1957; for more information, see volume 3, pp. 962–963), whose work provided the basis for game theory.

Color limits job opportunities

In 1942 Blackwell launched a job search by writing to each of more than 100 black colleges in the country. Because of prejudice toward African Americans in academic institutions at that time, he simply assumed he would be able to get a job only at a black institution. Nevertheless, he did obtain an interview with Jerzy Neyman, chair of the mathematics department at the University of California at Berkeley. Although Neyman supported hiring Newman, his advice would not be taken by the university until more than a decade later. Blackwell eventually found a job at Southern University in Baton Rouge, Louisiana, where he taught for a year before becoming an instructor at Clark College in Atlanta, Georgia. In 1944 he joined the faculty of Howard University, a prestigious and predominantly black institution in Washington, D.C. That same year Blackwell also married Ann Madison, with whom he later had three sons and five daughters.

Writes important papers on statistics

In 1945 Blackwell shifted the focus of his research to statistics after hearing mathematician Abe Girshick lecture on sequential analysis. (Sequential analysis involves analysis of an experiment that does not have a fixed number of trials). Intrigued by the presentation, Blackwell later contacted Girshick to offer an alternate example to a theorem Girshick had discussed in the lecture. The two mathematicians went on to form an enduring friendship and a fruitful working relationship. Blackwell's first statistical paper, "On an Equation of Wald," appeared in 1946. The following year he published "Conditional Expectation and Unbiased Sequential Estimation," which is perhaps his most significant contribution to modern statistics. In this paper he helped establish the Rao-Blackwell theorem, which relates to the sufficient statistic. (The sufficient statistic is a way of using information from a sample population to draw conclusions about the entire population). Blackwell was promoted to full professor at Howard in 1947 and served as head of the mathematics department until 1954.

Explores problems in game theory

Blackwell developed an interest in game theory while working at the RAND Corporation headquarters in Santa Monica, California, during the summers of 1948 to 1950. Blackwell, Girshick, and a few of their colleagues worked on the theory of duels, a form of two-player zero-sum game. (In a two-player zero-sum game, any amount of gain made by one player results in an equal amount of loss for the other.) The theory of duels involves predicting the outcome of a situation in which two players each hold a gun containing one bullet and walk toward one another. If one fires and misses, that player is required to continue moving toward the opponent. The specific problem Blackwell investigated was how a dueler should decide the best time to shoot. After developing the theory of that situation, he proposed and investigated a more challenging case: Each gun is silent and a dueler knows an opponent has fired only after being hit.

Although Blackwell's own work remained at the theoretical level, he became a well-known authority on game theory. His involvement began when an economist at RAND consulted him about making budget recommendations for the Air Force. The Air Force needed to determine the probability of war breaking out within a given period of time in order to calculate how much money would be required to mobilize troops and equipment.

Work leads to prestigious positions

In 1954 Blackwell and Girshick coauthored the book *Theory of Games and Statistical Decisions*. During that year Blackwell also accepted a professorship in statistics at Berkeley, going on to serve as chair of the department from 1956 to 1961. While he was at Berkeley he made another important contribution. Applying game theory to topology (a branch of mathematics concerned with geometrical configurations), he found a game theory proof for the Kuratowski Reduction Theorem (named after the Polish mathematician Kazimierz Kuratowski). From 1973 to 1975 Blackwell directed the University of California Study Center for the United Kingdom and Ireland. In 1974 he gave the prestigious Rouse Ball Lecture at the University of Cambridge in England.

An enthusiastic researcher and teacher

Blackwell has always been less interested in doing extensive research on a single topic than in exploring whatever problems intrigue him personally. "I guess that's the way scholars *should* work," Blackwell commented in an interview with Morris H. Degroot in *A Century of Mathematics in America*. "Don't worry about the overall importance of the problem; work on it if it looks interesting. I think there's probably a sufficient correlation between interest and importance." The problems Blackwell has found interesting have indeed proven to be important. In addition to being used for military strategy, his work has been applied in a variety of fields, including economics and accounting. Moreover, his enthusiasm for mathematical knowledge made him a thought-provoking and effective teacher who has inspired the careers of many young mathematicians. In his interview with Albers, Blackwell commented on the enjoyment he derived from teaching: "Why do you want to share something beautiful with somebody else? It's because of the pleasure he will get, and in transmitting it you appreciate its beauty all over again."

An active and honored mathematician

Blackwell has been a distinguished and active member of the mathematical community. He served as president of the Institute of Mathematical Statistics and the International Association for Statistics in the Physical Sciences. He is also a member of the American Statistical Association, the National Academy of Sciences (the first black mathematician to be elected), and the American Academy of Arts and Sciences. He has served on the Committee on National Statistics and the Mathematical Sciences Education Board. Retired from Berkeley since 1989, Blackwell has been awarded honorary degrees by Howard, Harvard University, and the National University of Lesotho, among other institutions.

Further Reading

A Century of Mathematics in America, Part III, American Mathematical Society, 1989, pp. 589–615 (reprinted from *Statistical Science,* February 1986, pp. 40–53).

Mathematical People, Contemporary Books, 1985, pp. 18–32.

The Rand Corporation: The First Fifteen Years, Rand, 1963.

Min-Chueh Chang

Born October 10, 1908
T'ai-yüan, China
Died June 5, 1991
Worcester, Massachusetts

Min-Chueh Chang was instrumental in developing oral contraceptives, or birth control pills.

Reproductive biologist Min-Chueh Chang was best known for helping to develop an oral contraceptive, which is commonly known as the birth control pill. Other scientists who worked with Chang were Gregory Goodwin Pincus (1903-1967), an American endocrinologist(a scientist who studies hormones), and John Rock (1890-1984), an American gynecologist and obstetrician (a physician who specializes in women's reproductive health and childbirth). Chang also did innovative work on in vitro fertilization (pregnancy begun by the fertilization of a female egg outside the body), which led to the first "test-tube baby."

Chang was born on October 10, 1908, in T'ai-yüan, China, to Gen Shu and Shih (Laing) Chang. In 1933 he received a bachelor of science degree in animal psychology from Tsing Hua University in Beijing. Shortly after graduating he moved to England, where he studied animal breeding at Cambridge University. Upon earning a Ph.D. in 1941, he went on to four more years of university work as a member of a research group at the

Cambridge University School of Agriculture. In 1945 Chang took a job as a research associate with the Worcester Foundation for Experimental Biology in Shrewsbury, Massachusetts. Nine years later he was named senior and principal scientist at the foundation. In 1951 Chang also joined the staff of Boston University in Boston, Massachusetts, where he became a full professor of reproductive biology in 1961.

Studies effects of progesterone

Soon after arriving at the Worcester Foundation, Chang began a study of progesterone with Pincus, who was an expert on reproduction in mammals. (Progesterone is the female hormone that is released in the body during ovulation, the time when an egg leaves the ovary.) By 1951 the scientists had determined that the role of progesterone in the female body could provide clues about how to create an oral contraceptive for humans. (An oral contraceptive is a substance taken by mouth to prevent fertilization of an egg.) Chang and Pincus realized that increasing blood levels of progesterone could stop ovulation. They experimented with more than 200 substances in order to find natural compounds that imitated the combined actions of estrogen and progesterone. At that point, they began a collaboration with Rock, who headed the Rock Reproduction Clinic in Brookline, Massachusetts. The team developed a pill made of three compounds, including estrogen and progesterone, derived from a wild Mexican yam. They began testing their pill on human subjects, using groups of women in Brookline as well as in Haiti and Puerto Rico.

The role of progesterone

Progesterone is a hormone that controls the process of menstruation in women. (Menstruation is the monthly dis-

Gregory Godwin Pincus, American Biologist

Gregory Goodwin Pincus (1903-1967) conducted research that advanced knowledge of hormones and animal physiology. He also participated in founding the Worcester Foundation for Experimental Biology (WFEB). He is best known, however, for helping Min-Chueh Chang develop the oral contraceptive pill. Having conducted research on sterility and hormones in the 1930s, Pincus turned to the problem of overpopulation in 1951. He had heard about the work of birth control advocate Margaret Sanger, and he wanted to find a way to curb escalating population rates, especially in underdeveloped countries. By 1953 Pincus was working with Chang at the WFEB, studying the effects of steroids (compounds containing hormones and other chemicals) on the fertility of laboratory animals.

Chang discovered a group of compounds called progestins, which are instrumental in stopping ovulation. Pincus took these findings to the G. D. Searle Company, a drug manufacturer, then shifted his research to humans instead of animals. He also brought human reproduction specialists John Rock and Celso Garcia into the project. After the team developed "the Pill," Pincus received the Albert D. Lasker Award in Planned Parenthood (1960), among other honors. He was elected to the National Academy of Sciences in 1965. Pincus died of myeloid metaplasia (a bone-marrow disease), which some speculate was caused by his work with organic solvents (liquids used for dissolving other substances).

charge of blood, secretions, and tissue from the uterus in a nonpregnant state.) Secretion (release) of the hormone into the body usually stops with pregnancy and lactation (the production of milk). Progesterone prepares the walls of the fallopian tubes and uterus for the implantation of a fertilized egg. (The fallopian tubes are a pair of tubes that connect the ovaries with the uterus, the organ in which a fetus will develop during pregnancy.) Progesterone is also the hormone that prevents ovulation (production of eggs) in pregnancy. During the menstrual cycle, the ovum (egg) matures through the action of hormones, including the female hormone estrogen. After the cycle begins, estrogen starts the process of preparing the uterus for pregnancy by developing a network of blood vessels. Blood flows to the area and then increases, causing the lining of the uterus to thicken. Ovulation occurs soon after estrogen levels reach their highest point. Then, as progesterone is secreted at increased levels, the amounts of other hormones decrease and the maturation of other ova (eggs) is temporarily halted.

Develops birth control pill

Although Chang and Pincus were successful in stopping ovulation, they decided to slightly alter the pill they had developed. They wanted to try to eliminate estrogen because they considered it to be unnecessary—they thought progesterone was the key ingredient they needed. Trials of the no-estrogen pill, however, had seriously negative results, including pregnancies and breakthrough bleeding (bleeding between menstrual periods) in the women they tested. Chang and Pincus restored estrogen to the pill, creating a form of contraception that was over ninety-nine percent effective and relatively safe. The combined estrogen-progesterone pill was approved by the U.S. Food and Drug Administration in 1960. It caused a revolution in birth rates and sexual practices in societies throughout the world. According to the London *Times* newspaper, Chang announced that "the pill made possible two sociological changes: the liberation of women and the separation of sex from child-bearing."

Researches in vitro fertilization

Besides producing safe and reliable oral contraceptives, Chang's work had a profound impact on two other areas of fertility research—embryo transfer (placing a fertilized egg into the uterus) and in vitro fertilization. In the 1950s his preliminary research on embryo transfer in rabbits with Cyril Adams created the opportunity for new methods of fertilizing farm animals. Their research also led to the development of in vitro fertilization in humans. Through in vitro fertilization, an infertile woman could have a fertilized egg implanted in her uterus and give birth to what has become known as a "test-tube baby." The first successful in vitro fertilization was conducted by a group led by English doctors **Patrick Steptoe** (1913-1988; for more information, see volume 3, pp. 882-888), and Robert G. Edwards. Their efforts led to the birth of Joy Louise Brown, the first "test-tube baby," on July 25, 1978. For his role in making this accomplishment possible, Chang was presented the Pioneer Award by the International Embryo Transfer Society in 1983. Four years later he was honored for his career achievements at the Fifth World Congress of the In Vitro Fertilization and Embryo Transfer.

Received other honors and awards

Chang married Isabelle C. Chin on May 28, 1948, and they had three children. Four years later he was naturalized as an American citizen. Having contributed to over 350 scientific studies throughout his career, Chang received the Ortho Award in 1950, the Lasker Foundation Award in 1954, and the Ortho Medal in 1961. He was also honored with the Marshall Medal by the British Society for the Study of Fertility in 1971 and was elected to the U.S. National Academy of Sciences in 1990. Chang died of heart failure on June 5, 1991, in Worcester at the age of 82.

Further Reading

Lamming, Eric, "Dr. Min-Chueh Chang," *Journal of Reproduction and Fertility,* January 1992.

"M. C. Chang; Obituary," *London Times,* June 14, 1991.

"M. C. Chang, Scientist, Dies at 82: A Developer of the Birth-Control Pill," *New York Times,* June 7, 1991.

Christine Darden

Born September 10, 1942
Monroe, North Carolina

hristine Darden has had a long and productive career as an aeronautical engineer (a scientist who studies the operation of aircraft) with the National Aeronautics and Space Administration (NASA). In 1989 she was appointed leader of the Sonic Boom Group, a research team that works on methods of reducing the impact of sonic booms from supersonic aircraft (airplanes and spacecraft that travel faster than the speed of sound). The U.S. government supports greater use of supersonic aircraft as a means of high-speed transportation. Nevertheless, disruptions and damage caused by sonic booms have thus far limited the use of faster-than-sound travel.

Christine Darden has conducted important research on how to reduce the effect of sonic booms.

Changes careers

Darden was born Christine Voncile Mann to Noah Horace and Desma Chaney Mann on September 10, 1942, in Monroe, North Carolina. Her father was an insurance agent and her mother was an elementary school teacher. For most of her early

Christine Darden has made advances in reducing the impact of sonic booms produced by aircraft that travel faster than the speed of sound. An aeronautical engineer for the National Aeronautics and Space Administration (NASA), Darden is involved in perfecting supersonic aircraft design. Her goal is to help solve environmental and commercial problems created by sonic booms, which can be damaging as well as disturbing. The work of Darden and other researchers could result in more extensive use of supersonic aircraft as a convenient means of high-speed travel.

schooling Darden attended the Winchester Avenue School in Monroe. She then transferred to Allen High School, a Methodist boarding school in Asheville, North Carolina, where she received her diploma. Darden then earned a bachelor's degree in mathematics from the Hampton Institute in Hampton, Virginia, in 1962, as well as a master's degree at Virginia State College in 1967. After pursuing a career as a mathematics teacher, she switched to engineering. Darden obtained a Ph.D. in that field from The George Washington University in Washington, D. C., in 1983.

Begins work with NASA

Upon graduating from college Darden taught mathematics at a series of high schools before becoming a research assistant in aerosol physics (the study of solids or liquids suspended in gas) at Virginia State College in 1965. When she earned a master's degree in 1967, she accepted a position with NASA at the Langley Research Center in Hampton, Virginia. Initially appointed as a data analyst, Darden was promoted to aerospace engineer within six years. In 1989 she was named leader of the Sonic Boom Group, a research team working on methods of reducing the sonic boom impact from supersonic aircraft.

How a sonic boom occurs

When an airplane accelerates beyond the speed of sound (called Mach 1), it creates a sonic boom—a loud, crashing noise that is caused by turbulent air. As long as the airplane is moving below Mach 1, the disturbed air remains well in front of the craft. But as the craft passes Mach 1 and is flying at supersonic (faster than sound) speeds, a sharp rise in air pressure occurs in front of the craft. In a sense the air molecules are crowded together and collectively collide, producing the supersonic bang. There are many shocks coming from a supersonic aircraft but these shocks usually combine to form two main shocks, one coming from the nose of the aircraft and the other from the tail. Each of the shocks moves at different speeds. If the time difference between the two shock waves is greater than 0.10 seconds, two sonic booms will be heard. This usually occurs when an aircraft like a space shuttle ascends quickly. If the aircraft ascends more slowly, the two booms will sound like only one boom to the observer.

Problems with sonic booms

Sonic booms can be so loud that they break windows and cause structural damage to buildings. Currently, the only supersonic aircraft permitted in the United States are military planes—and they are restricted to high altitudes so they will be create minimal disturbance. The Concorde, a supersonic commercial transport plane, is also allowed to fly, but only in limited areas. Operated by companies in Britain and France, the Concorde cannot fly over the continental United States and is permitted to land in restricted coastal areas. Although commercial supersonic flight is a desirable form of transportation because it saves time, noise problems have prevented it from being used more widely.

Researches new aircraft designs

In an effort to reduce noise problems from supersonic aircraft, Darden has used complex mathematical calculations to find ways to minimize sonic booms. Her research group designs and tests new wing and nose-cone shapes for aerodynamic quality. Monitoring the ability of a plane to travel through air with the least possible resistance, they look for sonic properties (the amount of sound created). Although sonic booms will not be entirely eliminated, advances in aerodynamic engineering may soften or redirect the sound so that it is less disturbing and damaging. Additionally, Darden is investigating other environmental impacts of supersonic flight, including the effects of sonic booms on the ozone layer (the layer of the atmosphere that shields the Earth from the Sun's harmful ultraviolet rays).

Advocates mentors for students

When an interviewer once asked Darden how and why she became interested in science, she responded: "The 'power' of mathematics and physical principles in understanding why things work has always fascinated me. I've had parents, teachers, and some supervisors who have encouraged me to pursue what I enjoyed. People often ask me if I have had a `mentor.' While I have never formally been in a mentor program, there have been many adults along the way who have offered words of advice [that] have helped me in my career. We must somehow get our students to accept mentorship whenever and however offered."

Darden is married to Walter L. Darden, Jr., a middle school science teacher, with whom she has two children. She has been active in local school systems, the Presbyterian Church, the National Technical Association, and the American Institute of Aeronautics and Astronautics. She has received numerous honors, among them the Dr. A. T. Weathers Technical Achievement Award from the National Technical Association in 1985. She was also chosen one of the 100 Top Black Business and Professional Women by *Dollars and Sense* magazine in 1986 and named Black Engineer of the Year in Government by the Mobile Oil Council of Engineering Deans in 1988. The Langley Research Center honored Darden with the Certificate of Outstanding Performance in 1989, 1991, and 1992. The author or coauthor of over 40 publications, Darden frequently gives presentations to professional and community groups.

Further Reading

"Sonic Boom," *McGraw-Hill Encyclopedia of Science and Technology,* Volume 16, McGraw-Hill, 1990, p. 680.

"Supersonic Flight," *McGraw-Hill Encyclopedia of Science and Technology,* Volume 17, McGraw-Hill, 1990, p. 674.

Van Sertima, Ivan, editor, *Blacks in Science: Ancient and Modern,* Transaction Books, 1985.

Philo T. Farnsworth

Born August 19, 1906
Indian Creek, Utah
Died March 11, 1971
Holladay, Utah

On a statue erected in honor of Philo T. Farnsworth in the U. S. Capitol Statuary Hall, a plaque commemorates the inventor as the "Father of Television." When Farnsworth was only 14, he sketched his ideas for harnessing electricity to transmit images and shared them with his high school chemistry teacher. He thus became the first person to propose that pictures could be televised electronically. By the time he was 21 he had proven his concept by televising the world's first electronically produced image. When he died in 1971, Farnsworth had been awarded over 100 television-related patents, some of which are still in use today.

Philo T. Farnsworth is considered by many to be the "father of television."

Early fascination with electricity

Farnsworth was born in Indian Creek, Utah, on August 19, 1906, the first of five children of Serena (Bastian) Farnsworth and Lewis Edwin Farnsworth. He was named after his grandfather, Philo Taylor Farnsworth I, a leader of Mormon pioneers

Inventor Philo T. Farnsworth was the first person to propose a way to transmit images electronically and to develop a working television system. Fransworth demonstrated his invention in 1927, when he was only 21 years old. While another inventor, **Vladimir Zworykin** (1889–1982; for more information, see entry in volume 3, pp. 1017–1022), claimed to have invented television even earlier, Farnsworth was given the patent for the idea. A productive inventor who also developed an early electron microscope and initiated the use of radar, Farnsworth is best remembered as "the father of television."

who settled in southwestern Utah. Although there was no electricity in Indian Creek, Farnsworth learned as much as he could about it from his father and from reading magazines. Edwin Farnsworth, who was a farmer, entertained his son with discussions about such modern inventions as the telephone, the gramophone, and locomotives. The family later moved to a farm in Idaho that had its own power plant. After poking and probing and eventually mastering the lighting system, Philo was soon put in charge of maintaining the plant. It had never run so smoothly. Even before Farnsworth entered high school he was adept at inventing gadgets, and he won a national invention contest when he was 13 years old.

Dreams of television

In 1920 Farnsworth read that inventors were attempting to transmit visual images by mechanical means. For the next two years he worked on an electronic version of the concept. He perfected the basic design for a device in 1922, then showed sketches of his appliance to his high school chemistry teacher, Justin Tolman. Little did they know that their discussions would later be critical in settling a patent dispute between Farnsworth and Vladimir Zworykin, his competitor at the Radio Corporation of America (RCA).

Investors support television research

Farnsworth took correspondence courses in physics from the University of Utah, then enrolled at Brigham Young University (BYU) in Provo, Utah. Largely self-taught, he so impressed two of his BYU chemistry professors with his ideas about television that they gave him the run of the chemistry and

Philo T. Farnsworth with one of his early television systems.

glass labs to start work on his theories. In 1924 Farnsworth's father died, leaving the young man with the responsibility of supporting the family. After a short time in the navy, he moved to Salt Lake City, Utah, to work as a canvasser (fundraiser) for the Community Chest, a local charity fund. Farnsworth became acquainted with George Everson, the businessman who was organizing the fund-raising effort, and his associate Leslie Gorrell. When Farnsworth told Everson and Gorrell about his ideas for television, they invested $6000 in his venture. With additional backing from a group of bankers in San Francisco, California, Farnsworth found a research lab and set a one-year deadline for proving his concepts.

Builds the first television system

On May 27, 1926, Farnsworth was married to his college sweetheart Elma Gardner, who was known as Pem. The next day they left for San Francisco, where Farnsworth would operate his lab. With assistance from Pem and her brother Cliff, Farnsworth designed and built all the components for his first television system—from the vacuum transmitter tubes (devices that transmit electromagnetic rays) to the image scanner (the camera that records images) and the receiver (a device that converts electromagnetic rays into images). The key invention was the Image Dissector camera, which scanned slowly in one direction and then more quickly in the opposite direction. The camera made possible much greater scanning speeds than had been achieved at the time. All television receivers today still use this basic scanning system. Farnsworth was granted a patent for his device. (A patent is a government grant stating that the inventor is the only person who can manufacture and sell the invention.)

On September 7, 1927, three weeks before his deadline, Farnsworth gathered his friends and engineering colleagues in a room adjoining the lab. He amazed them by showing an image of Pem on his new system. It became the first two-dimensional picture ever transmitted by television. Farnsworth's backers continued their support for another year, and in 1928 the first television system was unveiled to the world. In 1929 bankers who had invested in his research formed a company called Television Laboratories Inc. Farnsworth was named vice president and director of research.

Competes with RCA

Around the same time, however, RCA had begun aggressively competing for control of the emerging television market. RCA challenged Farnsworth's patent, stating that Zworykin had actually invented the first television system. The testimony of Tollman, Farnsworth's high school teacher, confirmed that Farnsworth had in fact documented his ideas one year before Zworykin's. This was only the first of many challenges from RCA, but in the end the corporate giant was forced to work out a cross-licensing (sharing) arrangement with Farnsworth. He eventually licensed his television patents to others working in the growing industry, letting them refine and develop his basic inventions. After his patents were first licensed in Germany and Great Britain, the U.S. Federal Communications Commission finally assigned broadcast channels in the United States.

Produces more innovations

During his early years in San Francisco, Farnsworth did other important work. He made the first cold cathode-ray tube (a vacuum tube that transmits electromagnetic rays) and designed the first simple electron microscope (a microscope that produces images with an electron lens). Farnsworth also perfected a means for using radio waves to sense direction, which is now known as radar (the acronym for radio detection and ranging). Farnsworth eventually established his own company, the Farnsworth Radio and Television Corporation. It boomed during World War II (1939–1946) while developing electronic surveillance equipment and other devices for the government. After the war the company took a downturn and was sold to the International Telephone and Telegraph Company (ITT) in 1949. Farnsworth remained with ITT for some time as a research consultant. Late in life he turned his attention to the field of atomic energy. Farnsworth died of emphysema on March 11, 1971, in Holladay, a suburb of Salt Lake City.

Honored for his achievements

Farnsworth received more than 300 patents during his career. For his pioneering work he was presented the First Gold Medal by the National Television Broadcasters Association in 1944. He was also awarded honorary doctorates in science from Indiana Technical College and Brigham Young University. Farnsworth's picture appeared on a 21-cent stamp, which was issued in 1983. He was honored with induction into the National Inventors Hall of Fame in 1984, and the Philo T. Farnsworth Memorial Museum was dedicated in Rigby, Idaho, in 1988.

Further Reading

Dedication of the Statue of Philo T. Farnsworth, Proceedings in the U.S. Capitol Rotunda, U.S. Government Printing Office, 1990.

Everson, George, *The Story of Television: The Life of Philo T. Farnsworth,* Norton, 1949.

Farnsworth, Elma, *Distant Vision: Romance and Discovery on an Invisible Frontier,* Pemberlykent, 1990.

May, Dennis, "Philo T. Farnsworth: The Father of Television," *BYU Today,* May 1989, pp. 33–36.

Sophie Germain

Born April 1, 1776
Paris, France
Died June 27, 1831
Paris, France

Sophie Germain was an internationally respected mathematician of the late 1700s and early 1800s. During her lifetime women were discouraged, often forbidden, from pursuing higher education and other intellectual activities. Despite the disapproval of her parents and a rule that barred females from technical school in Paris, Germain managed to learn high-level mathematics independently. Her skill and insight in math earned her the respect of prominent European mathematicians. She contributed important work to such fields as number theory and the mathematics of acoustics (the science of sound) and elasticity (the quality of a strained body to regain its shape). Germain wrote a prize-winning paper on elasticity that received an award from the French Academy of Sciences. As a result of her work in applied mathematics, she has been called one of the founders of mathematical physics (the science that deals with the interaction of matter and energy).

Sophie Germain was a leading French mathematician in the early 1800s.

43

Sophie Germain was a self-taught mathematician who earned the respect of many of Europe's greatest intellectuals in the 1700s and 1800s. She developed original concepts in number theory and the mathematics of acoustics and elasticity. Germain shared her ideas with other top mathematicians and made several new discoveries in the field. She also devised a partial solution to the problem known as Fermat's Last Theorem, which provided a basis for expansion of her work by twentieth-century mathematicians. Branching into an entirely new area, Germain developed a mathematical explanation for the unique motion of vibrations on elastic surfaces. She has since been given credit for helping to launch the field of mathematical physics.

Isolated by French Revolution

Germain was born on April 1, 1776, in Paris, France. She was the daughter of Marie-Madeleine and Ambroise-François Germain. Her father was a politically active merchant who helped to create the legislative body known as the Constituent Assembly. He later became a director of the Bank of France. Germain grew up during an extremely violent political period in France. She was 13 at the outbreak of the French Revolution(a chaotic and bloody event in which people fought to take political power away from the royalty and create a democratic government). During the Revolution the streets of Paris were filled with large demonstrations and public executions, and widespread hunger swept the city. Although Germain's parents were wealthy enough to protect her from these events, she was required to spend much of her time isolated in the family home.

Inspired by ancient mathematician

One of the few sources of information and entertainment for Germain was her father's library, which contained scores of books on a wide range of topics. Here she found material to occupy her curious, intelligent mind. Because girls were not allowed to attend public schools, her studies at home became her education. While reading a history of mathematics, she was inspired by the story of Archimedes, an ancient Greek mathematician. Archimedes was killed during a military invasion as he was deep in thought over a geometry problem. He was so preoccupied that he had not heard the approach of the soldier who dealt him the fatal blow. Deciding that such an engrossing subject must be a fascinating and important pursuit, Germain vowed to become a mathematician herself.

Discouraged by parents

Germain's parents did not approve of their daughter's decision—at the time it was considered unhealthy and unnatural for a young woman to devote too much time to intellectual activities. Taking extreme measures to prevent her from studying, they removed candles from her room. To ensure that she would stay in bed and sleep at night, they prohibited a fire being lit in her room. But a determined Germain hid the candles. On cold winter nights she wrapped herself in blankets so she could stay up reading and working on calculations. After her parents discovered her asleep at her desk one morning, they realized that fighting their daughter's ambition was useless. Now free to study as she pleased, Germain taught herself the Greek and Latin languages and mathematics. Her knowledge of Latin and math became sufficient enough for her to tackle the works of English mathematician and physicist **Isaac Newton** (1642-1727; for more information, see entry in volume 4, pp. 176-184) and Swiss mathematician Leonhard Euler (1707-1783).

Finds a mentor

By the age of 18, Germain realized she needed instruction beyond the books in her father's library. She began borrowing lecture notes from friends who were attending the École Polytechnique (technical school)in Paris. On the faculty of the school were some of the most important mathematicians of the day, including Joseph Louis Lagrange (1736-1813) and Gaspard Monge (1746-1818). Italian-born mathematician Lagrange had conducted work on the orbits of the Sun-Earth-Moon system as well as the planet Jupiter and its four suns. His calculations established regions now called Lagrangian points that are used to determine the equilibrium (state of balance) of celestial bodies. Monge was a French mathematician who was the first to liquefy sulfur dioxide, a substance that at room temperature is normally a gas but changes to a liquid at minus 98 degrees Fahrenheit. He was also the first director of École Polytechnique.

Leonhard Euler, Swiss Mathematician

Swiss mathematician Leonhard Euler (1707-1783) made significant accomplishments in trigonometry, algebra, and calculus. At the age of 16 he received a master's degree from the University of Basel in Switzerland, but he had a difficult time finding an academic position because he was so young. Finally, when he was 26, Euler was appointed professor of mathematics at the Petersburg Academy in Russia. During his years at the academy he did important work with the Dutch-born Swiss mathematician Daniel Bernoulli (1700-1782). Euler also devised a number of trigonometric and geometric theorems and rules known by his name. In 1735 he lost sight in his right eye as a result of his observations of the sun. In 1741, at the invitation of King Frederick H of Prussia (1712-1786), Euler left Russia to head the Academy of Science in Berlin (in present-day Germany). In 1760, during the Seven Years' War, invading Russian troops demonstrated they still remembered and respected Euler by sparing his Berlin home from destruction. He returned to St. Petersburg in 1766. That same year Euler lost sight in his left eye, but continued working until his death in 1783.

Germain sharpened her study of mathematics by following all of the classes at the school through her friends' notes. At the end of the term, when students were required to submit a paper to Lagrange, Germain did the assignment under the false name of Le Blanc. Lagrange was so impressed with her paper that he went in search of the author. Upon discovering the true identity of Le Blanc, he visited Germain's home to congratulate her personally and to encourage her work. Lagrange became Germain's mentor in mathematics, pointing her in new directions of study and discussing ideas with her.

Corresponds with European scholars

Lagrange was only one of several prominent mathematicians who assisted Germain in her career. She corresponded with a number of well-known scholars in order to further her education and independent work. They also exchanged letters about other topics such as biology, literature, and philosophy. One of Germain's major interests was number theory, an area in which she made many contributions during her correspondence with French mathematician Adrien-Marie Legendre (1752-1833). In the second edition of his book *Théorie des nombres* (*Theory of Numbers*), Legendre gave Germain credit for important discoveries. Under her pseudonym of Le Blanc, she also began exchanging letters with German mathematician **Karl Friedrich Gauss** (1777-1855; for more information, see entry in volume 2, pp. 371-375) after reading his book, *Disquisitiones arithmeticae* (*Disquisitions of Arithmetic*). Gauss complemented her for her understanding of the complex ideas of number theory. Once he discovered her true identity, he gave even more praise to the woman who had made so many accomplishments in a men's field.

Devises partial proof of Fermat's Last Theorem

A significant result of Germain's work in number theory was the partial solution to the "Last Theorem" of French mathematician Pierre de Fermat (1601-1665). The theorem stated that in the formula $x^n + y^n = z^n$, values for x, y, and z could never be found if n is a whole number greater than two. While Germain could not prove this to be true for all values of n, she was able to show that it was true when n was a prime number less than 100. On the basis of Germain's work, later mathematicians were able to prove the impossibility of the equation when values of n are prime numbers less than 41,000,000. Yet none were ever able to arrive at a complete solution. In 1993, however, English-born American mathematician Andrew Wiles (1953-)announced that he had arrived at a tentative proof of Fermat's Last Theorem.

Ventures into a new area

Germain also had an impact on the application of mathematics to the physical realms of acoustics and elasticity. In the early 1800s, the French Academy of Sciences sponsored a competition in which participants had to develop the best mathematical theory to explain the behavior of vibrations on an elastic surface. The challenge was inspired by the experiments of German physicist Ernst Chladni (1756-1824). Chladni found that when a powdery substance was placed on a glass or metal plate and the plate was made to vibrate, curves would be formed by the powder. These curves came to be called Chladni figures. Chladni's challenge was to explain how the figures were formed. Many scholars, including Germain's mentor Lagrange, did not attempt an explanation because they contended that the proper mathematical tools for the task had not yet been developed. But Germain decided to enter the competition.

Wins grand prize

Germain's first attempt at an explanation for the formation of Chladni figures, in 1811, was flawed as the result of mistakes she had made in her self-training in calculus. But Lagrange pointed out her errors, allowing her to submit an improved version when the competition was opened again in 1813 (no one had arrived at an acceptable solution during the first competition). This version earned Germain an honorable mention from the Academy, but a winning answer still had not been found. The Academy held yet another contest in 1815. This time, Germain submitted a revised solution and it earned the grand prize.

Publishes mathematical and philosophical works

Germain's accomplishment secured her rank among the top mathematicians in the world. She was celebrated with a special gathering at the prestigious Institut de France and invited to attend the group's meetings—an honor that had never before been given to a woman. Her prize-winning work was published in 1821. Germain went on to publish several other papers on the theory of elasticity. In addition, she wrote two philosophical books that were published after her death: *Pensées diverses* (*Diverse Thoughts*), a series of short essays on the lives of earlier scientists and mathematicians, and *Con-*

sidérations générales sur l'état des sciences et des lettres (*General Considerations on the State of Science and Letters.*) In the latter work she argued that there are many similarities between the sciences and humanities and that they should not be considered separate fields.

Selected for honorary degree

Germain's well-known brilliance in mathematics brought her invitations to join the circles of the greatest intellectuals in France. Outside her homeland, her friend Gauss arranged for her to receive an honorary doctorate degree from the University of Göttingen in 1831. Unfortunately, Germain had been stricken with breast cancer and she died on June 26, 1831, before the honor could be awarded. Eighty years later, a biographer wrote of Germain: "All things considered, she was probably the most profoundly intellectual woman that France has ever produced."

Further Reading

Dictionary of Scientific Biography, Volume V, Scribner's, 1972, pp. 375-76.

Ogilvie, Marilyn Bailey, *Women in Science: Antiquity through the Nineteenth Century,* MIT Press, 1986, pp. 90-92.

Osen, Lynn M., *Women in Mathematics,* MIT Press, 1974, pp. 83-93.

Lillian Gilbreth

Born May 24, 1878
Oakland, California
Died January 2, 1972
Phoenix, Arizona

Lillian Gilbreth pioneered the use of psychology in the field of industrial management.

Psychologist and industrial engineer Lillian Gilbreth was the first person to scientifically evaluate how the mental and physical health of workers influences productivity in business and industry. Before she introduced industrial management theory in the early twentieth century, most employers thought of workers primarily as machines—they were expected to perform even the most tiring or awkward tasks at the same speed all day, day after day. But this attitude prevented improvement in the production and quality of work. Gilbreth used scientific and psychological methods (observation and study of human behavior) to analyze the workplace. She found ways to make tasks less tiring and stressful so that workers would be more productive. Eventually becoming standard procedure in industrial management, her methods were adopted as a field of study at many universities in the United States.

Wants to be a teacher

Gilbreth was born Lillian Evelyn Moller on May 24, 1878, in Oakland, California. She was the oldest of nine children of William and Annie Delger Moller, who were strongly influenced by their German heritage and ran a religious household. Her mother was the daughter of a prominent Oakland businessman, and her father was a dedicated husband who had sold his New York business to become a partner in a hardware company in California. Because Annie Moller was in poor health, Gilbreth had responsibilities at home and did not start school until she was nine. She excelled academically, however, especially in literature and music, which she studied with composer John Metcalfe. Gilbreth was also well traveled as a teenager, visiting New York, Boston, and Chicago with her father.

Although Gilbreth's father was proud of her talents, he did not believe women should attend college. Nevertheless she convinced him to let her enter the University of California and live at home, where she continued to care for her sisters. She studied modern languages and philosophy, and her goal was to teach English. When Gilbreth received her bachelor's degree in 1900, she was the first woman in the university's history to speak on commencement day. She entered Columbia University in New York City to pursue a master's degree in literature, but illness forced her to return home during her first year. In 1902 Gilbreth completed her master's degree at the University of California, where she immediately began work on a Ph.D.

Changes direction of career

The following year Gilbreth took a break from her studies to travel abroad. On a stopover in Boston she met Frank Gilbreth (1868–1924), the owner of a construction business. At the time he was developing motion-study techniques (methods to minimize wasted time and energy and increase productivity in industry). They exchanged letters for 10

Lillian Gilbreth was one of the founders of modern industrial management (the study of how to improve productivity in the workplace). She combined psychology with the study of management in the early twentieth century, creating a method for businesses to help workers become more productive. Gilbreth broke new ground with her book *The Psychology of Management,* which concerned the health of the industrial worker. An outstanding scholar who introduced her theories to major universities throughout the United States, Gilbreth became widely known for making human relations an important part of management theory and practice.

months, then were married on October 19, 1904. The couple went on to have 12 children, two of whom later recorded their humorous memories of family life in the popular books *Cheaper by the Dozen* and *Belles on Their Toes.*

Work was the focus of Frank Gilbreth's life. Wanting an equal partnership with his new wife, he began teaching her about the construction business. When he saw that her interest in the human aspects of industry complemented his ideas, he encouraged her to work with him. The mental and physical health of workers was not an area of concern for businesses at that time. But Lillian Gilbreth saw that workers' health could have a great effect on the amount and speed of the work they could produce. Thus she shifted the focus of her doctoral studies from literature to psychology.

Becomes expert on worker fatigue

When the Gilbreths were married, Lillian took on several major responsibilities—continuing her academic work, starting a large family, and becoming acquainted with the business world. Beginning as a systems manager in Frank's consulting business, she was soon acknowledged as an expert in the study of worker fatigue and production. Her reputation was partially a result of her emphasis on precise measurement in data collection. Among Gilbreth's other contributions were analysis of machinery and tools in the workplace, invention of improved and simplified tools, and standardization of tasks. Most importantly, her work led to a greater understanding of the importance of the welfare of the individual in business operations. This concept was instrumental in wider acceptance of her husband's research on increasing productivity.

Introduces psychology in management

In 1910 the Gilbreths moved their growing family to Providence, Rhode Island, where Lillian entered Brown University to continue her doctoral studies in psychology. She wrote about industrial management from a scientific and psychological perspective. A lecture she delivered at the Dartmouth College Conference on Scientific Management in 1911 on the relationship between management and psychology became the basis for her doctoral dissertation.

In 1913 the Gilbreths started the Summer School of Scientific Management. They trained professionals to teach new ideas about management, emphasizing the study of motion and psychology. Tuition was free, admission was by invitation, and classes were well attended by professors and business people from the United States and around the world. The Gilbreths ran the school for four years. Gilbreth received her Ph.D. from Brown in 1915. Her dissertation had already been published as a book, *The Psychology of Management,* the previous year. She became the first theorist in industrial management to emphasize and document the importance of the use of psychology in supervising workers.

Becomes respected consultant

After her husband's death in 1924, Gilbreth moved her family to her home state of California. She continued a productive pace, providing a new home and college educations for her children, maintaining a consulting business, and teaching and conducting research. Gilbreth also became a highly respected businesswoman. The Johnson & Johnson Company hired her consulting firm to train their employees. For Macy's, the New York City department store, she studied the working conditions of salespeople to investigate techniques to reduce fatigue. Other clients included the Dennison Company and Sears, Roebuck and Company. She started a new school called Gilbreth Research Associates, which specialized in the needs and interests of retail businesses. By 1929, however, several universities were studying motion in their engineering schools,

Frank Gilbreth, American Engineer

During the early months of World War I (1914–1918) Frank Gilbreth (1868–1924) went to Germany to study industrial plants. This study became the basis of "Motion Study for the Handicapped," a paper he and Lillian Gilbreth wrote upon his return. While in Germany he introduced motion theories, conducted tests, installed new machines, and established laboratories. As injured soldiers returned from the war, Gilbreth developed improved surgical procedures. He was the first person to use motion-picture photography in operating rooms for the education of surgeons. He also became an expert in the rehabilitation of injured soldiers. He visited hospitals throughout Europe, watching the motions of injured soldiers, and developed ways to teach them to manage their daily activities.

The Gilbreths presented their paper at the Tenth Sagamore Sociological Conference in 1917. In addition to describing new methods of rehabilitation, the paper included other ideas for treatment of the handicapped. Among them was a typewriter with all capital letters, which eliminated the need for a shift key that requires two-handed operation. Perhaps the most interesting aspect of Frank Gilbreth's work during this period was the study of the 17 fundamental motions used to perform physical tasks, such as search, find, select, grasp, and position. He created a visual chart for adapting jobs to injured soldiers, which illustrated each fundamental motion. The chart facilitated the visual dissection of tasks and the substitution of motions from one task to another.

using laboratories complete with photographic devices and movement measurement tools. Convinced that her ideas would now be carried on, Gilbreth closed the school.

First woman engineering professor at Purdue

That same year Gilbreth traveled to Tokyo, Japan, to speak at the First World Power Congress. She was also invited to lecture at universities such as Stanford, Harvard, Yale, and the Massachusetts Institute of Technology. She joined the Purdue University faculty in 1935 as a professor of management, becoming the first woman professor in the engineering school.

When the United States entered World War II (1939–1945), Gilbreth worked as a consultant at the Arma Plant in Brooklyn, New York, which handled large navy contracts. As the staff grew from a few hundred people to 11,000, she managed personnel restructuring and worker training. Especially notable was Gilbreth's exercise program for the women employees. Although she was by then over 60 years old, Gilbreth kept up with the younger women in their exercises.

Remains active in later life

In 1948 Gilbreth began teaching at the Newark College of Engineering in New Jersey, where she stayed for two years. She went on to teach on the Pacific island of Formosa (also known as Taiwan) from 1953 to 1954 and at the University of Wisconsin in 1955. Gilbreth remained professionally active well into her eighties, speaking and writing on management issues. She was also a widely sought speaker on human relations problems in management. During her career Gilbreth received over a dozen honorary degrees. She was the recipient of the Hoover Medal from the American Society of Civil Engineers (1966). Numerous other engineering and management professional organizations around the world also recognized her pioneering work with honors and awards. Gilbreth died in Phoenix, Arizona, on January 2, 1972.

Further Reading

Carey, Ernestine G., and Frank B. Gilbreth, Jr., *Belles on Their Toes,* Crowell, 1950.

Carey, Ernestine G., and Frank B. Gilbreth, Jr., *Cheaper by the Dozen,* Crowell, 1948, expanded edition, 1963.

Gilbreth, Lillian, *The Psychology of Management,* Sturgis and Walton, 1914.

Gilbreth, Lillian, *The Quest of the One Best Way: A Sketch of the Life of Frank Bunker Gilbreth,* Society of Industrial Engineers, 1926.

Haas, Violet B., and Carolyn C. Perrucci, editors, *Women in Scientific and Engineering Professions,* University of Michigan Press, 1984.

"Lillian Moller Gilbreth: Remarkable First Lady of Engineering," Society of Women Engineers Newsletter, Volume 24, 1978.

Spriegel, W. R., and C. E. Meyers, editors, *The Writings of the Gilbreths,* Richard D. Irwin, 1953.

Yost, Edna, *Frank and Lillian Gilbreth, Partners for Life,* Rutgers University Press, 1949.

Hippocrates of Cos

*Born c. 460 B.C.
Cos, Greece
Died c. 377 B.C.
Larissa, Thessaly, Greece*

Hippocrates (pronounced "hih-POK-ruh-tees"), a famous Greek physician, is considered the "father of medicine." A leader of the medical school on the island of Cos in the fourth and fifth century B.C., he may also have been its founder. Under his influence Cos became the center of a new approach to medicine that rejected reliance on magic and superstition. Hippocrates and his followers developed the practice of observation and experimentation to determine the natural causes of disease. Surviving records from the Hippocratic school provided the basis for the scientific practice of medicine. The results of this method are evident today in the "Hippocratic Oath," a vow commonly taken by modern doctors.

Hippocrates has been called the father of medicine.

Receives medical education

Little is known about Hippocrates's life. According to historical accounts, he was born on the Greek island of Cos around 460 B.C. to Heraclides and Phenaretes. Several sources

The ancient Greek physician Hippocrates is credited with leading a revolutionary movement at the medical school at Cos. Rejecting the use of magic and superstition in the treatment of disease, he and his followers instead championed reliance on observation and experiments to learn about natural causes of disease. Although many of Hippocrates's beliefs about the body are now considered inaccurate, his insistence on removing magic from the practice of medicine helped pave the way for the scientific method in medical studies.

indicate that the men in his family had traditionally been magicians, while others suggest he was descended from a line of physicians. Because the practice of diagnosing and healing illness was largely based on magic at the time, both of these views could be close to the truth. Hippocrates supposedly received most of his medical education from his father and another man, Herodicos of Selymbria. Some stories claim that as a young man he also visited Egypt to study medicine.

Becomes a famous physician

Cos was the site of one of the great medical schools of ancient Greece. Hippocrates taught at the school for many years and was well known during his lifetime. He traveled widely, lecturing in Greece and probably throughout the ancient Middle East. References to him in the writings of the Greek philosopher Plato (c. 428-348 B.C.) indicate that he was also a famous doctor in the city of Athens. The height of Hippocrates's career apparently spanned the period of the Peloponnesian War (431 B.C. to 404 B.C.). He died around 377 B.C. in Larissa, Thessaly, an eastern region of Greece.

Ideas documented in *Corpus Hippocraticum*

Hippocrates is regarded as the father of medicine because he taught the separation of medical study and practice from myth and superstition. Evidence of his reliance on fact, observation, and clinical experience comes from the *Corpus Hippocraticum* ("Hippocratic Collection"). This series of 60 or 70 books appears to have been collected in the great Library of Alexandria after about 200 B.C. While few if any of the texts were written by Hippocrates himself, they are assumed to be an account of his medical teachings and philosophy. The *Corpus Hippocraticum* later served as a basis for Western medicine.

Rejects magic and superstition

According to the *Corpus Hippocraticum,* the Hippocratic approach emphasized that disease arises from natural causes, not from the whims of the gods. Since the books contain dozens of detailed clinical descriptions of diseases, it is clear that Hippocrates insisted on careful observation of medical conditions. He recommended as little interference as possible with the body's own ability to heal. Instead, his treatment focused on diet, rest, and cleanliness. Hippocrates also advanced the doctrine of the four humors, which stated that disease results from an imbalance among the four essential body fluids—blood, phlegm, black bile, and yellow bile.

Inspires Hippocratic Oath

Another important feature of Hippocrates's method was insistence on a high standard of behavior for physicians, a statement of medical ethics now known as the Hippocratic Oath. Developed over 2000 years ago, the oath probably reflects the views of Hippocrates while not actually having been written by him. When physicians took this pledge they vowed to serve only the benefit of the patient and to keep confidential anything seen or heard in the course of treatment. Many medical students today still take a form of the Hippocratic Oath upon receiving their degrees.

Further Reading

Asimov, Isaac, *Asimov's Biographical Dictionary of Science and Technology,* new revised ed., Doubleday, 1972, pp. 13-14.

Dictionary of Scientific Biography, Volume VI, Scribner's, 1972, pp. 418-31.

McGraw-Hill Dictionary of World Biography, Volume 5, McGraw-Hill, 1973, pp. 282-84.

Grace Hopper

Born December 9, 1906
New York City
Died January 1, 1992

"Most people are scared to death of change and I am not. Some of my most rewarding experiences have been in trying to do something in a new way."

Grace Hopper rose through U.S. Navy ranks to become a rear admiral at age 82, but she is best known for her contribution to the design and development of COmmon Business Oriented Language (COBOL) computer programming. Her professional life spanned the growth of modern computer science. As a young navy lieutenant Hopper programmed an early calculating machine, the forerunner of the modern computer. By the end of her career she had created sophisticated software programs for microcomputers. In 1991 President George Bush presented Hopper with the National Medal of Technology "for her pioneering accomplishments" in the field of data processing.

Fascinated by gadgets

Admiral Hopper was born Grace Brewster Murray on December 9, 1906, in New York City, the first of three children of Mary Campbell Van Horne Murray and Walter

Fletcher Murray. Hopper's parents encouraged her to develop her natural mechanical abilities. As a child she took apart household gadgets to see how they worked, but sometimes she could not put them back together. Once, after she had disassembled all seven clocks in the house in an effort to find one she could rebuild, her mother limited her to a single clock. Hopper's grandfather, who had been a senior civil engineer for New York City, inspired her enthusiasm for geometry and mathematics. An even greater inspiration was her father. When she was a teenager her father's legs were amputated because of severe arteriosclerosis (hardening of the arteries), and he had to walk on heavy wooden legs with the aid of canes. Seeing him resume his normal activities in spite of this inconvenience, Hopper, her sister Mary, and her brother Roger became determined to excel in their studies.

Becomes college professor

Hopper was a good student during her years at private girls schools in New York and New Jersey. In fact, she received a double promotion (skipped a grade) in grade school. After graduating from the Hartridge School in Plainfield, New Jersey, Hopper enrolled at Vassar College in Poughkeepsie, New York, to major in mathematics. Upon receiving a bachelor's degree in 1928, she went on to Yale University in New Haven, Connecticut. She received a master's degree in 1930 and a doctorate in 1934, both in mathematics. This was a rare achievement at the time, especially for a woman. Despite bleak prospects for female mathematicians in teaching beyond the high school level, Vassar hired Hopper first as an instructor then as a professor of mathematics. She taught at Vassar until the beginning of World War II (1939–1945). Her husband, Vincent Foster Hop-

IMPACT

Computer scientist Grace Hopper played an important role in the development of early computers. She is best known for perfecting the Common Business Oriented Language (COBOL). Throughout her career Hopper was concerned with making computers a useful tool for everyday work—not just a machine for scientists. In designing COBOL she utilized English-language commands instead of complex mathematical codes so that the program would work on any computer. By facilitating the sharing of information, Hopper's advances led to improved systems in both the military and private industry.

"Bug" and "Debug"

The problem of computer errors continued to plague the Mark team and led to the now-famous story of Grace Hopper being the first person to use the terms "bug" and "debug." One day in 1945, noticing that the Mark computer had failed, Hopper and her colleagues discovered a moth in the machine's circuits. Removing the insect, they taped it to a page in Hopper's log book. She labeled the moth "the first actual bug found." Since then the words "bug" and "debug," which are now familiar terms in the computer vocabulary, have been attributed to Hopper. Language experts have disputed this story, however, saying that both words had been in use among engineers long before Hopper and her team claimed to have originated them.

per, whom she had married in 1930, taught at New York University. They were divorced in 1945.

Works on earliest computer

In 1943 Hopper joined the U.S. Naval Reserve, attending midshipman's school and obtaining a commission as a lieutenant a year later. She was immediately assigned to the Bureau of Ships Computation Project at Harvard University in Cambridge, Massachusetts. Directed by noted American physicist and Harvard professor Howard Aiken (1900–1973), the project involved developing a machine that would assist the navy in making rapid, difficult computations (calculations) for wartime operations. It turned out that Aiken was in the process of designing what would become America's first programmable digital computer, the Mark I. For Hopper the experience was both frustrating and rewarding. Although she had no background in computing, she was handed a code book (instructions for the computer) and asked to begin making computations. Along with several other naval officers assigned to the project, Hopper plunged into the works of Charles Babbage (1792–1871), a British computer pioneer. In the 1830s Babbage had proposed an "analytical engine" that would operate with punch cards, and his plans helped Hopper learn more about Aiken's "computing engine."

Because the Mark I was the first digital computer to be programmed in number-code sequence (numerical order), Hopper experienced firsthand the failures and triumphs associated with the computer programming field. For instance, the code of machine language could be easily misread or incorrectly written. To reduce the number of programming errors,

Hopper and her colleagues collected programs that were free of error, producing a catalog that could be used to develop new programs. By this time the Mark II had been built, and Aiken's team used the Mark I and the Mark II side by side. They had thus created the first multi processor (a computer system that can do more than one operation simultaneously).

Works on UNIVAC

By the end of the war, Hopper had come to like navy life, but because of her age—she was 40—she could not be transferred into the regular navy from the women's reserve force, known as WAVES (Women Accepted for Volunteer Emergency Service). Remaining in the navy reserves, she stayed on at the Harvard Computational Laboratory as a research fellow, where she continued her work on the Mark computer series. In 1949 Hopper left Harvard to take the position of senior mathematician with the Eckert-Mauchly Computer Corporation. The company had just developed the Binary Automatic Computer (BINAC) and was in the process of introducing the first Universal Automatic Computer (UNIVAC). The UNIVAC, which recorded information on high-speed magnetic tape rather than on punched cards, was an immediate success. The company was later bought by the Sperry Corporation. Hopper stayed with the new organization, in 1952 becoming systems engineer and director of automatic programming for the UNIVAC division of Sperry.

Co-invents COBOL programming language

Hopper's association with UNIVAC resulted in several important advances in the field of programming. She developed an innovative program called "A-O" that would translate the human programmer's language into machine language. During the early 1950s, Hopper wrote articles, delivered papers, and co-authored a book on her achievements. She worked steadily to improve the design and effectiveness of programming languages. In 1957 she and her staff at UNIVAC created Flowmatic, the first program using English-language words, which was successfully incorporated into COBOL in 1960. This was a major advancement in the computing industry because COBOL was the first computer language developed for use by businesses. Hopper continued her work with Sperry, in 1964 becoming staff scientist of systems programming in the UNIVAC division.

Returns to navy life

While at Sperry, Hopper had remained active in the navy reserves. She reluctantly retired in 1966, but seven months later she was asked to direct efforts to standardize high-level computer languages in the navy. Returning to active duty in 1967, she was exempted from being required to retire at age 62. Although Hopper continued to work at Sperry until 1971, her activities with the navy brought her increasing recognition as a spokesperson for the usefulness of computers. In 1969 she was named "Man of the Year" by the Data Processing Management Association. During the next two decades Hopper received numerous other awards as well as honorary degrees. Having gained steady promotions during her navy career, she earned the rank of rear admiral in 1985, the year she retired. But her professional life did not end there. Immediately after leaving the navy Hopper became a senior consultant for the Digital Equipment Corporation, where she worked until her death on January 1, 1992.

Further Reading

Billings, Charlene W., *Grace Hopper: Navy Admiral and Computer Pioneer,* Enslow Publishers, 1989.

Byte, April 1994, p. 308.

Green, Laura, *Computer Pioneers,* Franklin Watts, 1985.

Hyde, Margaret O., *Artificial Intelligence,* Enslow Publishers, 1986.

Mompouollan, Chantal, *Voices of America: Interviews with Eight American Women of Achievement,* U.S. Information Agency, 1984.

Fred Hoyle

Born June 24, 1915
Bingley, Yorkshire, England

A prolific and talented author in the areas of both scientific fact and fiction, Fred Hoyle is best known for his public support of the controversial steady state theory of the creation of the universe. Early in his career he conducted ground-breaking research on the way stars produce energy and elements, which advanced understanding of the human body. He has also contributed to radar technology. More recently Hoyle has introduced other controversial theories that have caused extensive discussion in the scientific community.

Starts out in radar technology

Born on June 24, 1915, in Bingley, Yorkshire, England, Hoyle is the son of Benjamin Hoyle, a cloth salesman, and Mabel (Picard) Hoyle, a teacher. Attending Bingley Grammar School as a child, Hoyle frequently skipped school in order to watch barges float through the canals near his home. Despite these distractions, Hoyle excelled academically and was

"To achieve anything really worthwhile in research, it is necessary to go against the opinions of one's fellows."

accepted into Emmanuel College at Cambridge University. Studying mathematics and astronomy, he received a master of arts degree in 1939. On December 28, 1939, Hoyle married Barbara Clark, with whom he had two children.

During World War II (1939–1945), Hoyle served with the Admiralty in London, where he worked on British Navy radar (radio detection and ranging) technology projects. The Royal Air Force victory at the Battle of Britain has been credited to the navy's improvement of radar during this period. After the war, fledgling radio astronomers acquired numerous radar dishes and converted them into radio telescopes. Ironically, the amateur astronomers' discoveries in the 1960s helped to refute theories Hoyle developed in the 1940s and 1950s.

Examines Bethe's theory

In the early 1940s Hoyle focused his attention on a question first addressed in the work of American physicist Hans Bethe (1906–): How is energy produced in stars? In 1938 Bethe had suggested that stars are fueled by a sequence of nuclear reactions in which four hydrogen atoms are fused into a single atom of helium. As a result, a small amount of mass is converted into energy. This process is known as nuclear fusion. Although nuclear fusion was consistent with observations made by other scientists, Bethe's theory did not account for the production of elements heavier than helium. These heavy elements exist within other stars and are also abundant on Earth.

Explains what happens to elements

Hoyle expanded Bethe's findings by determining what would happen to elements at ever-increasing temperatures. He suggested that when a star has nearly exhausted its supply of hydrogen, nuclear fusion ceases. At this time the outward pressure of radiation, which is caused during the fusion process, also comes to a halt. Since energy is no longer flowing outward, the star begins to collapse because of the pull of gravity. The collapsing material then becomes more and more condensed, causing the core of the star to heat up and reach a temperature great enough to fuse helium atoms into an atom of carbon. The collapse of the star is then halted by the outward pressure of radiation energy coming from this new fusion. The star finally becomes stable.

The fusion cycle is repeated in the course of stellar evolution (changes in stars), creating oxygen, magnesium, sulfur and other heavier elements—until the element iron is formed. At this point, no more fusion reactions can occur, and the star implodes (goes through a catastrophic collapse), becoming a white dwarf (a star dimmer than the Sun but much more dense). During implosion, the star's outer layers start to burn, creating a supernova (an explosion with a brightness many times greater than the Sun). The supernova explosion creates elements heavier than iron, which are then hurtled into space by the force of the explosion. From such stellar debris, Hoyle hypothesized, a second generation of stars containing heavier elements is formed.

Becomes renowned astronomer

Hoyle further proposed that the Sun at the center of our solar system was once part of a binary (double) star system whose companion became a supernova eons ago. The resulting heavy elements that were ejected into space became the material from which planets were formed. Hoyle's remarkable theory of stellar evolution appeared to be correct. It agreed with other scientists' observations and accounted for the heavy elements in the solar system. However, astronomers are still disputing whether or not the Sun had a companion star or not. Some believe a passing star was the culprit in the explosion. Nevertheless, Hoyle's work in stellar evolution and the production of elements earned him a place among the world's top astronomers.

"Big bang" controversy explodes

Following the war, Hoyle returned to Cambridge University and became a professor of astronomy and mathematics. An important turning point in his career came in 1948 when American nuclear physicist George Gamow (1904–1968) published what became known as the big bang theory of the creation of the universe. The big bang theory states that billions of years ago all the matter of the universe was created by an enormous explosion. As a result of the explosion, galaxies formed and evolved from the remaining matter and are still moving away from each other at tremendous speeds. When Hoyle explained his new theory in a lecture in 1950, he became the first person to describe the central event of the theory as a "big bang." This popular name was adopted by other scientists and is still used today. Ironically, Hoyle would soon become one of the best-known critics of the theory.

An endless universe?

The concept that the universe had a specific beginning—and the implied idea that it will have an end—was rejected by many scientists and non-scientists. In response to the big bang theory, Austrian-born American astronomer Thomas Gold (1920–) and Austrian-born English mathematician Hermann Bondi (1919–) proposed the steady state theory. They offered the hypothesis that the universe is never-ending, an idea that appeared to agree with scientific observation. According to Gold and Bondi, matter is continuously being created in the universe. As galaxies drift apart, they proposed, new matter appears in the space that is left and evolves into new galaxies. Since the universe seemed to look the same no matter which direction or how far away scientists looked, Gold and Bondi suggested the cosmos was the same every "where" and every "when." That is, the physical state of the universe remains the same in the past, the present, and the future.

Walter Baade, German-born American Astronomer

In 1952 astronomer Walter Baade (1893–1960) pointed out serious flaws in the "yardstick" used by solid state theorists for measuring the cosmos. This "yardstick" was derived from the relationship between the brightness and the rate of pulsation of certain stars called Cepheid variable stars. According to Baade's findings, these stars are much farther away than had been previously calculated. This meant that the universe was therefore older and had been evolving longer. In addition, it was more than two times larger than had been believed. Baade suggested that if the steady state theory were to hold up, astronomers surveying space would expect to see "old" galaxies. Created billions of years ago, these galaxies would contain aging stars. Also there would be "new," recently created galaxies containing lighter elements and new stars. Yet known galaxies appeared to be similar in age, thus supporting the big bang theory.

As a result of Baade's conjecture, steady state theorists found it harder to prove that matter is continuously being created. The primary difficulty is that since space is so vast, the amount of matter created at a given moment is too small to support the theory. Therefore scientists have not been able to pinpoint the instant when the universe was formed.

Supports steady state theory

The steady state concept had several positive features. In particular, it avoided the troublesome issue of the beginning and end of creation. It was simple, presented a balanced universe, and attracted as many followers as the big bang theory. Hoyle became one of the most influential and talented supporters of the steady state theory. Since Gold and Bondi had not yet worked out a mathematical proof, Hoyle took on the job himself. He delved into the complex equations of German-born American physicist **Albert Einstein** (1879–1955; for more information, see entry in volume 1, pp. 260–269), made modifications, and produced a supporting mathematical model. Hoyle's explanation made the concept more believable and respectable in the scientific community. Now the official spokesperson for the solid state theory, he published several books on cosmology (an explanation of the origin and structure of the universe). Some of the books were highly technical, while others were aimed at the general public.

Many critics objected to the steady state theory because of the concept of the continual creation of new matter forming from nothing—an idea that seemed to violate the laws of nature. Hoyle responded to his opponents by saying it was easy to accept the notion of matter being created slowly and continuously over the eons. On the other hand, he said, believing that all matter in the universe was created in a single instant from a single blast was more difficult. For the next 15 years, scientists on each side of the argument interpreted new astronomical discoveries in ways that supported the theory they followed.

Modifies solid state theory

In light of new discoveries made by Walter Baade and other astronomers, Hoyle modified the steady state theory throughout the 1950s and 1960s. During this time he also founded the Institute of Theoretical Astronomy at Cambridge University and served as its first director. In 1954 Martin Baade revealed flaws in measuring methods used by solid state theorists. Then in 1963 the discovery of quasars by Martin Schmidt introduced another awkward complication. (Quasars are distant objects that release more light and energy than stars.) According to Schmidt, quasars could not fit into the steady state explanation of the universe. This tipped the balance toward the big bang theory, which had no trouble accounting for the existence of these "quasi-stellar." The following year, German-born American astrophysicist Arno Penzias (1933–) and American astronomer Robert W. Wilson (1936–) discovered background microwave radiation (electromagnetic radiations with wavelengths between one millimeter and 30 centimeters) in outer space. Claiming they had discovered the "remnants" of the big bang explosion with their radio telescopes, Penzias and Wilson sealed the fate of the steady state theory. Scientists once again embraced the big bang theory.

Introduces other controversial topics

In the following years, Hoyle found working with radio astronomers at Cambridge University increasingly difficult. When his proposed grant for a computer was rejected by the Science Research Council in 1972, he left the university to work elsewhere. Since then he has served as a visiting professor at various institutions, including the University of Manchester in England and the University of Cardiff in Wales. Hoyle has continued to draw attention in the scientific world by promoting controversial ideas. In 1981 he proposed that one-celled life could be found in dust that travels among comets. He suggested that life on Earth may have started from a close encounter with a comet. He also stated that the sudden appearance of global epidemics of disease could be caused by space-borne contaminants. This theory has not yet been verified by other scientists. In 1985 Hoyle ignited yet another controversy when he claimed that the British Museum's fossil of Archaeopteryx (an early form of bird) was a fake. So far his assertion has not gained the support of other experts. More recently, Hoyle has renewed his interest in the steady state theory by proposing a "quasi-state" theory. According to Hoyle, the universe was not created with a single big bang, but with many "little bangs," which occur in quasars and galaxies and create new elements.

Writes about scientific fact and fiction

A copious amount of information has flowed from Hoyle's pen during his career. Using his talent for simplifying complex theories for the general reading public, he has written technical treatises, textbooks, and science fiction stories. In collaboration with his son Geoffrey he wrote a radio play, *Rockets in Ursa Major,* and a television play, *A for Andromeda*. In 1994 Hoyle published his autobiography, *Home Is Where the Wind Blows: Chapters from a Cosmologist's Life*. He has also received numerous awards for his achievements in astronomy. Among them is the International Balzan Prize, which he shared with Martin Schwarzschild in 1955, for work on stellar evolution. Hoyle was honored by his country with a knighthood in 1972.

Further Reading

Abell, George, David Morrison, and Sidney Wolfe, *Exploration of the Universe,* 6th ed., Saunders College Press, 1991.

Devine, Elizabeth, *Thinkers of the Twentieth Century,* Gale, 1987.

Gamow, George, *The Creation of the Universe,* Bantam, 1952.

Hoyle, Fred, with John Elliot, *A for Andromeda,* Harper, 1962.

Hoyle, Fred, *Home Is Where the Wind Blows: Chapters from a Cosmologist's Life,* University Science Books, 1994.

Hoyle, Fred, with Geoffrey Hoyle, *Rockets in Ursa Major,* Harper, 1969.

Masakazu Konishi

Born February 17, 1933
Kyoto, Japan

Masakazu Konishi is a biologist who has spent most of his professional career studying the neurobiology of birds (the way the brain and nervous system of birds are structured and how they work). A professor at the California Institute of Technology in Pasadena, Konishi discovered that songbirds learn to sing by memorizing basic songs (templates) from other birds. Later he mapped the parts of a barn owl's brain to show how the owl hears sounds. This work has become a model for the study of animal sensory systems. As a result of observing the differences between the brains of male and female songbirds he also found that certain nerve cells are biologically programmed to die. Konishi's research on birds could provide valuable clues about the causes of neurological disorders in humans, such as Alzheimer's disease and Parkinson's disease.

Masakazu Konishi has made important discoveries about the brains of birds.

Specializes in animal studies

Konishi was born in Kyoto, Japan, on February 17, 1933. He is the only child of Shotaro and Hae Konishi, who were

73

Biologist Masakazu Konishi has advanced scientific understanding of the brains of birds. Among his contributions is the template of song learning among songbirds. Konishi discovered that when the bird hears the song of a "tutor" bird, its brain forms a song memory (template) from which the bird then creates its own songs. Konishi also mapped the parts of a barn owl's brain that are used for hearing sounds. He is perhaps best known, however, for his work on the nerve cells of birds. He identified programmed nerve cell death, which is believed to be responsible for the development of sex differences. Konishi's findings have had a significant impact on research into human brains.

both weavers. When the family experienced food shortages after World War II (1939–1945), Konishi decided to study agriculture in junior high school. By the time he entered high school in Kyoto, however, he found that animals were more interesting than agriculture. Turning his focus to zoology, Konishi finished high school and entered Hokkaido University in Sapporo. At Hokkaido he earned a bachelor's degree in zoology in 1956 and a master's degree in 1958. Upon completing his Ph.D. in zoology at the University of California, Berkeley, he pursued further academic work in Germany. He studied at the University of Tubingen and at the Max Planck Institute in Munich.

Konishi began his academic career as assistant professor of biology at the University of Wisconsin in 1965. A year later he moved to Princeton University in Princeton, New Jersey, where he became an associate professor in 1970. Then in 1975 he began a long association with the California Institute of Technology as a professor of biology. Five years later, he was appointed to his current position of Bing Professor of Behavioral Biology.

Finds songbirds need a tutor

While Konishi was at Berkeley he studied the central nervous system of birds. He became particularly interested in determining whether a bird learns to sing by listening to other birds. Konishi found that if a songbird is deafened before it becomes an adult, it will develop abnormal songs. Using this information, he developed the template theory, which explains how a younger bird learns from an adult tutor bird. The memory of the tutor's songs act as a guide, or template, that a songbird uses to shape its own songs. This was the first example of a non-human animal requiring vocal feedback to develop vocalization.

Makes discoveries about brains of birds

When Konishi moved to the California Institute of Technology he began exploring the neurophysiology (nervous system structure) of the barn owl's brain. After working for two decades, he unraveled the "wiring" of the brain to show two distinct pathways that enable the owl to hear. Konishi went on to study brain differences between male and female birds by observing another species, the Australian zebra finch. He discovered that the size and number of neurons (nerve cells) are smaller in female zebra finches. This finding contradicted a popular scientific belief at the time. The common assumption was that the hormone testosterone causes male nerve cells to grow while having no effect on female cells. Using radioactive tracers, Konishi found that brain cells related to song singing, a male characteristic, actually shrink and die in female finches. In male finches, however, the same cells grow. This discovery, called programmed cell death, is believed to be responsible for the development of differences between male and female finches. Other researchers have since found similar behavior in the cells of mammals.

Masakazu Konishi discovered that songbirds—like this yellow grosbeak—learn to sing by memorizing basic songs from other birds.

Honored for work

Konishi has published numerous articles in scientific journals and has been elected to the National Academy of Sciences. He has been recognized for his achievements with the Charles A. Dana Award for Pioneering Achievement in Health and the International Prize for Biology from the Japan Society for the Promotion of Science.

Further Reading

Konishi, Masakazu, with S. T. Emlen, R. E. Ricklefs, and J. C. Wingfield, "Contributions of Bird Studies to Biology," *Science,* October 27, 1989, pp. 465–72.

Jean Baptiste Lamarck

Born August 1, 1744
Bazentin-le-Petit, France
Died December 18, 1829
Paris, France

The work of French botanist Jean Baptiste Lamarck was generally ignored during his lifetime. Nevertheless he provided the basis for important—even revolutionary—changes in the classification of plant and animal life. Lamarck made his first contribution by creating a simple method for identifying plants. Turning to the study of animals, he improved on the work of Swedish naturalist **Carl Linnaeus** (1707-1778; for more information, see entry in volume 4, pp. 157-163). Lamarck found that when Linnaeus developed his classification system he did not designate a separate category for animals without backbones. Lamarck outlined many distinctive groups within this area, which he named "invertebrates." His study of fossils then led him to investigate the fate of ancient animals. (Fossils are remnants of organisms from past geologic ages that have been preserved in the Earth's crust.) Lamarck came to the conclusion that the animals had gradually changed over time, acquiring new traits. To explain how these changes took place, he developed the theory of the inheritance of acquired charac-

Jean Baptiste Lamarck was the first person to develop a theory of how plant and animal species gradually change over time.

Biologist Jean Baptiste Lamarck introduced the concept of the inheritance of acquired characteristics. Although Lamark's ideas were later proven incorrect, his work was an important step in the development of evolutionary thought. Beginning his scientific career as a botanist, Lamarck devised a simple method of identifying plants. When he expanded his work to include animals, he improved upon the original classification system of Swedish naturalist Carl Linnaeus. Lamarck is credited with giving the name "invertebrates" to animals without backbones. In his study of fossils and modern animals, Lamarck tried to determine whether ancient animals actually became extinct. This research led to his concept of acquired characteristics.

teristics. Although his explanation is now considered inaccurate, he was the first scientist to recognize the process of evolution (gradual change).

Family insists he become a priest

Jean Baptiste Pierre Antoine de Monet, Chevalier de Lamarck was born on August 1, 1744, in Bazentin-le-Petit, France. He was the youngest of 11 children born to Marie-Françoise de Fontaines de Chuignolles and Phillipe Jacques de Monet de Lamarck, a military officer. Although his parents belonged to the noble class, the family's life was hardly prosperous. At the age of 11, Lamarck enrolled in the Jesuit school at Amiens, France, because his father expected him to become a priest. He remained at the school until his father's death around 1760.

Joins the army and observes plants

When Lamarck was 16 he yearned for adventure, so he left school to join the army. After fighting in the Seven Years' War (1756–1763), he spent five years at various French ports on the Mediterranean Sea and the eastern borders of France. During his travels he observed the plants of various regions of France. In 1768 illness forced Lamarck to leave the military. Several years later he took a job in a Paris bank. For the next four years he studied medicine and became increasingly interested in meteorology (the study of weather patterns), chemistry, and shell collecting.

Becomes royal botanist

In 1778 Lamarck published *Flore française,* a carefully compiled catalog of French plant life. In the book he introduced a method for identifying plants according to a list of specifically defined characteristics. Lamarck's method soon attracted the attention of noted French naturalist Georges Buffon (1707–1788). Encouraging Lamarck's interest in plants, Buffon arranged his appointment as botanist (a scientist who studies plants) at the garden of King Louis XVI in 1781. The position gave Lamarck an opportunity to travel throughout Europe studying and collecting plant specimens. He continued to work at the royal garden until it was closed during the French Revolution (1789–1799; a movement to overthrow the monarchy and replace it with a democratic form of government).

Creates invertebrates classification

When the royal garden was reopened as the National Museum of Natural History in 1793, Lamarck was made a professor of zoology (the study of animals). He was placed in charge of organizing the museum's collection of animals and fossils without backbones. At that time zoologists relied on a classification system devised by Linnaeus in the early 1700s. He had grouped animals without backbones into two general categories: insects and worms. Lamarck did away with these categories, however, and named the entire group "invertebrates." He then set about classifying individual animals according to their physical similarities. For instance, he separated eight-legged arachnids (insects such as spiders) from six-legged insects. He also placed echinoderms (marine animals with circular shapes) such as starfish and sea urchins in a separate category from crabs, shrimp, and other crustaceans (marine animals with crust-like outer skeletons). Lamarck eventually published the results of his efforts in a seven-volume work, *Natural History of Invertebrates* (1815-22). Today it is considered his most important contribution to botany.

Develops revolutionary theory

Lamarck had earlier believed that all species of animals and plants remain the same through time. (A species is a group of living organisms that can all interbreed to produce fertile

Lamarck's Four Laws

In 1809 Jean Baptiste Lamarck published *Zoological Philosophy,* in which he described his theory that living creatures had developed from the simplest life forms to more complex organisms. To explain how this process took place he set forth four laws: (1) Organisms possess an in-born drive toward perfection; (2) they can adapt to the environment; (3) spontaneous generation (the process of life arising out of non-living matter) occurs frequently; and (4) acquired characteristics can be passed from one generation to the next. Lamarck is best known for the last law, the theory of inheritance of acquired characteristics (later found to be incorrect). To illustrate this law he gave the example of the giraffe. He hypothesized that the giraffe was originally a primitive antelope-like animal that had to keep stretching its neck to reach leaves high on trees for food. According to Lamarck, stretching caused the primitive animal's neck to grow longer, and this acquired characteristic was then passed on to its offspring.

offspring.) While doing research for his classification system, however, he noticed differences between living animals and ancient fossils. After ruling out the possibility of extinction (the death of all members of a species), Lamarck realized that the fossil species had not disappeared. Instead, he surmised, they had gradually changed over time. He also concluded that living creatures had developed from the simplest life forms into more complex organisms, with the most highly developed and complex creatures being humans.

Ignored during his lifetime

Lamarck had been elected to the French Academy of Sciences in 1779, yet during his lifetime his theories were virtually ignored by the scientific community. Although he lost his eyesight at age 65, he continued writing with the help of his daughter, who took his dictation. When Lamarck died in severe poverty in 1829, his family was forced to sell his papers and scientific collections to pay for his funeral. During the mid-1800s critics of English naturalist **Charles Darwin** (see entry) briefly revived interest in Lamarck's work in hopes of disproving Darwin's theory of natural selection. (Darwin's theory of natural selection states that evolutionary change is produced by adaptation of living species to their environment.) The attempt failed, and natural selection became the first widely accepted theory of evolution. Nevertheless, Lamarck has earned a place in history as the first scientist to recognize the process of evolution.

Further Reading

Asimov, Isaac, *Asimov's Biographical Encyclopedia of Science and Technology,* new revised ed., Doubleday, 1972, pp. 203–4.

Dictionary of Scientific Biography, Volume VII, Scribner's, 1972, pp. 584–94.

McGraw–Hill Encyclopedia of World Biography, Volume 6, McGraw–Hill, 1973, pp. 306–8.

Henrietta Leavitt

Born July 4, 1868
Lancaster, Massachusetts
Died December 21, 1921
Cambridge, Massachusetts

Henrietta Leavitt developed a method for accurately measuring the distance of remote stars and galaxies from the Earth.

As a researcher at the Harvard College Observatory for almost 20 years, Henrietta Leavitt made a number of important contributions to astronomy (the study of celestial bodies). Her most famous discovery was the period-luminosity relation of variable stars (stars that show changes in brightness). This method made it possible to determine the distances of far-off stars and galaxies. She also established brightness scales for stars, enabling astronomers to categorize the types of stars they observed. When Leavitt was a young adult she became severely deaf as the result of an illness. Consequently she was never allowed to choose her own path of research, yet her colleagues recognized her as a brilliant scientist. In addition to her other accomplishments, Leavitt identified 2400 new variable stars during her career.

Class creates interest in astronomy

Henrietta Swan Leavitt was born in Lancaster, Massachusetts, on July 4, 1868, one of the seven children of Henrietta Swan Kendrick and George Roswell Leavitt. Her father was a Congregationalist minister who had a parish in Cambridge, Massachusetts. After attending public school in Cambridge, Leavitt moved with her family to Cleveland, Ohio. She attended Oberlin College from 1885 to 1888 before transferring to the Society for the Collegiate Instruction of Women (now Radcliffe College)in Cambridge. During her senior year, she took an astronomy course, which fired her interest in the subject. After receiving a bachelor's degree from Radcliffe in 1892, Leavitt took another astronomy course. Then she was forced to remain at home for a number of years because of an illness that left her severely deaf.

Begins career at Harvard Observatory

Leavitt's handicap, however, did not dampen her interest in astronomy. After spending some time traveling, she volunteered as a research assistant at Harvard College Observatory in Cambridge in 1895. Seven years later she was appointed to the permanent staff by astronomer and observatory director Edward Charles Pickering (1846–1919) at a salary of thirty cents an hour. Leavitt worked at Harvard until her death in 1921. While Pickering gave her little chance to plan her own research projects, she eventually rose to a position as chief of the photographic photometry department at the observatory. (Photometry is the method of determining the brightness, or magnitude, of stars)

IMPACT

Henrietta Leavitt achieved a major breakthrough in astronomy. By carefully observing the changing brightness of variable stars (stars that show changes in brightness), she developed the period-luminosity relation theory. This theory describes the mathematical relationship between the overall brightness of a variable star and the time it takes for the star to complete one pulsation (change in brightness). Leavitt's finding was immediately adapted by other astronomers, who now had a completely new idea of the size and shape of the universe. Leavitt's period-luminosity relation resulted in several scientific advances. One of her most important discoveries was that the Earth's sun is not the center of the galaxy. Leavitt's new method also proved for the first time that there are galaxies outside of our own.

Establishes scale of star brightness

In 1907 Pickering asked Leavitt to establish a "north polar sequence." (Also known as a standard, a sequence is the

Magnitude of Stars

When Henrietta Leavitt worked on the "north polar sequence," she was establishing a way to determine the magnitude (brightness) of stars. The lower the magnitude, the brighter the star. Leavitt compared stars ranging from mangitudes +4 to +24. On a clear night, stars of about magnitude +6 can be seen with the naked eye. Large telescopes can detect objects as faint as +27. Very bright objects have negative magnitudes. The sun is –26.8.

ranking of stars in a certain area of the sky according to brightness.) She was to devise a standardized system for determining the brightness (magnitude) of stars in the northern sky, which could then be used for the entire sky. A new method was needed because taking pictures of stars with photographic telescopes was complex and unreliable. A major problem was that photographs did not show the actual brightness of stars. In addition, each telescope gave different results. If a standard of star brightnesses could be created, however, the brightness of an individual star could be estimated by comparing it with another star. To accomplish her task, Leavitt used 299 photographic plates from 13 telescopes and compared stars according to magnitude.

The results of Leavitt's research were published in the *Annals of Harvard College Observatory*. In 1913 her system was adopted by the International Committee on Photographic Magnitudes, which was creating a map of the sky. Making this work a lifelong project, Leavitt went on to establish brightness sequences for 108 areas in the sky. She also derived brightness standards for the forty-eight "Harvard standard regions" developed by Pickering. Her work was used throughout the world until astronomers developed improved methods.

Discovers period-luminosity relation

Leavitt discovered 2400 new variable stars, about half the number known at the time. Most notably, she studied photographs of the Magellanic Clouds (the Milky Way's two companion galaxies) taken at Harvard's observatory in Arequipo, Peru. Of the 1800 variable stars Leavitt detected on the Magellanic Cloud pictures, some were Cepheid variables, whose change in brightness is extremely regular. (Cepheids were named after Delta Cephei, the first star of this type to be discovered.) In 1908 Leavitt found that the brighter the Cepheid, the longer it took to change its magnitude. Leavitt reasoned that since the Cepheids in the Magellanic Clouds were nearly all the same distance from Earth, their periods were related to their light output (luminosity). In other words, the longer the period of pulsation, the brighter the star. By 1912 Leavitt had proven that Cepheids' apparent brightness was mathematically related to the length of their periods. That year, she published a table of the length of 25 Cepheid periods and their apparent luminosity. The periods ranged from 1.253 days to 127 days, with an average of five days.

Work leads to important discoveries

Leavitt's discovery of the period-luminosity relation was a major leap forward for astronomers. Astronomers could now directly calculate the true (absolute) brightness of a Cepheid by measuring its period of pulsation. They could also determine the distance to the star. Before Leavitt had established the period-luminosity relationship, cosmic distances could be determined only as far as about 100 light years. (A light year is a measure of distance, not time. It is the distance that light can travel in a year (365 1/4 days) in a vacuum, at the rate of 186,000 miles or 300,000 kilometers per second.) Now, astronomers were able to calculate distances of ten million light years.

Leavitt's work produced other significant results. Danish astronomer Ejnar Hertzsprung (1873–1967) adapted the period-luminosity relation in order to determine the actual distance of stars from Earth. Hertzsprung and American astronomer Harlow Shapley (1885–1972) found that the Magellanic Clouds were actually separate galaxies in the range of 100,000 light years from Earth. Leavitt and others had thought the Magellanic Clouds were bodies inside our Milky Way galaxy.

Honored by colleagues

Leavitt never gained the recognition given some of her fellow female astronomers at the Harvard College Observatory. Among these women were **Annie Jump Cannon**

(1863–1941; for more information, see volume 1, pp. 131–136) and Williamina P. Fleming (1857–1911). These women made important advances in the new field of stellar spectroscopy (determining characteristics of a star from the pattern of colors and dark lines in its spectra, or color range). But Leavitt's talents did not go unnoticed. One of her colleagues, Margaret Harwood, described her as possessing the best mind at the observatory. Contemporary astronomer Cecilia Payne-Gaposchkin called Leavitt the most brilliant woman at Harvard. She was also recognized for her scientific abilities with acceptance into professional associations. She was a member of both the American Associaton for the Advancement of Science and the Astronomical and Astrophysical Society of America. In addition, she was named an honorary member of the American Association of Variable Star Observers.

Further Reading

Bailey, Martha J., *American Women in Science: A Biographical Dictionary,* ABC-Clio, 1994, p. 205.

Dictionary of Scientific Biography, Volume VIII, Scribners, 1970, pp. 105–6.

James, Edward T., et al., editors, *Notable American Women, 1607–1950: A Biographical Dictionary,* Belknap Press, 1971, pp. 382–83.

Kass-Simon, G., and P. Farnes, editors, *Women of Science,* Indiana University Press, 1990.

Ogilvie, Marilyn Bailey, *Women in Science: Antiquity through the Nineteenth Century,* MIT Press, 1986, p. 121.

Aldo Leopold

Born January 11, 1886
Burlington, Iowa
Died April 21, 1948
Wisconsin

Aldo Leopold was an early environmentalist who laid the groundwork for many current conservation laws and policies. In addition to teaching about conservation and campaigning for environmental laws, he wrote several books that changed public attitudes about nature. Leopold's *Game Management* (1933)has guided generations of biologists in protecting North American wildlife. In *A Sand County Almanac* (1949), a collection of essays that was published a year after his death, he stressed the interdependence of humans and nature.

Aldo Leopold helped shape many conservation policies now in effect in the United States.

Learns outdoor skills from father

Born in Burlington, Iowa, on January 11, 1886, Leopold developed an early appreciation for the outdoors from his father, Carl Leopold. As a boy, Leopold learned how to hunt and read tracks left by wild animals, a practice he continued throughout his life and later passed on to his wildlife management students. Leopold's father also introduced him to the

Aldo Leopold was instrumental in bringing about U.S. government involvement in protecting natural resources and wildlife. Through teaching, writing, and political action, he increased the appreciation of nature as being valuable for its own sake and not simply as a resource for exploitation and profit. Leopold's idea, which became known as the "conservation ethic," was unpopular among many politicians during his own time. Nevertheless, his philosophy led to the creation of the first national wildlife reserve in the Gila Wilderness of New Mexico. Twenty-five years after Leopold's death, the U.S. Congress passed the Endangered Species Act.

writings of American authors Henry David Thoreau, Jack London, Stewart Edward White, and Ernest Thompson Seton. His mother, Clara Starker Leopold, was a home-maker who instilled in her son an appreciation of literature, philosophy, and poetry.

Studies forestry at Yale

In 1908 Leopold graduated from the Sheffield Scientific School at Yale University, in New Haven, Connecticut. He then stayed on at Yale to study for a year at the new school of forestry, which was based on the conservation philosophy of Gifford Pinchot (1865–1946). A 1898 Yale graduate, Pinchot had become the chief of the U.S. Department of Agriculture's Division of Forestry (an early forerunner to the U.S. Forest Service). He supported the utilitarian approach to conservation (the view that people have the right to use natural resources wisely) and he believed that forests should not be set aside as reserves but maintained to produce timber indefinitely. Like his Yale colleagues, Leopold accepted Pinchot's philosophy, but he kept his mind open to ideas that in a few years would bring him into conflict with the forest service chief.

Works as forest ranger

In 1909 Leopold went to work for the Division of Forestry as a ranger in a district that included territories that are now the states of New Mexico and Arizona. He was promoted quickly, becoming deputy supervisor and then supervisor of Carson National Forest, and finally, in 1913, assistant district forester at Albuquerque, New Mexico. While living in New Mexico, Leopold met Estella Bergere, a Santa Fe native who shared his love for the outdoors. They were married in Santa Fe on October 9, 1912. All five of their children would eventually follow in Leopold's footsteps by entering careers in science.

Promotes controversial conservation ideas

As early as 1915 Leopold began shaping his conservation values when he wrote a handbook about wild game (animals hunted for sport or food) for forest rangers and officials. He believed that preserving nature provided its own rewards—the beauty of a protected natural system and the personal satisfaction humans could derive from being a part of its continued existence. This idea contrasted with more popular theories, such as Pinchot's philosophy of "wise use" and the view that nature and wildlife are valuable only in terms of financial profit.

Organizes game protection group

That same year Leopold organized Albuquerque sportsmen interested in protecting wildlife into a game protection association. To communicate with the members, he established a newsletter called *The Pine Cone*. In 1916 Leopold became secretary of the New Mexico Game Protection Association, and he gave the organization a powerful voice in state politics. The issue he emphasized most strongly was protection of big game, which he believed could be improved by taking the choice of a state game warden away from politicians. Big game was disappearing, he argued, because the warden failed to enforce game laws. The issue became so popular that in the New Mexico race for governor, both candidates pledged their support for it. The winner, Ezequiel de Baca, later broke his promise and appointed a poorly qualified game warden, but the governor died before his candidate could be confirmed for the job. The new governor selected a game warden supported by the Game Protection Association.

Leopold's Legacy

Conservationist Aldo Leopold and his wife Estella Bergere Leopold had five children, all of whom eventually entered careers in science. Among them are Luna Bergere Leopold (1915–) and Estella Bergere Leopold (1927–). Luna Bergere Leopold is the foremost authority in the field of hydrology (the study of water distribution and flow on and below the earth's surface and in the atmosphere). One of the first scientists to be educated in environmental conservation, he has influenced scientific ethics and public policy. He worked with the U.S. Geological survey from 1950 until 1973, when he was appointed professor of geology and landscape architecture at the University of California at Berkeley. During his career he has called for stronger pro-conservation leadership from government, improvement of water engineering practices, and establishment of single environmental perspective for both the scientific community and government. He was the first hydrologist elected to the National Academy of Sciences.

Estella Bergere Leopold worked as a paleobiologist (a biologist who studies fossils) with the U.S. Geographical Survey for 21 years. Her research revealed that patterns of evolution were influenced by changes in landscape and climate. Extinction and evolution are highest in the middle of the continent, Leopold concluded. She also discovered that coastal areas, with their more moderate climates, are able to sustain older species such as the giant redwood. In 1976 she joined the faculty of the University of Washington at Seattle, where she is a professor of botany. Estelle Leopold and Luna Leopold, with their brother Starker, set an American record when all three were elected to the National Academy of Sciences.

Campaigns for nature reserves

Leopold remained politically active throughout his career, although not so strongly as during his early years in Albuquerque. When his innovative ideas about conservation nearly cost him his job as an assistant district forester in Albuquerque, he ignored the opposition. In response, he launched a vigorous campaign to preserve large, ecologically sound regions. He promoted his philosophy in a series of articles directed at different audiences—sportsmen, fellow foresters, citizen conservationists, economists, and the general public.

First wilderness reserve created

Leopold's conservation campaign eventually succeeded. In 1924 the U.S. Forest Service set aside a half million acres of the Gila Wilderness in New Mexico. This was the first officially designated wilderness reserve on federal land. That same year Leopold left field work to become the associate director of the United States Forest Products Laboratory in Madison, Wisconsin. He left the Forest Service in 1928 to become a private forestry and wildlife consultant. In 1931 he was awarded a gold medal by *Outdoor Life* magazine for his conservation efforts. (The award is given annually to one conservationist from the East and another from the West in the United States.)

Publishes influential conservation book

Leopold's famous "conservation ethic" drew widespread attention in 1933 when he published *Game Management.* Considered his most important work, the book argues that people should see the environment as a community for all of life. Furthermore, Leopold maintained, nature should not be regarded simply as an economic resource that can be exploited at will. His views influenced the development of several federal wildlife conservation laws during his lifetime, including the 1934 Fish and Wildlife Coordination Act. But his ideas had the greatest impact two and three decades after his death, as national concern about the environment increased. For example, Leopold's work shaped the landmark 1969 National Environmental Policy Act, which required the federal government to consider the environmental impact of planned development.

Another important result of Leopold's teachings was the Endangered Species Act of 1973. It recognized the need to conserve the ecosystem (an entire natural community and its environment) of endangered plants and animals. Other government laws influenced by Leopold include the Forest and Rangelands Renewable Resources Planning Act of 1974, the National Forest Management Act of 1976, and the Federal Land Policy and Management Act of 1976. All of these measures focused on preserving ecosystems, rather than individual species. (A species is a group of living organisms that can all interbreed to produce fertile offspring.)

Appointed first professor of wildlife management

In 1933, when *Game Management* was published, the University of Wisconsin hired Leopold to fill a newly created professorship in wildlife management. He held the position until his death. At Wisconsin, Leopold and his students developed the "inversity principle," which states that the average production of a breeding population decreases as the number of individuals increases. Realizing that textbooks could not teach all skills, he tried to instill in his students the ability to "read the landscape" and "read sign" of wild creatures. One of Leopold's former students, Robert A. McCabe, recalled in *Science* journal that his teacher "had a way of looking at a landscape and telling you its history and its future fifty years hence."

Through his academic post Leopold played a leading role in several environmental organizations. In 1934 President Franklin D. Roosevelt (1882–1945) named him to the Special Committee on Wild Life Restoration. The following year Leopold became a director of the Audubon Society as well as a founder of the Wilderness Society. In 1947 he was elected honorary vice president of the American Forestry Association and president of the Ecological Society of America. He was also appointed to the advisory council of the newly formed Conservation Foundation.

Writes *A Sand County Almanac*

In 1934 Leopold bought an abandoned farm on the Wisconsin River (50 miles north of Madison), where he wrote a series of poetic essays that were inspired by the change of seasons. Month by month, he recorded his observations of nature's ways in simple, non-scientific prose. In 1949, the year after Leopold death, the essays were published as *A Sand*

County Almanac. Leopold died of a heart attack in 1948, while battling a brush fire at a neighbor's farm. He was put to rest where his life had begun, in Burlington, Iowa, overlooking the Mississippi River.

Further Reading

Carter, Luther J., "The Leopolds: A Family of Naturalists," *Science,* March 7, 1980, pp. 1051–55.

Leopold, Aldo, *Game Management,* Scribners, 1933.

Leopold, Aldo, *A Sand County Almanac, and Sketches Here and There,* Oxford University Press, 1949.

Meine, Curt, *Aldo Leopold, His Life and Work,* The University of Wisconsin Press, 1988.

Seed, John, and others, *Thinking Like a Mountain: Toward a Council of All Beings,* New Society Publishers, 1988.

Gilbert Newton Lewis

Born October 23, 1875
Weymouth, Massachusetts
Died March 23, 1946
Berkeley, California

Gilbert Newton Lewis increased understanding of basic concepts of modern chemistry.

Gilbert Newton Lewis is best known for his theory of the nature of acids and bases, and for his explanation of chemical bonding. He also made contributions to thermodynamics (a branch of physics concerned with the properties of heat), photochemistry, and isotope separation (the sorting out the different varieties of an element that have the identical atomic number but different atomic mass). In addition, Lewis devised "electron dot" symbols for chemical structures that illustrate the way molecules hold together.

Lewis's ideas about chemical bonding are among the first theories taught to beginning chemistry students. When he began his career, theories of energy and energy flow (thermodynamics) were almost never applied to practical problems in the classroom. Lewis was instrumental in revolutionizing chemical education in the United States. He argued that students could not learn anything by simply memorizing information from a textbook. Teachers should therefore encourage students to think for themselves, he said, and students should be allowed to conduct chemistry experiments in class.

Enjoys home education

Gilbert Newton Lewis was born on October 23, 1875, in Weymouth, Massachusetts, to Francis Wesley and Mary Burr (White) Lewis. He learned to read at an early age and was educated at home until he was 13. He then he enrolled in a school affiliated with the University of Nebraska. J. H. Hildebrand noted in the *Annual Review of Physical Chemistry* that Lewis regarded his unusual schooling as "an advantage that ... occurred frequently in the careers of distinguished men, that of having 'escaped some of the ordinary processes of formal education.'" In 1894 Lewis transferred from the University of Nebraska to Harvard University in Cambridge, Massachusetts. After receiving a bachelor's degree in chemistry two years later, he continued his studies at Harvard. Under the direction of American chemist Theodore William Richards (1868–1928), Lewis pursued a Ph.D. in chemistry while teaching part time at the Phillips Academy in Andover, Massachusetts. He received his doctorate in 1899, at the age of 24.

Begins Berkeley career

Lewis returned to Harvard to teach, then studied in Germany with German chemists Friedrich Wilhelm Ostwald (1853–1932) and Walther Hermann Nernst (1864–1941). He also worked for a year at the Bureau of Science in Manila, the Philippines. During this period Lewis began formulating ideas that later became his most important contributions to chemical theory. While in Germany, he made the acquaintance of the famous German-born American physicist **Albert Einstein** (1879–1955; for more information, see volume 1, pp. 260–269). Lewis went on to publish several papers on Einstein's theories, but his work did not draw much attention. Unhappy with the fact that new ideas were discouraged at Harvard, Lewis moved to neighboring Massachusetts Institute of Technology (MIT) in 1905. He started as an associate professor in a research group

Chemist Gilbert Newton Lewis conducted research that resulted in several basic concepts of modern chemistry. His contributions include the description of covalent bonds, the definition of acids and bases, and the use of thermodynamics in explaining chemical reactions. Lewis also created a new method of teaching chemistry, which encourages students to engage in research and to openly discuss ideas with their teachers. He is credited with revolutionizing chemistry education in the United States.

headed by chemist Arthur Amos Noyes (1886–1936). Within five years he had become a full professor and acting director of research, a remarkable achievement in such a short period of time. In 1912 Lewis was appointed dean of the College of Chemistry at the University of California, Berkeley, where he remained for the rest of his career. During World War I (1914–1918) he served with the Army Chemical Warfare Service in France.

Revolutionizes chemistry education

At Berkeley, Lewis inspired both students and professors. Although he was too nervous to stand in front of a class himself, he had a direct influence on the teaching of chemistry. He redesigned chemistry courses and included such subjects as thermodynamics, which was not part of a student's chemistry education at the time. In order to make chemistry more attractive, he also involved first-year students in research. He further insisted that teachers and students discuss and debate topics (an unusual practice in the early twentieth century). Then Lewis and coauthor Merle Randall wrote a textbook, *Thermodynamics and the Free Energy of Chemical Substances,* which was published in 1923. Since then the book has been studied by generations of pupils.

In addition to creating a better learning environment for students, Lewis gave his professors and researchers great freedom of choice in their projects. He encouraged them to gain a broad knowledge of chemistry rather to specialize in a single area. Demanding that the university provide funds for facilities and equipment, he gradually built one of the best chemistry programs in the world. Nearly 300 Ph.D. degrees in chemistry were awarded at Berkeley during Lewis's tenure. Several graduates went on to become Nobel Prize winners. Among them were Glenn Seaborg (1912–), Willard Libby (1908–1980), and Melvin Calvin (1911–).

Explains free energy

Lewis's own research has had a significant impact on the field of chemistry. In particular, he has increased scientific understanding of thermodynamics. Until he began research in the area the theory was entirely mathematical and almost no work had been done with actual experiments. While Lewis was at MIT, he began to carefully measure "free energy" in both organic (compounds that make up living things) and inorganic processes. Free energy is a basic theory of thermodynamics. Measurement of free energy tells the chemist several things: how likely a chemical reaction is to occur, how a reaction takes place, and how complete the reaction is likely to be. Lewis also showed how free energy data could be applied to problems in chemistry. For example, he introduced the concept of "activity," which describes how chemical reactions occur in a solution (a liquid in which a chemical substance has been dissolved). Between 1913 and 1923, Lewis and Randall summarized nearly everything known about free energy in several papers and a book.

Proposes a theory of chemical bonding

Lewis also introduced the theory of chemical bonding. By the time he began thinking about chemical bonding (the joining of elements), the electron had been discovered. (An electron is a charged atomic particle). The electron was believed to participate in bonding, and several different ideas had been advanced to explain how atoms hooked together to make molecules. But none of them seemed to be correct. For some time Lewis had been contemplating a distinctive feature of the periodic table. (The periodic table is an arrangement of chemical elements in order of the number of atoms contained in them). On the table, certain properties (traits) are repeated in every eighth element. Lewis surmised that there is a relationship between these repetitions and the number of electrons in an element. Furthermore, he hypothesized, this relationship could explain how chemical bonding takes place. He did not formally propose his theory of bonding, however, until 1916.

Lewis first needed to elaborate on a theory proposed by German chemist Richard Abegg (1869–1910). According to Abegg, atoms are most stable when they have eight electrons around them on the outside. Elements with fewer than eight electrons tend to gain or lose electrons to reach a stable form. This process is known as ionic bonding. Lewis added to Abegg's theory by stating that there is a second way atoms may achieve a complete set of eight electrons. In some cases, Lewis said, pooled electrons from two atoms pair up and the atoms share a pair of electrons. The sharing of pairs of electrons enables each atom in a molecule to obtain the greatest stability. Lewis gave the term covalent bonding to the sharing of paired electrons. He symbolized covalent bonding with patterns of dots, a notation that is still used today.

Langmuir expands Lewis's theory

No one took Lewis's covalent bonding theory seriously when he first proposed it. Finally, in 1919 the noted American chemist and physicist Irving Langmuir (1881–1957) further developed the idea of the covalent bond. He was more persistent and articulate in convincing the chemical community that the theory was important, and so it was for a time called the Lewis-Langmuir electron dot theory. Lewis took issue with this name, feeling that he had originated the theory. Historians generally agree, however, that Langmuir made important contributions. The theory probably would have remained unused even longer if he had not promoted it to other scientists. In 1923 Lewis published a book on the theory, *Valence and the Structure of Atoms and Molecules.*

Creates "heavy water"

In 1933 Lewis suddenly changed the course of his research and started working on a completely new subject, isotope separation. Isotopes are differently weighted forms of a single element, and isotopes of the same element are very difficult to separate because their chemistry is identical. Working with isotopes of hydrogen, Lewis managed to prepare nearly pure water (consisting only of oxygen and hydrogen) that contained only the deuterium isotope of hydrogen (the isotope that is twice the weight of regular hydrogen). He thus produced "heavy water," which is now used in nuclear reaction research. The creation of heavy water was Lewis's only contribution to nuclear chemistry, for his later investigations on isotopes were largely unsuccessful.

Defines acids and bases

When Lewis published *Valence and the Structure of Atoms and Molecules* in 1923, he examined the concept of valence (the number of electrons a substance can donate or gain to reach stability). He had successfully applied his chemical bonding theory to the chemical compounds known as acids and bases (compounds that can accept a hydrogen ion from an acid). Yet once again his idea had received little notice in the scientific world. At that time, chemists thought acids must have a hydrogen ion to donate and, correspondingly, a base must be able to receive a hydrogen ion. (An ion is an atom or group of atoms that has become electrically charged by gain or loss of a negatively charged electron.) Scientists were at a loss, however, to explain the behavior of acids in compounds that had no hydrogen to donate. In 1938, Lewis gave a lecture at the Franklin Institute in Philadelphia, Pennsylvania, in which he insisted he had removed this obstacle. He proposed that an acid could be defined as any electron-pair recipient and a base could be defined as any electron-pair donor. These definitions would cover almost all chemicals in any reaction, including hydrogen ion transfers. Lewis's concepts are still being used today.

Pursues various interests

In the last years of his life, Lewis became interested in the study of photochemistry (the interaction of light energy with chemical compounds to cause reactions). As with most of his areas of interest, he had begun to investigate light and color early in his career, but his most important published work on the subject appeared later. Lewis collaborated with Berkeley graduate Melvin Calvin on a paper about photochemistry. He then experimented in the areas of fluorescence and phosphorescence (the release of light from different substances). Eventually, he began to connect these experiments with the rapidly developing field of quantum mechanics (the explanation of the behavior of subatomic particles). Once again he combined theory and practice, as he had with thermodynamics and chemical reactions decades earlier.

Lewis's interests outside of chemistry included economics and prehistoric glaciation (formation of glaciers) in the Americas. His last paper, which was published after his death, analyzed the thermodynamics of ice ages (times of widespread glaciation). Although Lewis officially retired in 1941, he continued his scientific work until his death from a heart attack in his Berkeley laboratory on March 23, 1946. He left behind his wife, Mary Hinckley Sheldon Lewis, whom he had married in 1912, and three children. His two sons followed him into careers in chemistry.

Further Reading

Hildebrand, J. H., "Fifty Years of Physical Chemistry in Berkeley," *Annual Review of Physical Chemistry,* Volume 14, 1963, p. 1.

Tiernan, N. F., "Gilbert Newton Lewis and the Amazing Electron Dots," *Journal of Chemical Education,* Volume 62, July 1985, p. 569.

Fang Lizhi

Born February 12, 1936
Hangzhou, China

F ang Lizhi (pronounced "fong lee-*jur*") is known as a lead-ing astrophysicist (a scientist who studies matter in space) and an outspoken critic of the Chinese Communist gov-ernment. A supporter of human rights and intellectual free-dom since his student days, he was sentenced to manual labor in the 1950s. During his confinement Lizhi read a smuggled book that introduced him to the field of cosmology (a branch of astronomy concerned with the origin and development of space and time). In 1972 he published a paper on the big bang theory, a forbidden topic in China. (The big bang theory states that the universe began with a single large explosion of matter at a certain point in time.) In 1989 Lizhi sought political asy-lum (protection from punishment for political reasons) at the United States Embassy in China. He took this step when Communist forces massacred anti-government protesters at Tiananmen Square in Beijing. In 1992 Lizhi took a position in the physics department at the University of Arizona in Tuc-

Fang Lizhi is a world-renowned astrophysicist and a prominent activist for human rights in China.

Chinese astrophysicist Fang Lizhi is known equally for his scientific work and for his support of human rights reform in China. Lizhi has contributed to the big bang theory of the origin of the universe and to the study of the shape of the universe. He became a political activist because he wanted Chinese scientists to be able to study current theories, not simply ideas supported by the Communist Party. Lizhi's fight for intellectual freedom has inspired others to push for reforms in China. Conflicts with the Communist government finally forced Lizhi to leave the country in 1990.

son, where he teaches cosmology and quantum theory. (Quantum theory is an area of physics based on the subdivision of light energy into quanta, or units.)

Fascinated by radios

Fang Lizhi was born on February 12, 1936, in Hangzhou, China, to Fang Chengpu and Shi Peiji. His father worked as an accountant for the railroads in China, so the family enjoyed a middle-class life. Nevertheless Lizhi experienced the difficulties of growing up in a politically unstable era. At that time China was occupied by Japanese forces, and schoolchildren were forced to wear Japanese-style uniforms and attend ceremonies in honor of the Japanese emperor. After the Japanese were defeated in World War II (1939-1945), American soldiers assisted in the transfer of power to the Chinese Nationalist government. Radios used by the U.S. Army sparked Lizhi's interest in science. Determined to build his own radio, the 12-year-old spent his lunch money to buy radio parts. He also started reading books on electronics.

By the time he was a student at Beijing's top high school, Lizhi realized he needed to study physics if he wanted to learn how radios work. He began reading physics books, including works about the structure of the atom by Danish physicist **Niels Bohr** (1885-1962; for more information, see entry in volume 1, pp. 98-104). During this period Lizhi also developed his political beliefs. After witnessing the beating of students by police, he joined a secret Communist organization that supported the downfall of the Nationalist government. In 1949 the Communists took control of mainland China, forming the People's Republic of China under leader Mao Zedong.

Joins Communist party

At the age of 16, Lizhi entered Beijing University to study theoretical and nuclear physics. After graduating with high honors four years later, he took a job on a secret government project to build a nuclear reactor. That same year he also joined the Chinese Communist Party (CCP), a position he had hoped would gain him acceptance among Chinese scientists and advance in his career.

Almost immediately, however, Lizhi encountered conflicts with the government, which tried to control scientific ideas that were studied in China. Lizhi voiced his objections to the oppressive Communist influence on physics. In 1956, when Mao invited comments from intellectuals about how to improve the country, Lizhi promptly called for educational reform and intellectual freedom. Along with thousands of other academics, Lizhi was expelled from the party in 1957 and forced to work for eight months on a farm in the country.

Returns to teaching and writing

After serving his sentence, Lizhi was allowed to help organize a new physics department at the University of Science and Technology (Keda) in Beijing. While teaching electromagnetics (how magnetism is developed by a current of electricity) and quantum mechanics (the theory of small-scale physical processes), he conducted research in solid-state and laser physics. But because of his earlier statements, government officials would not allow his name to appear on any publications. Therefore the *Journal of the Chinese Academy of Sciences* anonymously printed Lizhi's first paper, which analyzed the nature of the proton (the elementary particle found in the nucleus of all atoms). A year after returning to Beijing, Lizhi began working with the Academy of Sciences' Institute of Physics, which was building the first lasers in China. ("Laser" is an acronym for light amplification by stimulated emission of radiation. The device produces intense light with a precisely defined wavelength.) For three years his career flourished, and he published ten scientific papers. He also married physicist Li Shuxian in 1961; the couple has two sons.

Imprisoned during Cultural Revolution

During China's Cultural Revolution (1966-1976), Mao sought to eliminate Western and traditional Chinese influences. His tactics included closing schools and libraries and forbidding people to read scientific literature. Mao also punished intellectuals for their beliefs, so in 1966 Lizhi was arrested once again—but this time by his own political party. After enduring a year of solitary confinement, he was sentenced to manual labor in Anhui Province. He worked in rice paddies, in a coal mine, and on the construction of a railroad tunnel.

Even though all literature except Communist documents was banned at this time, Lizhi managed to smuggle one book with him to the countryside. It was *Classical Theory of Fields* by the Russian physicist and Nobel Prize winner Lev Landau (1908-1968). In an interview for *Popular Science* magazine, Lizhi recalled: "The first half of the book was about electrodynamics, the second half about gravitation and relativistic astrophysics. For six months, I read it over and over again. That's what decided me to enter the field of cosmology. So what began as a punishment for being an intellectual turned out to be responsible for my whole future scientific career."

Promotes big bang theory

In 1969 Lizhi was sent to a new Keda branch at Hefei in the Anhui Province. He taught courses on astrophysics (a branch of physics dealing with the physical properties and behavior of celestial bodies). He also began writing again, but now he published his articles under a pseudonym because the political climate was still dangerous. Publications about cosmology had been forbidden by the CCP since 1949, but the ban was lifted in 1972. Taking advantage of their freedom, Lizhi and others published an article on the big bang theory. It was immediately condemned by the Communists because it contradicted the government-supported view that the universe is infinite, with no beginning or end. But Lizhi and his colleagues were not punished. He continued to work throughout the 1970s in a gradually improving academic and political environment. In 1978 he was readmitted to the CCP and won

China's National Award for Science and Technology. He also became the youngest full professor at Keda. When Lizhi was allowed to travel in 1979, he spent six months at Cambridge University in England. In 1986 he worked at the Institute for Advanced Study Princeton University in New Jersey.

Speculates on shape of the universe

Lizhi has spent most of his career conducting theoretical research on the shape of the universe. He is particularly interested in topology (a mathematical discipline concerned with sets of geometric points). He has compared cosmology to archaeology (the study of ancient cultures) because it reconstructs the history of the universe from physical evidence such as light, radiation, matter, and antimatter (matter composed of antiparticles). Lizhi has used topology to speculate on the shape the universe might have taken in the first fraction of a second after the big bang. As Hans Christian von Baeyer put it in *The Sciences* journal, Lizhi's question is whether the universe is "a ball or a doughnut." His work could advance scientific insight into whether the universe will continue to expand or whether gravity will eventually begin to pull it back together again. In 1985 Lizhi won the International Gravity Foundation Prize for a paper he coauthored with Humitako Sato on quasars (star-like objects that release enormous amounts of light and radio waves) and the history of the universe.

Lectures on human rights

Despite offers from universities and research institutions throughout the world, Lizhi remained in China during the 1980s. In *Current Biography Yearbook* he is quoted as saying, "The democracies have many astrophysicists, and China not so many. I love China.... I want to stay where I can both have an impact on science and help to import democracy." Lizhi was appointed vice president of Keda in 1984. He and Guan Weiyan, the president of Keda, drafted a plan to increase the power of the faculty and to encourage freedom of speech on campus. Consistent with national policy, they invited foreign visitors and arranged for students to study abroad. Lizhi lectured throughout the country on freedom of expression, becoming a well-known public figure and capturing the attention of students. By now he was also a world-renowned astrophysicist. Because of Lizhi's reputation, the government did not try to stop his campaign for human rights and democratic reforms.

Then in 1986 a student protest for free elections and other democratic reforms grew into massive demonstrations in Beijing and spread to other cities. Though Lizhi and Weiyan had actually discouraged the marches, they were blamed by the CCP for the activities. Lizhi was punished by being reassigned to a research position at the Beijing Observatory, and in 1987 he was again expelled from the party.

Receives political asylum

Repression did not stop Lizhi from continuing to promote democracy and human rights. In 1989 he made the daring move of writing personally to Chinese leader Deng Xiaoping to request the release of political prisoners. Soon afterward, Chinese police prevented Lizhi from attending a dinner with visiting American President George Bush, to which he had been invited. Lizhi made the most of the situation, speaking with foreign reporters about human rights in China. He became an international celebrity. Then the government turned against him when student demonstrations broke out in Beijing's Tiananmen Square. Although Lizhi did not express support of the protest, the CCP considered him to be one of the instigators. On June 5, 1989, the day after government troops massacred students in the square, Lizhi and his wife sought refuge in the United States Embassy in Beijing. The Chinese government immediately called for his arrest.

Lizhi and his wife remained in the embassy for 13 months. During that time Lizhi wrote a number of scientific papers and received the Robert F. Kennedy Memorial Human Rights Award. He received permission to leave the country only after intense diplomatic pressure from the United States. In 1990 he served as a visiting researcher at Cambridge University, where his family joined him. He then accepted a position at the Institute for Advanced Study in 1991.

Builds T3 model

In 1991 Lizhi published, in English, a book of political and philosophical essays titled *Bringing down the Wall: Writing on Science, Culture, and Democracy in China.* The following year he took his current position as associate professor of physics at the University of Arizona. Since then Lizhi's research has focussed on building the T3 model, a new topographical description of the universe. Maintaining his loyalty to China, he has expressed hope for progress in human rights in the country. In a profile in *Scientific American,* Lizhi explained that his scientific and political beliefs are closely related: "If you study anything, you must raise questions.... But authorities in communist countries do not like you to raise questions."

Further Reading

Aikman, David, "Interview: The Science of Human Rights," *Time,* August 20, 1990, pp. 12-15.

Brown, William, "A Dissident View on Life, the Universe and Democracy," *New Scientist,* July 21, 1990, p. 19. Fisher, Arthur, "Man without a Country," *Popular Science,* August 1996, pp. 62-66.

Lizhi, Fang, *Bringing down the Great Wall: Writings on Science, Culture, and Democracy in China,* Knopf, 1991.

Lizhi, Fang, "The Chinese People Must Participate in a Universe of Rights," *Los Angeles Times,* November 26, 1989.

Lizhi, Fang, "A Chinese Tom Paine Speaks out on Democracy," *Washington Post,* January 18, 1987, p. C1.

Lizhi, Fang, with J. Ruffini, *Cosmology of the Early Universe,* Taylor & Francis, 1985.

Lizhi, Fang, "First Word," *Omni,* March 1990, p. 8.

Lizhi, Fang, "Human Rights Must Be Part of New China," *Los Angeles Times,* April 13, 1989, p. 7.

Yam, Philip, "Fundamental Rights, Fundamental Physics," *Scientific American,* May 1994, pp. 39-40.

Jan Ernst Matzeliger

Born September 15, 1852
Paramaribo, Dutch Guiana
(now Surinam)
Died August 24, 1889
Lynn, Massachusetts

Jan Ernst Matzeliger revolutionized the shoemaking industry with the invention of the shoe–lasting machine.

Jan Ernst Matzeliger was a nineteenth-century inventor and machinist who revolutionized the shoemaking industry and made a fortune for his financial backers. Over a period of several years he made personal sacrifices in order to perfect a shoe–lasting machine, which performed the most difficult part of the shoemaking process—fitting and sewing the upper part of a shoe to the inner sole. After designing, patenting, and building working models, Matzeliger factory-tested the device. The shoe–lasting machine became as revolutionary and beneficial as the cotton gin designed by American inventor Eli Whitney (1765–1825) and the sewing machine introduced by another American inventor, Elias Howe (1819–1867). As a result of Matzeliger's innovation, shoe manufacturers could make 150 to 700 pairs of shoes a day, compared with the 50 pairs previously produced by hand-lasting methods.

Jan Matzeliger was born on September 15, 1852, in the port city of Paramaribo in Dutch Guiana (the present–day country of Surinam in South America). His mother was a native Surinamese of African descent, and his father was a Dutch engineer. Matzeliger's father had been sent to the island colony to take charge of the government machine works. A well-educated man, he was a member of a wealthy and aristocratic Dutch family.

Becomes a skilled machinist

Starting out as an apprentice in a government machine shop supervised by his father, Matzeliger eventually became a skilled machinist. Then at the age of 19 he signed on as a sailor on a steamship with the Dutch East Indies Company. During voyages he helped repair the engines on the steamship. After sailing for two years in the Far East, the ship went to North America. When it docked in Philadelphia, Pennsylvania, in 1873, Matzeliger left the Dutch East Indies Company and looked for work as a machinist. Philadelphia was a busy commercial center at the time, with many factories offering opportunities to skilled machinists. Yet the segregated job market was not open to blacks. Matzeliger, who was of mixed race, was at a particular disadvantage because Dutch was his native language and he spoke little English.

Eventually Matzeliger found a job at a shoemaker's shop, where he learned to use a McKay machine that sewed the seam of a shoe sole. Now fascinated with the shoemaking process, he was advised to go to Lynn, Massachusetts, the shoe manufacturing center of North America. Matzeliger left his job in Philadelphia and arrived in Lynn on a winter day in 1877. At first the social climate for African-Americans in his new home made it difficult for him to settle into the community. He also had a hard time finding a job in the shoe facto-

IMPACT

Inventor Jan Ernst Matzeliger designed a machine to perform shoe–lasting, the most difficult part of the shoemaking process. Prior to his innovation, shoe–lasting—fitting and sewing the upper part of a shoe to the inner sole—had been done by hand by skilled laborers. Because the process was so slow, factories could produce only about 50 pairs of shoes per day. After Matzeliger introduced his machine, work time was greatly reduced and output was increased to 150 to 700 pairs of shoes each day. Consequently, manufacturers were able to cut their prices and more people could afford to buy factory–made shoes.

ries. Finally, the Harney Brothers company hired him to sew shoes on the familiar McKay sole-sewing machine. At night he went to school to improve his English.

Studies shoemaking machines

Soon Matzeliger became interested in learning more about the machines. He saved his money and bought a set of drawing instruments for drafting designs of new machines. To increase his knowledge, Matzeliger observed the automated process of shoemaking in the factory. Each worker had his or her own part of the shoe to work on and a machine to operate. There were specialized machines for each step of the process, but there was no machine for shoe–lasting, the final and most difficult task.

Matzeliger concentrated his observations on shoe–lasting. He noticed that lasters (workers who did shoe–lasting) often could not keep up with the machines. Since their work was so challenging, lasters had a strong union and were considered kings of the shoemaking trade. It was said they sometimes worked slowly on purpose, and they frequently went on strike. One day, Matzeliger announced that he could make a machine to do their job. The lasters greeted his claim with skepticism.

Matzeliger was determined to learn as much as possible so he could invent a shoe-lasting machine. He requested a job as a millwright at Harney Brothers. Circulating throughout the factory, he checked and repaired the machinery. The new position also gave him the opportunity to watch the lasters at work.

Secretly designs invention

Matzeliger took an inexpensive, barely heated room in the old West Lynn Mission, where he worked on his plans for a shoe-lasting machine in secret. (Historians speculate that poor living conditions contributed to Matzeliger's early death from tuberculosis.) Within six months he had made a model of his machine. Although the model was constructed simply of old cigar boxes, wire, nails, and scrap wood, another inventor offered him $50 for the device. Wisely, Matzeliger refused the offer. His next step was to make a working model out of metal. Some parts he was able to salvage from junkyards, others he had to fashion himself from pieces of scrap metal. To do this, he needed a forge to heat the metal and a lathe to shape it.

Creates working model of machine

Matzeliger found a forge at Beal Brothers shoe factory, so he left Harney Brothers and went to work for Beal Brothers. His new employer gave him a workspace and use of the forge and lathe. Both machines were old and cumbersome, but Matzeliger was determined to complete his project. He also took a part-time job as a coach driver, transporting young people to a local park for recreation.

By 1882 Matzeliger had completed the scrap-metal model. He knew he was on the right track when another inventor offered him $1,500 for only a part of the model. He again refused the offer. Since a scrap-metal version of his machine would not stand up to factory testing, he needed to make parts that met exact specifications. Knowing the project would be expensive, he approached several businessmen in Lynn and asked them to finance his invention. They turned him down. One investor had already lost $100,000 on a failed shoe-lasting machine.

Finally, Matzeliger found two backers, C. H. Delnow and M. S. Nichols, who agreed to give him funds in return for two-thirds of any future profits. Together the three men formed the Union Lasting Machine Company, and Matzeliger set about constructing his third model. When he had made sufficient progress he applied for a patent (a government statement that the inventor has the exclusive right to make and sell his invention for a certain period of time). This process involved submitting detailed drawings and a complete description of the invention.

Awarded patent

Government patent officials in Washington, D.C., could not understand Matzeliger's complicated drawings. Furthermore, they did not believe the machine could fulfill its inventor's claims. As a result, the patent office sent an examiner to Lynn to inspect the machine. Matzeliger demonstrated how his invention worked: It held the last, gripped the leather, drew the leather over the last, fitted the leather at the heel and toe, moved the last forward, fed the nails, and drove the nails. The patent official was satisfied, and on March 20, 1883, Matzeliger was granted U.S. Patent No. 274,207 for his shoe-lasting machine.

The machine proved itself in a factory test on May 29, 1885, by lasting 75 pairs of women's shoes. Later, the machine would turn out 150 to 700 pairs of shoes in one day. To begin manufacturing the machine, Delnow and Nichols needed more money. They obtained funds from George W. Brown, the northeast agent for the Wheeler Wilson Sewing

Machine Company, and Sidney W. Winslow, who became known as the machinery king of New England. In exchange for their investment, Winslow and Brown took over the patent from Matzeliger. He was given a block of stock in the new enterprise, the Consolidated Lasting Machine Company.

Revolutionizes shoe industry

Production of the shoe-lasting machine began in the mid-1880s and expanded rapidly. Soon every shoe manufacturer in Lynn wanted to buy one of Matzeliger's new machines. Before long, the shoe business was booming throughout New England. Shoe prices were cut in half, and sales to other countries were reaching a new high. Matzeliger had caused a revolution in the industry. Rather than putting the shoe lasters out of work, his machine actually provided more work—which had now become much easier.

By 1897 Winslow was the "machinery king." Bringing together the major shoe–lasting machine manufacturers in the Northeast, he organized the New York Machine Company. Two years later he completed the consolidation of machine manufacturing companies to form the United Shoe Machinery Corporation, with himself as president. From 1899 to 1910, the United Shoe Machinery Corporation earned over $50 million and held 98 percent of the shoe machinery business. In 1955 the company was worth more than a billion dollars.

Contracts tuberculosis

Demand for Matzeliger's machine had spread worldwide by 1889. The inventor continued to improve the machine and received four additional patents. In spite of his success, he made few changes in his simple lifestyle. He taught oil painting classes and became the leader of Christian Endeavor (a religious group for young adults) at the North Congregational Church in Lynn. It was the only church in the town that would accept him—the others turned him away because he was black. During a church picnic in the summer of 1886,

Matzeliger developed a cold that was later diagnosed as tuber-culosis. Unable to afford more expensive treatment at a sanito-rium, he went into a hospital. He was bedridden for three years and died on August 24, 1889, at the age of 37. Matzeliger had never married, but he had a foster son named Perrie Lee, to whom he left many of his paintings and papers. He willed much of his stock in the shoe company to the North Congrega-tional Church, which was able to pay off a mortgage when the stock value doubled in 1904. Matzeliger was buried in the Pine Grove Cemetery in Lynn.

Further Reading

Dictionary of American Biography, Volume VI, edited by Dumas Malone, Scribners, 1961, pp. 426–27.

Dictionary of American Negro Biography, edited by Rayford W. Logan and Michael R. Winston, W. W. Norton, 1982, pp. 429–30.

Annie Russell Maunder

Born April 14, 1868
County Tyrone, Ireland
Died September 15, 1947

Annie Russell Maunder conducted sunspot research with her husband, Edward Walter Maunder. The astronomers (scientists who study celestial bodies) specialized in detecting dark spots appearing on the Sun's surface. In 1898 she obtained a photograph of a solar prominence (a cloud of gas rising from the atmosphere of the Sun) that was six times the radius of the Sun in length. It was the largest image of the phenomenon to be captured on film up to that time. Maunder was also active in the British Astronomical Association, serving as vice president of the organization several times until 1942. She also planned the format of the official journal, the *Journal of the British Astronomical Association.* Maunder was editor of the publication from 1894 to 1896 and from 1917 to 1930. She held a paid position at the Greenwich Observatory, an unusual situation for a woman during the late nineteenth and early twentieth centuries.

Annie Russell Maunder was a pioneering female astronomer who specialized in photographing the Sun.

115

Annie Russell Maunder was a professional astronomer during the late 1800s and early 1900s. Working with her husband, astronomer Edward Walter Maunder, she took photographs that advanced scientific understanding of such phenomena as sunspots and solar eclipses. In 1898 one of her photographs showed the largest solar prominence ever captured on film up to that time. In addition to her research, Maunder was also active in professional associations, publishing a number of articles with her husband and serving as vice president of the British Astronomical Association.

Hired as "computer"

Annie Russell was born on April 14, 1868, in County Tyrone, Ireland. The daughter of Rev. W. A. Russell, she was educated at Victoria College in Belfast, Ireland, and Girton College in Cambridge, England. In 1889 she received a Senior Optime in the Mathematical Tripos, the highest mathematical honor available to women at Girton. Two years later she was hired as a "computer" to assist astronomer Edward Maunder, head of the solar photography department at the Royal Observatory in Greenwich and founder of the British Astronomical Association. Russell's job was to examine and measure daily sunspot photographs. She and Maunder became friends and were married in 1895. In 1897 and 1898 Annie Russell Maunder was a Pfeiffer student for research at Girton College. Throughout her career she worked in close collaboration with her husband on a variety of astronomical subjects, though her own favorite was the Sun. Among Maunder's contributions were eclipse observations and photographs made during expeditions to Lapland in 1896, India in 1898, Algiers in 1900, Mauritius in 1901, and Labrador in 1905. The Maunders coauthored a number of articles published in the *Monthly Notices of the Royal Astronomical Society* and the *Journal of the British Astronomical Association.*

Takes picture of longest coronal streamer

Traveling to India to see the eclipse of the Sun in 1898, Maunder obtained on film the longest solar prominence (also known as a coronal extension or coronal streamer) ever captured on film at that time. She equipped a camera to photograph the greatest possible extension of coronal streamers,

and she did in fact photograph one with a length of six solar radii (the distance from the center to the outer edge of the Sun). In related work Maunder proposed that the Earth influenced the number and areas of sunspots, and that the frequency of sunspots decreased from the eastern to the western edge of the Sun's disk as viewed from the Earth. She also suggested that changes in the Sun caused changes in the Earth's climate. With support from a research grant from Girton College, she also contributed to a photographic survey of the Milky Way.

In 1892 Maunder failed to obtain membership in the Royal Astronomical Society, but she did become a member of the British Astronomical Association, which welcomed female members. On several occasions she was asked to be president of the association, but she refused on account of her soft-spokenness. She was a representative at the Women's International Congress in London in 1899.

Stellar constellations in the night sky over Providence, Rhode Island. Annie Russell Maunder was especially interested in the origin of the 48 ancient constellations.

Studies history of astronomy

Maunder was interested in the history of astronomy, especially the origin of the 48 ancient constellations. (A constellation is a group of stars forming a pattern in the sky.) She noted that the southern limit of those constellations gave clues to the latitude (a "line" parallel to the Earth's equator) of their observers. Maunder shared with her husband a fascination for the astronomy of the early Hindus and Persians, and wrote several articles on the subject. Surviving Edward by 19 years, she died on September 15, 1947.

Further Reading

Maunder, Annie Russell, with Edward Maunder, *The Heavens and Their Story,* R. Culley, 1908.

Ogilvie, Marilyn Bailey, *Women in Science: Antiquity through the Nineteenth Century,* MIT Press, 1986, pp. 129-230.

Journal of the British Astronomical Association, December 1947, p. 238.

Ernst Mayr

Born July 5, 1904
Kempten, Germany

onsidered one of the most important evolutionary biologists of the twentieth century, Ernst Mayr has made major contributions to ornithology (the study of birds), evolutionary theory, and the history and philosophy of biology. He is best known for his work on speciation, or the way one species arises from another. (A species is a group of living organisms that can all interbreed to produce fertile offspring.) Having lived in the United States for over 60 years, Mayr has published hundreds of articles and more than a dozen books. Through his writing he has not only clarified earlier scientific thought, but he has also proposed new theories that have changed the course of biological research.

Ernst Mayr is considered one of the most important evolutionary biologists of the twentieth century.

A bird-watcher since childhood

Ernst Mayr was born on July 5, 1904, in Kempten, Germany, near the borders of Austria and Switzerland. He was one of three sons of Helene Pusinelli Mayr and Otto Mayr,

Evolutionary biologist Ernst Mayr has been called the "Darwin of the twentieth century." Mayr's work has contributed to scientific understanding of the process of evolution, a theory made popular by naturalist Charles Darwin in the nineteenth century. In his book *Systematics and the Origin of Species* (1942), Mayr explained the evolution of new species, which involves his theory of "geographic speciation." According to Mayr, change begins when an organism is separated by geography from its original population. Over the course of many generations the organism will become an entirely new species.

who was a judge. As a boy, Mayr enjoyed bird watching, and he and his parents spent their weekends hiking and observing wildlife. In an interview for *Scientific American* magazine, Mayr remembered his early enthusiasm for birds: "All my high school days, as soon as I was done with my homework, I would be out with my bicycle in a park or someplace, bird-watching. That was the foundation for my whole career."

Mayr received an extensive education that included the study of Latin and Greek. Following in the footsteps of several physicians in his family, he entered the University of Greifswald to a medical degree in 1923. Within two years, however, he had become so interested in the evolutionary theories and exploratory voyages of nineteenth-century British naturalist **Charles Darwin** (1809–1882; for more information, see entry in volume 1, pp. 203–210) that he switched from medicine to zoology (the study of animals). Mayr then moved to the University of Berlin, where he had once worked at the zoological museum during summer vacations. In 1926 he received his Ph.D. in zoology with honors. Soon afterward, he became the assistant curator (superintendent) at the museum.

Leads ornithological expeditions

While still working at the museum, Mayr went to Budapest, Hungary, in 1928 to attend a zoological conference. There he met Lionel Walter Rothschild (1868–1937), a British baron (nobleman) and well-known zoologist. Impressed by the young man, Rothschild asked him to lead an ornithological expedition to Dutch New Guinea, in the southwest Pacific. Mayr jumped at the chance. At that time New Guinea had not been extensively explored by Europeans, so traveling was extremely difficult. Nevertheless, Mayr was eager to investigate the birds of several remote mountain ranges on the island. Predictably, the trip was not easy, and Mayr's party suffered a variety of illnesses and injuries. But his determination remained strong. Deciding to stay in the region, he made a second expedition, which was sponsored by the University of Berlin, to mountain ranges in the Mandated Territory of New Guinea. Then in 1929 and 1930, Mayr participated in the American Museum of Natural History's Whitney South Sea Expedition to the Solomon Islands. The experiences and insights crowded into these few years in the South Pacific would stimulate Mayr's thinking about biology and the development of species for decades to come.

Publishes evolutionary ideas

When the expedition to the Solomon Islands was over, Mayr was invited to be a Whitney research associate in ornithology at the American Museum of Natural History in New York City. Upon his promotion to associate curator of the museum's bird collection in 1932, he decided to stay in the United States. Eventually he became an American citizen. Over the next decade, Mayr worked at identifying and classifying bird species, studying the effect of geographical location on bird populations. This research resulted in two of his most influential books.

In 1941 Mayr published the *List of New Guinea Birds,* in which he explores the ways closely related species can be distinguished from one another. The book also accounts for physical variations within a species. Evolutionary biologist **Stephen Jay Gould** (1941–; for more information, see entry in volume 2, pp. 415–421) noted in *Science* journal that by writing the *List of New Guinea Birds,* Mayr "sharpened his notion of species as fundamental units in nature and deepened his understanding of evolution."

Scientists unclear about evolution

Most biologists in the 1930s and 1940s accepted the validity of natural selection, the basic argument of Darwin's theory of evolution. (Natural selection is the idea that species change and evolve; it is sometimes loosely called "the survival of the fittest.") At the same time, however, few scientists understood how the process of natural selection actually worked. According to Darwin, the fittest members of an animal populations were the ones that survived. But, many biologist wondered, where did those especially well-adapted creatures come from in the first place? During this period the question was complicated by a lack of understanding of exactly what constituted a plant or animal species. Scientists took two conflicting approaches: one school of thought tried to classify species by their shape and appearance, and another tried to identify species through their genes (units of hereditary information carried on chromosomes).

Disturbed by Goldschmidt theory

In December 1939, Mayr attended a lecture series at Yale University presented by Richard Benedikt Goldschmidt (1878–1958), a well-known German geneticist. Goldschmidt argued that new species can arise through sudden genetic mutation (a change in the structure of a gene, resulting in new physical characteristics in a creature). He believed that these changes could take place within a single generation. Mayr was appalled by what he heard. As Fred Hapgood explained in *Science 84* journal, "What Mayr heard in those lectures seemed so wrong that he decided, in his own words, to 'eliminate' those ideas 'from the panorama of evolutionary controversies.'" Convinced that extremely long periods of time were required for the development of a new species, Mayr set out to demolish Goldschmidt's argument.

Proposes theory of geographic speciation

The result was the book *Systematics and the Origin of Species,* which Mayr published in 1942. Relying on his research in the South Pacific, Mayr argued that geographic speciation is basic to the formation of new species. This concept had been advanced more than 100 years earlier—even before Darwin—but it had never taken hold. Mayr showed how the process works: A few animals become separated from their original population and they breed among themselves for many generations. They eventually change so much that they can no longer breed with their original group. For example, birds from the mainland who settled on an island may look like their mainland ancestors, with which they share similar genetic traits. Yet the two groups will not be able to interbreed because the island birds have become a new species. This concept, which Mayr continued to develop through his career, was to form the core of his thinking.

Mayr's ideas about speciation gained acceptance and respect within most of the scientific community. *Systematics and the Origin of Species* has been called the "bible" of a generation of biologists. American zoologist **Edward O. Wilson** (1929–; for more information, see entry in volume 3, pp. 969–979) noted in *Science 84* journal that Mayr offered him and other scientists the "theoretical framework on which to hang facts and plan enterprises." Wilson continued, "He gave taxonomy [the classification of living things] an evolutionary perspective. He got the show on the road."

Appointed professor at Harvard

Over the next several years, Mayr continued to expand and refine his ideas about speciation. In 1946 he founded the Society for the Study of Evolution, becoming the first secretary and later president of the organization. In 1947 he founded the group's official journal, *Evolution,* and served as the first editor. In 1953 he was named Alexander Agassiz Professor of Zoology at Harvard. From 1961 to 1970 he was director of Harvard's Museum of Comparative Zoology. During those years he expanded the museum, which is now a major center of biological research. By this time, Mayr was a recognized leader of "the modern synthetic theory of evolution." Three other prominent researchers in the field were American paleontologist George Gaylord Simpson (1902–1984), Russian-born American biologist Theodosius Dobzhansky (1900–1975), and English zoologist Julian Huxley (1887–1975).

In 1963 Mayr published *Animal Species and Evolution,* in which he wrote of man's place in the natural world. In an interview with *Omni* magazine in 1983, Mayr discussed concerns about humanity's role in nature that he has addressed throughout his career: "Man must realize that he is part of the ecosystem and that his own survival depends on not destroying that ecosystem."

Becomes historian of biology

Although Mayr retired from Harvard as emeritus (honorary) professor of zoology in 1975, he has continued to work intensely and expand his interests. Among his new projects was an ambitious history of biology. In 1982 he published *The Growth of Biological Thought,* which he intended to be the first of two volumes. Then in 1991, at the age of 87, he published yet another careful discussion of evolution, *One Long Argument.* In the book he outlines the differences between modern evolutionists and Darwin. Mayr observes that "The modern evolutionist realizes how great a role chance plays in evolution." In 1997 he released a general history of biological thought for non-scientists, titled *This Is Biology: The Science of the Living World.*

Honored for influential career

Mayr married Margarete Simon on May 4, 1935, and they have two daughters. For many years Mayr, a lean man with brown eyes and white hair, was a familiar figure around Harvard. People noted that Mayr's natural assertiveness and strong writing style add to the persuasiveness of his arguments. During an exceptionally long career, Mayr has been awarded ten honorary degrees from such prominent institutions as Oxford University, Cambridge University, and the University of Paris. In 1954 he was elected to the National Academy of Sciences. Among his numerous prizes are the Darwin-Wallace Medal (1958), the Linnean Medal (1977), the Gregor Mendel medal (1980), and the Darwin Medal of the Royal (1987). In 1983 Mayr received the Balzan Prize, which has been called the equivalent of the Nobel Prize in the biological sciences. He was awarded an equally prestigious honor in 1994 with the Japan Prize from the Committee on the International Prize for Biology. When Mayr received the Balzan Prize and the Japan Prize, fellow scientists applauded his accomplishments. Many have acknowledged him as the greatest evolutionary biologist of the twentieth century.

Further Reading

Gibbons, Ann, "Ernst Mayr Wins the Japan Prize," *Science,* October 21, 1994, p. 365.

Gould, Stephen Jay, "Balzan Prize to Ernst Mayr," *Science,* January 20, 1984, pp. 255-57.

Hapgood, Fred, "The Importance of Being Ernst," *Science 84,* June 1984, pp. 40-46.

Johmann, Carol A., "Interview: Ernst Mayr," *Omni,* February 1983, pp. 73-78, 118-19.

Mayr, Ernst, *Animal Species and Evolution,* Belknap Press-Harvard University Press, 1963.

Mayr, Ernst, "Evolution," *Scientific American,* September 1978, pp. 47-55.

Mayr, Ernst, *Evolution and the Diversity of Life,* Belknap Press-Harvard University Press, 1976.

Mayr, Ernst, *The Growth of Biological Thought,* Belknap Press-Harvard University Press, 1982.

Mayr, Ernst, *List of New Guinea Birds,* American Museum of Natural History, 1941.

Mayr, Ernst, *One Long Argument,* Harvard University Press, 1991.

Mayr, Ernst, *Systematics and the Origin of Species,* Columbia University Press, 1942.

Mayr, Ernst, *This Is Biology: The Science of the Living World,* Harvard University Press/Belknap, 1997.

Rennie, John, "Darwin's Current Bulldog," *Scientific American,* August 1994, pp. 24–25.

Yoon, Carol Kaesuk, "Ernst Mayr: Long Evolution of `Darwin of Twentieth Century,'" *New York Times,* April 15, 1997.

Walter Munk

Born October 19, 1917
Vienna, Austria

A leading oceanographer and geophysicist, Walter Munk has contributed to scientific understanding of ocean currents and circulation, tides, the formation of waves, and irregularities in the rotation of the Earth. Munk's work was instrumental to predicting ocean tides for the D-Day invasion of Normandy during World War II (1939–1945). He also headed a long-range international project to detect global warming by measuring ocean temperatures with sound waves. During his career Munk has been a pioneer in adapting new technology to oceanographic and geophysical research. He was an early user of scuba diving equipment, and he was among the first scientists to use computers for analyzing geophysical data.

Goes to California

Walter Heinrich Munk was born on October 19, 1917, in Vienna, Austria, the son of Hans and Rega Brunner Munk. In an interview with *Scientific American* magazine he admitted he never considered becoming a scientist when he was young: "I

really grew up being interested in only skiing and tennis. Certainly not science." In 1932 he family moved to New York City, where Munk was expected to enter his grandfather's banking business. Becoming bored at the bank, he began taking physics courses at Columbia University, but then decided he wanted to move as far as he could from New York. Impressed by pictures of California in travel brochures, he settled on that state as his new home. Arriving on the west coast, he went to the California Institute of Technology (Cal Tech) in Pasadena, where he was accepted after an unusual application process. "I was terribly naive," Munk recalled in an interview with *Scientific American* magazine, "I hadn't applied. I just showed up and knocked on the dean's door. I thought that was all it took." Munk was given an entrance exam, which he barely passed.

High tide at Big Pine Key, Florida. Walter Munk has contributed greatly to scientific understanding of ocean currents and tides.

Starts career at Scripps

Munk earned a bachelor's degree in physics from Cal Tech in 1939, the same year he became a U.S. citizen. (Physics is the

Oceanographer Walter Munk has made important advances in the understanding of ocean currents, waves, and tides. He used his knowledge of ocean movement to help develop a method of predicting conditions on beaches during World War II (1939–1945). This information was critical to military landings such as the D-Day invasion by Allied forces at Normandy, France. He also conducted first-hand research on the effect of atomic bombs on ocean waves and currents. A pioneer in the use of sound waves to monitor ocean patterns, Munk has used the technology to test for evidence of global warming in ocean waters.

science that explores the physical properties and composition of objects and the forces that affect them.) He received a master's degree in geophysics (the physics of the Earth) from the school in 1941. He had planned to continue working in geophysics, but then he took a summer job at the University of California's Scripps Institution of Oceanography in La Jolla. Munk became so interested in oceanography (the study of oceans and seas) that he decided to complete his doctoral studies at Scripps. Working under Norwegian meteorologist and oceanographer Harald Sverdrup (1888–1957), he earned a Ph.D in oceanography in 1947.

Conducts World War II ocean research

During World War II, Munk enlisted in the U.S. Army, but he was later allowed to move to the navy so he could work with Sverdrup on ocean-related military projects. One of their jobs was to develop a method for forecasting the height of breaking waves and the condition of surf on beaches. This system was extremely important to preparations for the ultimately successful Normandy invasion. Munk's work was used in a number of other military landings on shores in North Africa and the South Pacific. During the war Munk went on to serve in the U.S. Army's Ski Battalion. He was also a meteorologist for the Army Air Force as well as an oceanographer with the University of California Division of War Research.

Following the war, in 1946, Munk participated in nuclear weapons testing at the Bikini Atoll in the South Pacific Ocean. He studied ocean currents and waves created by nuclear explosions. He observed one test from a raft anchored just ten miles from ground zero (the site where the nuclear blast occurs).

Munk described the blast to in an interview with the *Orange County Register* newspaper: "It's stunning; it's horrible. It's not dark, it's quite white. You see the boiling and the water vapor above you, like a curtain coming down all around you."

Founds Institute of Geophysics branch

In 1947, after earning his Ph.D., Munk was appointed assistant professor of geophysics at Scripps Institution. Within seven years he had become a full professor and a member of the University of California's Institute of Geophysics, which had its headquarters in Los Angeles. During the 1950s Munk helped to explain why the axis of the Earth wobbles and why the Earth's spin has small variations. In 1960 he established a branch of the institute in La Jolla, which later became the University of California at San Diego. The new branch was created to study the atmosphere, oceans, and interior of the Earth using experimental and mathematical physics. Munk served as associate director of the system-wide University of California Institute (later renamed the Institute of Geophysics and Planetary Physics) until 1982.

Studies ocean swells and tides

In the early 1960s, Munk began studying attenuation (loss of intensity) in ocean waves. Using pressure-sensing devices that were lowered to the ocean floor at six different locations, he and colleague Frank Snodgrass were able to track very long ocean swells. The swells extended over 12,000 kilometers across the Pacific Ocean from Australia to Alaska. As a result of the tracking, Munk found that storms taking place near Antarctica create the long swells that arrive at Southern California in the summer.

In 1969 Munk began exploring ways of improving tide prediction. He developed sophisticated pressure-sensing instruments that could be placed in capsules and dropped to the ocean floor. An acoustical (sound-wave) signal would then return the capsule back to the sea surface. When Munk retrieved the instruments, they allowed him to precisely measure tides in the deep sea. He has conducted measurements off the coast of California, in the Antarctic Ocean, and in the Atlantic Ocean in the Bay of Biscay in Europe and south of Bermuda. Munk has done further research in using sound waves as a tool to monitor the seas.

Attempts to confirm global warming

Still fascinated by the ocean, Munk is involved in the effort to detect global warming by measuring ocean temperatures with sound waves. The $35-million project, which involves scientists from seven nations, is called Acoustic Thermometry of Ocean Climate (ATOC). It resulted in part from a successful experiment Munk headed in 1991 off Heard Island in the southern Indian Ocean. The experiment proved that low-frequency sounds produced by underwater speakers could be transmitted and picked up by listening devices up to a distance of 18,000 kilometers. Munk also learned that sound waves cross the Earth's oceans in sound channels—3,000-foot-deep bands of water that are not affected by weather conditions on the surface. Acting as a kind of superhighway, the channels restrict and focus sound waves to particular paths. Thus the waves do not easily break apart and can be heard over long distances.

The ATOC has been put on hold as a result of environmental concerns about the effect of sound waves on ocean life. If allowed to proceed, the project will duplicate the Heard Island work on a much larger scale. Transmitting stations off California and Kauai, Hawaii, will send pulses of sound to listening stations throughout the Pacific Ocean. Scientists will then use the ocean channels to take water-temperature measurements over the entire Pacific. In this way they hope to gain enough information to detect whether the Earth's surface, 70 percent of which is ocean, has become measurably warmer over a period of one to two decades.

Wins highest honor

Munk's work has won international recognition. He was elected to the National Academy of Sciences (1956) and to the

Royal Society of London (1976). In 1993 he was awarded the Vetlesen Prize, which is considered the highest honor in the earth sciences. A member or fellow of more than a dozen professional societies, Munk has held three Guggenheim Fellowships. He has also published more than 200 scientific papers. Munk and his wife, Judith, an architect, have two children.

Further Reading

Cass, Connie, "Life at Sea," *Orange County Register,* April 21, 1993.

Modern Men of Science, McGraw-Hill, 1968.

Modern Scientists and Engineers, McGraw-Hill, 1980, pp. 339–40.

Yam, Phillip, "The Man Who Would Hear Ocean Temperatures," *Scientific American,* January 1995, pp. 37–40.

Yoichiro Nambu

January 18, 1921
Tokyo, Japan

Yoichiro Nambu has made a number of important contributions to the field of particle physics.

Yoichiro Nambu is a ground breaking theoretical physicist (a scientist who develops ideas about physical objects and the forces that affect them). His research has contributed to the understanding of subatomic particles (particles that make up atoms). In addition to helping to discover a number of new elementary particles (particles that cannot be broken down into smaller objects), he has developed explanations of the creation and behavior of particles. In 1982 he was awarded the National Medal of Science by President Ronald Reagan "for seminal contributions to the understanding of elementary particles and their interactions." Since 1991 he has been Professor Emeritus of Physics at the University of Chicago. According to Nambu's colleagues, he is a scientist who is continually ahead of the times. One friend was quoted in *Scientific American* magazine as saying, "people don't understand him, because he is so farsighted."

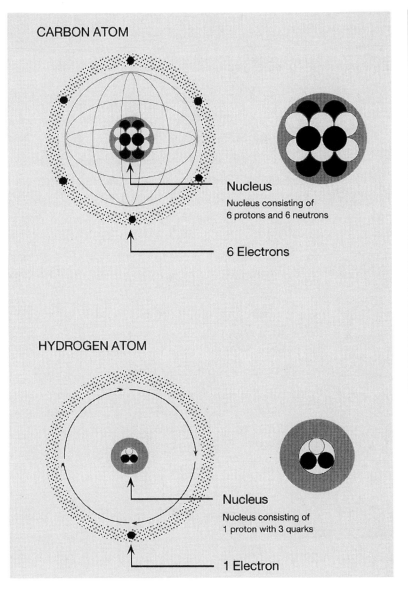

CARBON ATOM

Nucleus
Nucleus consisting of
6 protons and 6 neutrons

6 Electrons

HYDROGEN ATOM

Nucleus
Nucleus consisting of
1 proton with 3 quarks

1 Electron

Subatomic particles. Yoichiro Nambu's research has led to a more complete understanding of subatomic particles (particles that make up atoms).

Seeks challenge of physics

Yoichiro Nambu was born in Tokyo, Japan, on January 18, 1921, to Kichiro and Kimiko Nambu. His father, Kichiro, was a schoolteacher. An independent thinker, Kichiro had run away from his home in Fukui, near Kyoto, to attend the university in Tokyo. After a major earthquake destroyed Tokyo when his son Yoichiro was only two years old, Kichiro took

Theoretical physicist Yoichiro Nambu's ability to imagine the unusual world of subatomic particles has allowed him to make a number of significant discoveries. Not only has he helped to define new particles such as bosons, pions, and gluons, he has also given new explanations of the behavior and creation of particles. Nambu is particularly known for the idea that subatomic particles do not always observe the rules of symmetry that apply to larger physical bodies. For instance, he found that the number of subatomic particles in a superconducting material does not remain the same in a reaction. Instead, the number actually increases. Nambu also originated the "string theory," the observation that some particles act like they are connected by strings.

his family back to Fukui and built a house outside the town. Yoichiro Nambu attended a strict military-style school, but his father's belief in the importance of thinking for oneself helped to keep the extreme ideas of the school in perspective. He often escaped by reading his father's books.

In 1937 Nambu followed in his father's footsteps and attended a college in Tokyo. He found an open environment where people freely discussed and investigated a wide range of ideas—something he had not experienced in his rural hometown. Ironically, Nambu's worst subject was physics because he had a hard time grasping concepts like entropy (the loss of energy that occurs in any closed system). In fact, he flunked his class in thermodynamics (the study of heat). Perhaps inspired by one of his professors, Nambu decided to pursue a career in physics in spite of this weakness. He earned a bachelor of science degree in 1942, then completed his Ph.D. at the University of Tokyo in 1952.

Starts career after war

World War II (1939-1945) broke out while Nambu was studying in Tokyo, so he was drafted into the Japanese army for much of the war. During his first year in the military he was given difficult physical tasks such as digging trenches and carrying boats. But then he was assigned to a scientific group that was trying to develop a short-wave radar system. While working on this project he fell in love with one of his research assistants, Chieko Hida, whom he married after the end of the war. They have two sons.

After the war, Nambu returned to Tokyo, where he accepted a research position. Conditions in Tokyo were harsh:

Nambu was forced to live in his office because housing was so difficult to find, and he spent much of his time searching for food. But in his spare moments, he was able to turn to ideas about physics. He kept up on developments in the field by reading *Time* magazine and other materials brought in by American forces that had occupied the city after Japan's defeat in the war.

Nambu was appointed professor of physics at Osaka City University in 1949, three years before his doctorate was granted. In 1952 he moved to the Institute for Advanced Study in Princeton, New Jersey, and two years later he joined the physics department at the University of Chicago as a research associate. Nambu has remained affiliated with the University of Chicago for most of his career. Achieving the rank of professor in 1968, he was chair of the department of physics from 1974 until 1977, when he was appointed a Henry Pratt Judson Distinguished Service Professor. Nambu became a U.S. citizen in 1970.

Leads particle physics research

Despite difficult conditions for scholars and scientists in Japan in the late 1940s and early 1950s, Nambu began developing ideas in particle physics. He created a mathematical formula that showed how two particles can bind together. He was also one of several scientists who proposed that new particles are created in pairs. In Chicago in 1957, he was the first person to predict the existence of the omega particle. Although other scientists did not accept his idea at first, the particle was discovered within the next year. Nambu later played an important role in the prediction of boson, pion, and gluon particles.

Throughout Nambu's career he has directed his research not only toward predicting the existence of various subatomic particles, but also making sense of their behavior. His ideas and explanations have contributed to a body of intellectual work known as grand unification theories. Also called "GUTs," these theories are an attempt to explain the fundamental forces of nature in a single framework.

Proposes "broken symmetry" theory

Nambu's best-known contribution to GUTs is his concept of "spontaneous symmetry breaking" in particle physics. The laws of physics predict that subatomic particles should behave symmetrically. That is, the number of particles at the beginning of an event should equal the number of particles at the end of an event. But experiments show that subatomic particles in superconductors (materials that conduct electricity with very little loss of energy) do not keep such a balance. Nambu showed that the magnetic field of a superconductor makes certain particles heavy, causing the breakdown of symmetry and the creation of new particles. He called these new particles "bosons." In the mid-1980s physicists built on Nambu's work to advance a GUT explanation that describes at least two of nature's forces, weak force (which is responsible for particle decay) and electromagnetism (magnetism created by a current of electricity). This theory, now widely accepted by physicists, is known as the electroweak theory.

Advances knowledge of quarks

Nambu next turned to the study of quarks (subatomic particles that carry a certain type of charge). One of his important contributions in this area was suggesting that quarks are held together by even smaller particles called gluons. Nambu's study of quarks also led to the "string theory" of particle movement. String theory is the idea that quark particles act as if they are connected by strings. This concept may open doors to new discoveries in the field of particle physics.

According to Nambu's colleagues, the physicist's ideas are always ten years ahead of their time. His work is so forward-thinking and complex that it takes that long for other scientists to understand and appreciate what he has done. His fellow scientists consider him a shy and modest man who has an unusual gift for imagining the three-dimensional motions of physical systems. Nambu continues to focus his research on quarks, trying to determine why individual quarks seem to have different masses. (Mass is the amounts of matter in a body.) He is also studying biological issues and entropy, including the behavior of virus-sized particles.

Honored for influential career

Nambu has been honored for his contributions to the understanding of elementary particles and their interactions. His awards include the Dannie Heineman Prize for Mathematical Physics from the American Institute of Physics (1970), the J. Robert Oppenheimer Prize (1976), the Max Planck Medal (1985), and the P. A. M. Dirac Medal (1986). Nambu holds honorary degrees from universities in the United States and Japan. He has published numerous professional articles as well as a *Quarks,* a popular book on particle physics.

Further Reading

Mukerjee, Madhusree, "Strings and Gluons—The Seer Saw Them All," *Scientific American,* February 1995, pp. 37-39.

Nambu, Yoichiro, *Quarks,* World Scientific, 1985.

Emmy Noether

Born March 23, 1882
Erlangen, Germany
Died April 14, 1935
Bryn Mawr, Pennsylvania

Emmy Noether is considered one of the world's greatest woman mathematicians.

Emmy Noether was a world-renowned mathematician whose innovative approach to modern abstract algebra inspired colleagues and students. (Rather than working with specific problems, abstract algebra is concerned with general concepts.) She was dismissed from her university position at the beginning of the Nazi era in Germany because she was both Jewish and female. Noether then moved to the United States and taught at Bryn Mawr College and other institutions. When she died, German-born American physicist **Albert Einstein** (1879–1955; for more information, see entry in volume 1, pp. 260–269) remembered her in a letter to the *New York Times* newspaper as "the most significant creative mathematical genius thus far produced since the higher education of women began."

Comes from scientific family

Amalie (Emmy) Noether was born on March 23, 1882, in the small university town of Erlangen in southern Germany.

Her mother, Ida Amalia Kaufmann Noether, came from a wealthy family in Cologne. Her father, Max Noether, a professor at the University of Erlangen, was an accomplished mathematician who worked on the theory of algebraic functions. Two of her three younger brothers also became scientists. Noether's childhood consisted of the usual activities of going to school, learning household skills, and taking piano lessons. Since girls were not allowed to enroll in the gymnasium (college preparatory school), she attended the Städtischen Höheren Töchterschule, where she studied arithmetic and languages. In 1900 she passed the Bavarian state examinations with evaluations of "very good" in French and English (she received only a "satisfactory" evaluation in practical classroom conduct). This certified her to teach foreign languages at female educational institutions.

Begins teaching career

Instead of seeking a language-teaching position, Noether decided to pursue university studies. Since she had not graduated from a gymnasium, however, she first had to pass an entrance examination. She unofficially sat in on courses at the University of Erlangen from 1900 until 1902, then in 1903 she passed the entrance exam and enrolled at the University of Göttingen. There she encountered such notable German mathematicians as Hermann Minkowski (1864–1909), Felix Klein (1849–1925), and **David Hilbert** (1862–1943; for more information, see entry in volume 2, pp. 454–462). In 1904 she entered the University of Erlangen, which admitted women. At Erlangen, Noether studied with Paul Gordan, a mathematics professor who was also a family friend. She received her Ph.D. with honors in 1908.

Noether worked without pay at the Mathematical Institute of Erlangen from 1908 until 1915. Her university duties included doing research and serving as a dissertation adviser for two students. Occasionally she delivered lectures in the absence of her father, who was in poor health. In addition, Noether began to work with Ernst Otto Fischer (1918–), an algebraist who directed her toward a broader theoretical style. Noether not

Mathematician Emmy Noether provided the foundations for important developments in mathematics and science during the early twentieth century. She helped establish the importance of the general theory of relativity originated by German-born American physicist Albert Einstein. Later in her career she became a pioneer in the field of abstract algebra, developing a system that allowed practical mathematics to be applied to theoretical fields such as logic and number theory. Noether's work led to new and creative uses of mathematics in chemistry and physics.

only published her doctoral thesis, but she was also elected to membership in the Circolo Matematico di Palermo in 1908. The following year she was admitted to the German Mathematical Society. She addressed the society's 1909 meeting in Salzburg, Austria, and its 1913 meeting in Vienna, Austria.

Formulates mathematics of relativity

In 1915 Klein and Hilbert invited Noether to join them at the Mathematical Institute in Göttingen. They were working on the mathematics of the general theory of relativity that had been newly announced by Einstein, and they believed Noether's expertise would be helpful. In the general theory of relativity, Einstein attempted to explain the relationship between measurements made in any two systems (frames of reference) that are in motion. The general theory states that a body affects the shape of the space that surrounds it, so that a second body moving near the first body will travel in a curved path. In this way, general relativity uses the curvature of space to explain gravity (the force of attraction between all matter). Mathematicians wanted to develop exact formulas that could be used to calculate such relationships and determine if Einstein's theory was correct. In 1918 Noether mathematically proved two propositions that form a cornerstone for the theory of general relativity. One is now known as Noether's Theorem.

University refuses to hire women

While Noether was making important mathematical contributions, she worked without pay at Göttingen because women were not admitted to the faculty. Hilbert tried unsuccessfully to secure a position for her. He finally arranged for her to teach, however, by announcing a class in mathematical physics under his own name and then letting her lecture in his place. By 1919 university rules were loosened and she was designated a Privatdozent (a licensed lecturer who could receive fees from students but not from the university). Three years later Noether was given the unofficial title of associate professor. Nevertheless, she was actually hired as an adjunct (part-time) teacher and paid a modest salary without fringe benefits or tenure.

Lays foundations of abstract algebra

Brilliant mathematicians often make their greatest contributions early in their careers. Noether was a notable exception to that rule. She began producing her most powerful and creative work around the age of 40. In 1920 she wrote a paper on noncommutative field theory. (This theory pertains to a system in which an operation such as multiplication yields a different answer for a x b than for b x a). The following year she produced a paper on the theory of ideals in rings, which is considered her most important accomplishment. Expanding on the work of German mathematician Julius Wilhelm Richard Dedekind (1831–1916) on solutions of polynomials (complex algebraic expressions), Noether's work laid the foundation for modern abstract algebra.

Rather than working with specific problems, abstract algebra is concerned with the general concepts. Logic and number theory are connected with applied (practical) mathematics by abstract algebra. This connection makes abstract algebra useful in chemistry and physics.

Recognized by professional associations

During the winter of 1928-29, Noether was a visiting professor at the University of Moscow and the Communist Academy in Russia. The following summer she taught at the University of Frankfurt. The International Mathematical Congress of 1928 recognized her contributions to mathematics by inviting her to be the principle speaker at a meeting in Bologna, Italy. In 1932 she was chosen to address the Congress's general session in Zurich, Switzerland.

Noether was on the mathematics faculty at Göttingen when it enjoyed the highest reputation for mathematical research and teaching in the world. Yet she was unable to secure a teaching position equivalent to that of her male counterparts. Such prominent mathematicians as Hermann Weyl (1885–1955) could not even use their influence in Noether's behalf. Weyl once commented: "I was ashamed to occupy such a preferred position beside her whom I knew to be my superior as a mathematician in many respects." In 1932, on Noether's fiftieth birthday, the university's algebraists held a celebration in her honor. Later that year she was named cowinner of the Alfred Ackermann-Teubner Memorial Prize for the Advancement of Mathematical Knowledge.

Removed from university for being Jewish

The supportive scholarly environment at the University of Göttingen ended in 1933 with the rise of the Nazi Party in Germany. (The Nazi Party enforced political and economic doctrines based on totalitarian government, state control of all industry, and the rule of groups considered to be racially superior.) Within months, anti-Jewish policies spread through the country. On April 7, 1933, Noether was formally notified that she could no longer teach at the university. She was a dedicated pacifist (an individual opposed to the use of violence), and Weyl later recalled, "her courage, her frankness, her unconcern about her own fate, her conciliatory spirit were, in the midst of all the hatred and meanness, despair and sorrow surrounding us, a moral solace."

For a time, Noether continued to meet informally with students and colleagues, inviting groups to her apartment. Then the Emergency Committee to Aid Displaced German Scholars entered into an agreement with Bryn Mawr, a women's college in Pennsylvania, which offered Noether a professorship. Her first year's salary was funded by the Emergency Committee and the Rockefeller Foundation.

Teaches in America

In the fall of 1933, Noether was supervising four graduate students at Bryn Mawr. Early the following year she began delivering weekly lectures at the Institute for Advanced Study at Princeton University in New Jersey. She never expressed any anger toward Germany for forcing her out of her position and her home, and she maintained friendly ties with her former colleagues. With her characteristic curiosity and good nature, she settled into her new home in America. Noether learned enough English to successfully converse and teach, although she occasionally lapsed into German when concentrating on technical material.

In 1934 Noether visited Göttingen to arrange shipment of her possessions to the United States. When she returned to Bryn Mawr, she had received a two-year renewal on her teaching grant. In 1935 she underwent surgery to remove a tumor in her uterus. The operation successfully removed the tumor, but four days later Noether suddenly developed a high fever and lost consciousness. She died on April 14, 1935, apparently from a post-operative infection. Her ashes were buried near the library on the Bryn Mawr campus.

Honored after death

Over the course of her career, Noether supervised a dozen graduate students and wrote 45 technical papers. She also inspired countless scientific discoveries through her habit of suggesting topics of investigation to students and colleagues. Attempting to show Noether the honor she had not received during her lifetime, the University of Erlangen held a conference on the fiftieth anniversary of her doctorate in 1953. In 1982 the university commemorated the hundredth anniversary of her birth by dedicating a memorial plaque at the Mathematics Institute. During the same year, the Emmy Noether Gymnasium, a coeducational school emphasizing mathematics, the natural sciences, and modern languages, was opened in Erlangen.

Further Reading

Brewer, James W., *Emmy Noether: A Tribute to Her Life and Work,* edited by Martha K. Smith, Marcel Dekker, 1981.

Kimberling, Clark H., "Emmy Noether," *The American Mathematical Monthly,* February 1972, pp. 136-49.

Kramer, Edna E., *The Nature and Growth of Modern Mathematics,* Princeton University, 1981, pp. 656-72.

Magill, Frank N., editor, *Great Events from History II,* Books International, 1991, pp. 650-54, 716-19.

Noether, Emmy, *Collected Papers,* Springer-Verlag, 1983.

Osen, Lynn M., *Women in Mathematics,* Massachusetts Institute of Technology, 1979, pp. 141-52.

Perl, Teri, *Math Equals: Biographies of Women Mathematicians,* Addison-Wesley, 1978, pp. 172-78.

John P. Parker

Born 1827
Norfolk, Virginia
Died February 4, 1900
Ripley, Ohio

Through hard work and ingenuity, John P. Parker rose from slavery to become a successful inventor and the owner of a prosperous iron foundry. His accomplishments are significant because in the nineteenth-century, United States patents were rarely granted to black inventors, and even fewer black people operated thriving businesses. Parker was one of only fifty-five African Americans to obtain more than one patent in the United States by 1900. In fact, according to the African American writer and educator W.E.B. Du Bois, Parker owned at least three of the seventy-seven patents issued to African Americans before 1886.

"... a plow made by a black man, tells us more than a hundred first class speeches."

Sold into slavery at age eight

The son of a black slave mother and a white plantation owner, John Percial Parker was born in Norfolk, Virginia, in 1827. At the age of eight he was sold by his master (who may have been his father) to an agent in Richmond, Virginia, who

John P. Parker was a prominent nineteenth-century African American inventor who held patents for numerous tools that contributed significantly to the growing agricultural industry after the Civil War (1861-1864). Parker's inventions included a screw for a tobacco press, a portable screw press, and a harrow known as the Parker Pulverizer. Prior to the Civil War, Parker was also a prominent Underground Railroad "conductor" who is credited with leading nearly one thousand African American slaves to freedom.

took him for resale to Mobile, Alabama. In his autobiography Parker later described the humiliating experience. In Norfolk he and another slave were tied together and forced to walk to Richmond. After he was sold a second time, Parker was marched in chains the entire distance to Alabama with a large slave caravan. In Mobile he was purchased as a household servant by a physician.

Although laws known as slave codes prohibited slaves from being educated, the doctor's sons smuggled books into their home and taught Parker to read and write. When Parker was sixteen he was sent with two of the sons to be their servant while they attended Yale University in New Haven, Connecticut. Fearing that Parker would try to escape once he reached the North, however, the doctor ordered him to return to Mobile. He then apprenticed Parker to craftsmen. Among the craftsmen was a plasterer who, enraged at Parker for not doing a job correctly, beat the young man so severely that he was hospitalized. While recovering from his injuries Parker managed to escape and flee to New Orleans, Louisiana, where he stowed away on a river boat. He had several other adventures before the doctor eventually found him and took him back to Mobile. This time Parker was apprenticed to an iron molder (a person who shapes objects from liquefied iron ore in molds) at a local foundry (a factory where iron ore is processed and made into products), and he discovered his future career.

Buys his freedom

Parker quickly proved his talents as a highly productive molder. "Being of an inventive mind," he recalled in *His Promised Land,* "I soon rigged up my bench so I could do more and better work than any man in the shop." But, he added, "This fact naturally caused some ill-feeling among the other workmen toward me." To make matters worse, he was extravagant and could not manage his money. "My master gave me what I made," Parker said, "so I very foolishly spent my money on myself. I remember I paid twenty dollars for a hat." His problems increased when he had a fight with his foreman, so the doctor sent him to a foundry in New Orleans. Again the other workers were hostile to his superior talents, and he lost his job.

When it appeared that Parker would be sold as a field hand on a sugar plantation, he conceived a unique plan. He persuaded one of the doctor's patients, a widow named Mrs. Ryder, to purchase him and let him buy his freedom. At the last minute she agreed to pay $1800 for him—reportedly the fee was so high because of Parker's reputation for stubbornness—and he went to work as a molder in another Mobile foundry. According to one account, while Parker was employed at this foundry, he invented a circular harrow (an instrument that breaks up and smooths soil). His foreman then stole the idea and fired Parker. By 1845, however, Parker managed to pay off his debt to Mrs. Ryder. He was a free man.

An Underground Railroad Conductor

For many years prior to the Civil War (1861-1864), John P. Parker was a prominent "conductor" on the Underground Railroad, a network of white and black abolitionists in the North and South who helped African Americans fleeing from slavery. Yet, Parker did not receive wide recognition for his achievements—either as an inventor or an abolitionist—until the 1970s. Parker dictated his autobiography to Frank Moody Gregg, a journalist, in 1880. More than a century later, in 1996, Parker's fascinating story was published as *His Promised Land*.

Becomes involved in the Underground Railroad

Upon gaining his freedom Parker asked for a pass to Indiana, and he took a job at a foundry in New Albany. But he stayed there only briefly before moving to Cincinnati, Ohio, which, he said, "lured [him] away to other adventures." In Cincinnati, Parker became involved in the Underground Railroad, helping slaves cross the border from Kentucky, then a territory in the South. In 1848 Parker married Miranda

Boulden, with whom he would eventually have six children. Two years later the Parkers moved to Ripley, Ohio, home of the famous abolitionist John Rankin, a Presbyterian minister whose house on the bank of the Ohio River was a way station for escaping slaves. Rankin allegedly sheltered the woman who was the inspiration for the character "Eliza" in Harriet Beecher Stowe's novel *Uncle Tom's Cabin* (1852).

According to Gregg, when Parker moved to Ripley he "entered into one of the most adventurous careers of any slaverunner along the entire border." For almost fifteen years Parker helped to liberate nearly one thousand slaves. Since slaverunning was against the law, however, he told no one about his activities. Working as an iron molder during the day and transporting slaves across the river at night, Parker led a double life. Gregg was a young boy growing up in Ripley at the time, and he remembered Parker "as the man who was afraid to walk on the sidewalk. Winter or summer, rain or shine, he invariably walked in the middle of the street. The reason he did was Ripley was an old town with many narrow alleys, out of which enemies could leap at him unawares. This habit he formed when there was a reward on his head, dead or alive."

Starts his own company

Parker had another reason for secrecy: He was becoming a successful businessman. In 1854 he established the Ripley Foundry and Machine Company, a small plant for the manufacture of castings (iron products cast in molds). In 1863 Parker acted as a recruiter of soldiers to serve in the 27th Regiment of the United States Army, a black unit, in the Civil War. His foundry also made castings for the war effort, and during this time he patented several inventions. After the war, in 1865, Parker and his partner William Hood bought a foundry and blacksmith shop. Within three years they nearly doubled their investment of $6000. Employing twenty-five workers, the company manufactured engines ranging from ten to twenty-five horsepower, a reaper and mower (a machine for harvesting grain), a sugar mill (a device for grinding sugar cane or sugar beets into table sugar), steel plows, and even iron frames for schoolhouse desks. Parker marketed his agricultural implements specifically to African American buyers throughout the South, who were now able to farm their own land. As a result of his entrepreneurial spirit, Ripley began to thrive. A local history notes that no one "was more prominently identified with the prosperity of the town than John Parker."

Patents best-known inventions

Although many African American businesses failed during economic hard times known as the Panic of 1873, Parker's enterprise survived. In 1876 he formed another partnership, Belchamber & Parker, to manufacture threshers (machines for separating seed from harvested plants such as wheat). The company dissolved two years later, but by that time Parker was a wealthy man. He went on to patent his best-known inventions. In 1884 he obtained the patent for a screw (the principal operating part) for tobacco presses (devices that cut tobacco), and the following year he was issued a patent for a portable screw press. In 1890 he patented a type of harrow called the Parker Pulverizer. All of these items were produced in his foundry.

Overcomes adversity

The 1880s was also a period of setbacks and disasters. In 1885 Parker nearly went bankrupt as the result of a failed venture into milling (the processing of flour from grain), a trade in which he had no experience. The following year the mill burned down, totally wiping out his investment. In 1889 another fire destroyed Parker's home and damaged his foundry. Fortunately the fire department saved his machine shop, where he manufactured the tobacco presses, his main business at the time. In less than a year Parker had built a new home, foundry, and woodworking shop. He called his company the Phoenix Foundry (the phoenix is a legendary bird that lived for 500 hundred years, burned itself, and arose from the ashes to live again).

Leaves a legacy

The Phoenix Foundry was the largest business of its kind between Portsmouth, Ohio, and Cincinnati. At least one of Parker's sons worked as a sales agent for the company, marketing the Parker Pulverizer in the West. The foundry remained in operation until 1918, well after Parker's death, but it was not run by any of his children. He had stipulated in his will that they were forbidden to carry on the family business because he wanted them to go to college and pursue professions. His three sons and three daughters all fulfilled his wishes. In the late 1990s restoration was begun on Parker's home—which still has the original cast iron front steps made in his foundry—in Ripley as a memorial museum to his inventive and humanitarian spirit. Both the Parker and the Rankin houses became National Historical Landmarks in 1997.

Further Reading

Bernstein, Mark, "Freedom's Ferryman," *Ohio Magazine,* April, 1997, pp. 44-8; 108-110.

James, Portia P., *The Real McCoy; African American Invention and Innovation from 1619 to 1930,* Smithsonian Institution, 1989, p. 48.

Sprague, Stuart Seely, ed., *His Promised Land: The Autobiography of John P. Parker,* Norton, 1996; paperback edition, 1997.

Weeks, Louis, "John P. Parker: Black Abolitionist Entrepreneur, 1827-1900," *Ohio History,* Spring, 1971, pp. 155-62.

Mary G. Ross

Born in 1908
Oklahoma

M ary G. Ross has made notable contribution as an aerospace engineer, particularly in areas related to space flight and ballistic missiles. As a member of the original engineering team at Lockheed's Missile Systems Division, she worked on a number of defense systems. She also contributed to space exploration efforts with her work for the *Apollo* program, the *Polaris* reentry vehicle, and interplanetary space probes.

Mary G. Ross has contributed to the engineering of defense systems and space programs.

Early interest in math and physics

Mary G. Ross was born in Oklahoma in 1908 into a distinguished Cherokee Indian heritage. Her great-great-grandfather, John Ross, was the principal chief of the Cherokee Nation between 1828 and 1866. Mary Ross was later to remark that she had been brought up in the Cherokee tradition of equal education for both boys and girls. She was, however, the only girl in her math class, which did not seem to bother

Aerospace engineer Mary G. Ross has assisted in important U.S. government defense and space programs. During the 1950s she was one of the original members of the Lockheed Missile Systems Division. Assisting in the design of ballistic missiles and other national defense systems, Ross also worked as an engineer on the U.S. space program. Among the projects on which she participated were the Agena rockets used in the *Apollo* space program, the *Polaris* reentry vehicle, and the space probes to Mars and Venus.

her. Indeed, her early interests were math, physics, and science.

Armed with these interests and a sense of purpose, Ross graduated from high school when she was 16. She attended Northeastern State Teacher's College, graduating in 1928. She then taught mathematics and science in public schools. She also served as a girls' advisor at a Pueblo and Navajo school for boys and girls. After teaching for nearly a decade, Ross returned to school herself, this time to Colorado State Teachers College (now the University of Northern Colorado at Greeley). She graduated with a master's degree in mathematics in 1938.

Begins work with Lockheed

The aviation industry underwent considerable growth at the beginning of World War II (1939–1945). In 1942 Ross found a position as an assistant to a consulting mathematician with Lockheed Aircraft Corporation in Burbank, California. Her early work at Lockheed involved engineering problems having to do with transport and fighter aircraft. Meanwhile, with the support of Lockheed, Ross continued her education at the University of California, Los Angeles, where she took courses in aeronautical and mechanical engineering.

Selected for new missiles division

When Lockheed formed its Missiles Systems Division in 1954, Ross was selected as one of the first 40 employees. She was the only female engineer among them. As the U.S. missile program developed, Ross became increasingly involved in researching and evaluating the performance of ballistic (projectile) missiles and other defense systems. She also studied the distribution of pressure caused by ocean waves and how it affected submarine-launched vehicles.

In 1958 Ross concentrated on satellite orbits and the Agena series of rockets that played a prominent role in the *Apollo* program to land astronauts on the moon during the 1960s. As an advanced systems engineer, Ross worked on the *Polaris* reentry vehicle and engineering systems for manned space flights. Before her retirement from Lockheed in 1973, she conducted research on flyby space probes (exploratory missions that involve flying near the planets) that would study Mars and Venus. After Ross retired she remained active in engineering by delivering lectures to high school and college groups. She concentrated particularly on encouraging young women and Native American youths to train for technical careers.

Recognized for work

During her career, Ross wrote a number of classified publications and received several honors. In 1961 she won the *San Francisco Examiner* award for Woman of Distinction, and the California State Federation of Business and Professional Clubs recognized her contributions with the Woman of Achievement Award. Ross was elected a fellow and life member of the Society of Women Engineers, whose Santa Clara Valley Section established a scholarship in her name. She has also received achievement awards from the American Indian Science and Engineering Society and from the Council of Energy Resource Tribes. In 1992 she was inducted into the Silicon Valley Engineering Hall of Fame.

Miriam Rothschild

Born August 5, 1908
Ashton Wold, England

"I think that if you had to describe any talent I might have, it is that I am a good observer. And that means that you don't only notice things, but you think about what you have noticed."

Miriam Rothschild's best-known work has been her studies of insects and parasites (organisms that live in or on another organism). Considered the world's foremost authority on fleas, she has made numerous other scientific contributions. She has written more than 350 papers in a variety of fields such as marine biology, chemistry, horticulture (the science of growing plants), and zoology (the study of animals). Rothschild is also the author of 12 books. Although she is widely respected for her research on fleas, however, Rothschild did not have a typical education in the sciences. In fact, her scientific accomplishments are entirely a result of a natural curiosity about the physical world and a positive learning environment provided by her family.

Family inspires interest in natural history

Miriam Louisa Rothschild was born into the wealthy Rothschild banking family on August 5, 1908, at Ashton Wold,

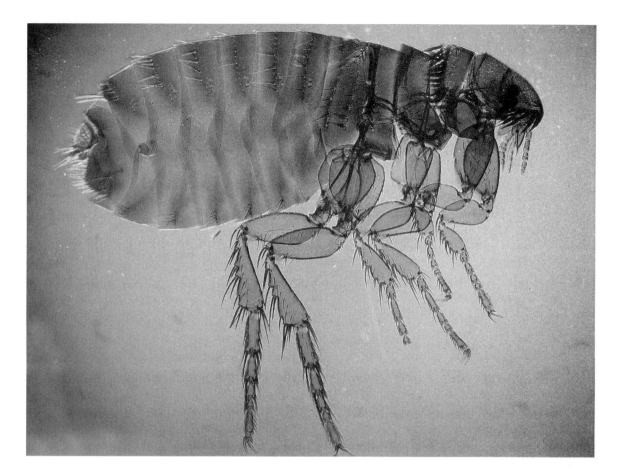

her parents' estate near Peterborough, England. She is the oldest of four children of Nathaniel Charles and Rozsika von Wertheimstein Rothschild. Her grandfather was the first Baron Rothschild. Although Miriam's father was a banker by profession, zoology was his true passion. He founded the Society for the Promotion of Nature Preserves and for years he studied moths, butterflies, and fleas. During his lifetime he put together an astounding collection of fleas that numbered in the millions. He also identified the type of flea that carries the bubonic plague (an epidemic disease caused by a bacterium). Rothschild's mother, who was Hungarian by birth, had her own unique talents and interests. In addition to possessing a sharp business sense, she was a champion in women's lawn tennis.

As a child, Rothschild spent six months of every year with her grandparents and her uncle Walter at their estate outside

A flea magnified 50 times. An authority on the insect, Miriam Rothschild showed how fleas reproduce and how and why they choose their hosts.

Zoologist and naturalist Miriam Rothschild is perhaps best known as a world authority on fleas. She made important discoveries about fleas while cataloging and studying the enormous collection of fleas put together by her father. Rothschild also studied other parasites and helped to discover why monarch butterflies are poisonous to birds and animals. Although she had little formal education, Rothschild has made significant contributions to the fields of zoology, chemistry, marine biology, and horticulture.

London. Although all the Rothschilds expressed an interest in nature, Walter Rothschild was most responsible for sparking Miriam's interest in science. Like his brother, he was an enthusiastic collector of natural specimens. His collection included more than two million butterflies, 300,000 bird skins, 200,000 bird eggs, and numerous other animals. Surrounded by such influences, Rothschild began her own collection of ladybugs and caterpillars when she was four years old.

Receives unusual education

Rothschild did not attend school while she was growing up because her father believed formal education discouraged creativity and natural curiosity. She read a great deal and was tutored by her governess. When her father committed suicide after several years of chronic illness and depression, she lost interest in natural history for a while. But Rothschild's enthusiasm eventually returned, and at 17 years of age she enrolled in several evening classes at a local university.

Rothschild initially planned to work toward degrees in both English literature and zoology. After taking a trip to the marine biological station in Plymouth, England, however, she decided to focus her efforts on zoology. While she was in Plymouth in the late 1920s she met naturalist G. C. Robson, who invited her to work as a researcher at the University of London's Biological Station in Naples, Italy. At the station she studied marine life. Rothschild later recalled in an interview with *Scientific American* magazine, "My trouble at Naples was that I merely went into everything because it was all so fascinating."

Begins scientific career

Rothschild continued her studies when she went to work at the Marine Biological Station in Plymouth in 1932. She became interested in parasites after discovering mollusks (invertebrate animals encased in shells) that were infested with flatworms. For the next seven years she worked tirelessly, studying the flatworm parasites and their mollusk hosts. Rothschild also studied other marine animals and collected numerous specimens. At the beginning of World War II in 1939, however, the Germans bombed the research station. Rothschild's laboratory was completely destroyed.

Rothschild returned to Ashton Wold, which had been converted to a military hospital and air field. In the early 1940s, she was asked to work with British mathematician **Alan Turing** (1912–1954; for more information, see entry in volume 4, pp. 228–234) and other scientists on the *Enigma* project. This was a top-secret British effort to crack German codes. In 1943 she left *Enigma* to marry George Lane, a British soldier who had emigrated from Hungary. The couple had four children and adopted two others. Around the time she was married, Rothschild became a member the agricultural council and began studying wood pigeons. She found that some pigeons with darker feathers were not a different strain of bird, as some believed, but were actually infected with tuberculosis. Soon after the war ended in 1945, she published *Fleas, Flukes, and Cuckoos,* a book about parasites. Rothschild and her husband were divorced in 1957.

Becomes world authority on fleas

During the war Rothschild and her family had opened their home to Europeans refugees, and she continued to help relocate refugees after the war. Despite this work and the challenge of raising several children, Rothschild continued her scientific pursuits. She began a lengthy project to catalog her father's enormous flea collection, which was the most comprehensive in the world. Taking 20 years to compile, her findings eventually filled six volumes. Through her extensive research, Rothschild showed how fleas reproduce and how and why they choose their hosts. She also discovered how fleas can leap enormous distances: They have an elastic-like substance at the back of their knees that allows them to jump up at 150 times the force of gravity. Rothschild explained to *Scientific American* why the study of fleas was valuable: "I discovered, just by accident, that if you knew the histology [microscopic structures] of the flea, you could pretty much know the histology of any other insect."

Pursues other interests

During research on rabbits in Australia, Rothschild found that fleas on rabbits relied on the rabbits' hormones to control their own reproductive cycles. Later Rothschild and Swiss organic chemist Tadeus Reichstein (1897–1996) studied the monarch caterpillar's diet of milkweed plants. They found that a chemical in the milkweed makes the adult monarch butterfly distasteful and possibly poisonous to birds and other animals. Rothschild has been interested in butterflies since she was a child, and she continues to study them. In 1991 she published *Butterfly Cooing Like a Dove,* which combines scientific observations with personal reflections, art, poetry, and philosophy.

As she grew older, Rothschild's eyesight was no longer strong enough to work with the microscope. Rather than ending her scientific pursuits, however, she has simply turned to new projects. One of her major interests has been preserving and restoring the natural landscapes of the British Isles. On the grounds near her home, for example, she has recreated a medieval hayfield filled with native wildflowers. This accomplishment has inspired others to buy seeds from her fields and grow native plants as well. She also actively supports more humane treatment of animals.

Named to Royal Society

In addition to science, Rothschild's other interests include travel, reading, and philanthropy. She has been recognized for her wide-ranging scientific achievements, particularly her studies of fleas. She has served as a visiting professor of biology at London's Royal Free Hospital Medical School, and she was named a fellow of the Royal Society—one of the highest scientific honors in Britain.

Further Reading

Gibson, Helen, "Britain's Quirky Samaritans," *International Wildlife,* July-August 1993, pp. 38–43.

Holloway, Marguerite, "A Natural History of Fleas and Butterflies," *Scientific American,* August 1990, p. 116.

Sullivan, Walter, "Miriam Rothschild Talks of Fleas," *New York Times,* February 10, 1984, p. C2.

Susan Solomon

Born January 19, 1956
Chicago, Illinois

Susan Solomon helped to discover how certain chemicals destroy the protective ozone in the Earth's atmosphere.

S usan Solomon played a key role in discovering the cause of a major threat to the Earth's environment—the loss of the protective ozone layer in the upper atmosphere. Ozone protects all life on Earth from large amounts of damaging ultraviolet radiation from the Sun. An atmospheric chemist (a scientist who studies chemical reactions in the atmosphere), Solomon was the first person to propose that chlorofluorocarbons (gases used in refrigerators and aerosol spray cans) could in some places on the globe lead to ozone destruction in clouds in the stratosphere (an upper level of the Earth's atmosphere).

TV sparks interest in science

Susan Solomon was born on January 19, 1956, in Chicago, Illinois. Her father, Leonard Solomon, was an insurance agent, and her mother, Alice Rutman Solomon, was a fourth-grade teacher. She has one brother, Joel. As a child

Solomon enjoyed watching natural history programming on television. She said in an interview that she recalls "exactly what got me first interested in science. It was the airing of [French marine explorer and naturalist] **Jacques Cousteau** (1910-1997; for more information, see entry in volume 1, pp. 168-173) on American TV when I was nine or ten years old." Although she was especially interested in biology, she commented in the interview that she learned "biology was not very quantitative [easily measured in specific quantities, or amounts],"

By the time Solomon entered the Illinois Institute of Technology, she had met her need for quantitative study by choosing chemistry as a major. During her senior year she was assigned a project that became the basis of her scientific career. The project called for measuring the reaction of the chemical compounds ethylene and hydroxyl radical, a process that occurs in the atmosphere of the planet Jupiter. While compiling the data she read about the atmosphere of planets, which led her to focus on atmospheric chemistry.

Studies ozone layer

In 1977, just before entering graduate school at the University of California at Berkeley, Solomon worked at the National Center for Atmospheric Research (NCAR) in Boulder, Colorado. She met research scientist Paul Crutzen, who introduced her to the study of ozone in the upper atmosphere. As soon as she arrived at Berkeley, Solomon sought out atmospheric chemist Harold Johnston (1920–), who did pioneering work on the effects of supersonic transport (aircraft) on the atmosphere. Solomon credits Crutzen and Johnston with encouraging her interest in atmospheric chemistry. After

≥IMPACT≥

Atmospheric chemist Susan Solomon has significantly advanced scientific understanding of the ozone layer of the Earth. After other scientists discovered that a hole was developing in the ozone layer above the Southern Hemisphere, Solomon traveled to Antarctica to investigate what was causing the problem. She found that cholorofluorocarbons (chemical compounds used in a variety of manmade products) were responsible for producing high levels of chlorine dioxide in the atmosphere. Her findings have led to severe limitations on the use of chlorofluorocarbons in products such as aerosol cans and refrigeration fluids.

completing graduate work at Berkeley, she moved to NCAR to do her doctoral research with Crutzen.

After receiving a Ph.D. in chemistry in 1981, Solomon accepted a research position at the National Oceanic and Atmospheric Administration (NOAA) Aeronomy Laboratory in Boulder, Colorado. Initially, her research focused on developing computer models of ozone in the upper atmosphere. Ozone is a highly unstable molecule made up of three atoms of oxygen. By comparison, the oxygen used in the metabolism (creation of energy through biological processes) of living things is a fairly stable combination of two oxygen atoms. In the upper atmosphere, between altitudes of about 32,000 and 100,000 feet, a layer of ozone absorbs much of the Sun's deadly ultraviolet radiation, thereby protecting all life on Earth.

Discovers danger of chlorofluorocarbons

In 1985 scientists first reported that, during the spring (September and October) in the Southern Hemisphere, the density of the ozone layer over Antarctica had been decreasing rapidly in recent years. The cause of this "hole" in the ozone layer was unknown. The following year scientists decided to send a research team and equipment to Antarctica to measure atmospheric levels of ozone and nitrogen dioxide. Much to the surprise of her colleagues, Solomon volunteered to travel to Antarctica to make the measurements. Previously she had been concentrating on theoretical studies, but the chance to understand the cause of the ozone hole prompted her to turn to experimental work.

Solomon led an expedition to Antarctica during August, September, and October of 1986. She and a team of co-workers measured the amounts of several atmospheric components, including chlorine dioxide. The level of this chemical was much higher than anyone expected, and it provided an important clue to the appearance of the ozone hole.

When Solomon returned to the NOAA lab in Boulder, she wrote a report that provided a theoretical explanation for the ozone hole. She showed how the high level of chlorine dioxide was linked to the rapid chemical destruction of ozone that occurred in reactions on stratospheric clouds. The extra chlorine dioxide, she concluded, came from chlorofluorocarbons. These compounds were released into the atmosphere by such products as foams from aerosol cans and coolants leaking from refrigeration equipment. In 1987 Solomon returned to Antarctica for more measurements, which confirmed her initial findings. Her explanation for the cause of the ozone hole is now generally accepted by scientists. Solomon's discovery has led many countries to limit the production and use of chlorofluorocarbons.

Becomes expert on ozone policy

In recognition of her achievement, Solomon received the gold medal for exceptional service from the U.S. Department of Commerce (the agency that oversees the NOAA). She has testified several times before congressional committees about ozone depletion and is increasingly sought out as an expert on ozone science and policy. Although Solomon has raised the awareness of humans' affect the ozone, she prefers to avoid political activity. She says that she considers herself a scientist and not a policy expert. Solomon married Barry Lane Sidwell on September 20, 1988, and has a stepson by the marriage. Her most recent research concerns ozone levels in the Arctic.

Further Reading

Bylinsky, Gene, "America's Hot Young Scientists," *Fortune,* October 8, 1990, p. 56.

Glanz, James, "How Susan Solomon's Research Changed Our View of Earth," *R & D,* September 1992, p. 46.

Mary Somerville

Born December 26, 1780
Jedburgh, Roxburghshire, Scotland
Died November 29, 1872
Naples, Italy

Mary Somerville wrote a number of successful books that popularized new scientific ideas in the 1800s.

Mary Somerville was one of the best-known women of science in the nineteenth century. Her books on scientific topics were best sellers throughout Europe and in the United States, bringing the new scientific ideas of the 1800s to a wider audience. Somerville's earliest papers were based on experiments she conducted herself on the effects of solar radiation on various substances. She received a number of awards and honors for her work, and she used her role as a respected intellectual to speak out in favor of giving women equal rights and the opportunity for higher education. Earning the respect of other scientists, she became one of the first two women to be named honorary members of the Royal Astronomical Society in 1835.

Receives little education

Mary Fairfax Somerville was born on December 26, 1780, in Jedburgh, Roxburghshire, Scotland. She was the fifth of seven children in her family, but only three lived to adulthood. Her mother, Margaret Chambers Fairfax, was the daughter of an official in the Scottish government. Her father, William George Fairfax, was a vice-admiral in the Royal Navy who had once earned fame as a hero of the Battle of Camperdown. Somerville was raised in the seaport village of Burntisland, Scotland. Margaret Fairfax was often left in charge of the family for long periods of time while her husband was at sea. She did not concern herself with the education of her daughters because at that time girls were expected to learn only domestic and social skills. Somerville was required to help with household chores and was taught to read the Bible, but otherwise she was free to do as she liked. She did not enjoy playing with dolls, so she spent her time exploring the seashore and moors near her home.

When Somerville was about ten years old, her father arrived home from a long absence to find that his daughter could barely read and could not write or do arithmetic. Concerned that his daughter had become a "savage" without even the basics of education, he sent her to a prestigious boarding school in the town of Musselburgh. Somerville had become accustomed to having freedom, however, so she found the school restrictive and uninteresting. She particularly disliked the metal contraptions the girls were required to wear during their lessons to improve their posture. Although she learned some arithmetic, grammar, French, handwriting, and spelling, she was not a good student. After a year her parents withdrew her from the school. When Somerville was 13 she was sent to a school in Edinburgh.

Investigates mysteries of algebra

During her teenage years, Somerville learned all the skills expected of a young woman from an upper-middle class family. She could sew, cook, paint, play the piano, and read poetry. But she had also become an enthusiastic reader, studying everything she could find in the family's small library and teaching herself Greek and Latin. But most of her time was filled with social activity. Ironically, she discovered her interest in mathematics at a party. As she was looking through a popu-

Science writer Mary Somerville introduced important scientific developments of the 1800s to general readers, students, and fellow scientists in Europe and the United States. Her talent for explaining mathematical and scientific concepts made her the most famous and respected woman in science of her time. An inspiration to other women, she won prestigious awards and honors that had previously been reserved only for men. She also supported granting women equal rights and giving them opportunities for higher education. Somerville"s work led to new scientific research, including the discovery of the planet Neptune.

lar magazine with a friend, she noticed mysterious figures on a page. Her friend told her they were "algebra." Somerville was immediately intrigued by the subject, but she could find no one to explain algebra to her.

Somerville therefore decided to investigate algebra on her own. Then she learned that *Elements of Geometry,* a book by the ancient mathematician Euclid (c. 300 B.C.), would give her an explanation of algebra and other forms of mathematics. After convincing her brother's tutor to find a copy of the book for her, Somerville began her study of mathematics. But when her family learned about her new interest, they ordered her to cease her project. At that time people believed a woman could be harmed physically and mentally by intense intellectual concentration. Now forbidden to pursue her studies openly, Somerville simply did her reading and math calculations in secret.

Marriage allows freedom

In 1804, at the age of 24, Somerville married Samuel Grieg, a cousin who had served with her father in the navy. The couple moved to London, where Samuel took a job. As a married woman, Somerville had more freedom to study as she pleased, but her husband did not encourage her interests. They had two sons, one of whom died in infancy. After Samuel died in 1807, Somerville returned to her family in Burntisland.

As a financially independent widow, Somerville could ignore her family's disapproval of her academic work. She began to study openly, eventually mastering higher mathematics. She also read *Philosophiae Naturalis Principia Mathematica,* a book on the laws of gravity and motion by the famous English mathematician **Isaac Newton** (1642-1727; for more information, see entry in volume 4, pp. 176-184). Somerville received public recognition for her mathematical skills when she won a second place medal for finding a solution to a problem published in a mathematics journal. The editor of the journal, William Wallace, was so impressed with her work that he became her mentor.

Somerville received even more support for her intellectual pursuits from her second husband (and cousin), William Somerville, whom she married in 1812. An open-minded surgeon, he joined her in learning about other scientific topics, including geology and mineralogy. William's work for the Army Medical Board, and later for the Royal Hospital, took the couple to London, where they lived for nearly 20 years. They had four children together, but only two survived to adulthood.

Conducts experiments on solar radiation

Somerville kept a busy schedule in London. In addition to raising her children, she maintained an active social life, which brought her in contact with some of the great thinkers of England and Europe. Energized by this rich environment, she began her own scientific research—a series of experiments on the effects of the Sun's radiation on the Earth. In 1826 Somerville published her first scientific paper, "On the Magnetizing Power of the More Refrangible Solar Rays." Her husband also presented the paper to the Royal Society, the prestigious scientific organization of which he was a member. Widely praised by scientists, Somerville's work inspired others to conduct experiments on her idea that the Sun's radiation could magnetize materials. (The theory was later proved incorrect.)

Over the next several years Somerville continued her study of solar radiation. In 1836 she published "Experiments on the Transmission of Chemical Rays of the Solar Spectrum across Different Media," and in 1845 she completed "On the Action of Rays of the Spectrum on Vegetable Juices." Both papers appeared in scientific journals. During this time she also published an essay on comets that was printed in the popular magazine *Quarterly Review* after the sighting of Halley's comet in 1835.

Women's Rights Champion

In her later years, Mary Somerville became involved in the campaign for granting women equal rights, as well as opportunities for higher education. She was the first person to sign a famous petition to give women the right to vote in England. After Somerville's death at the age of 91 on November 19, 1872, in Naples, Italy, many of her books were donated to a women's college in England. In recognition of Somerville's role as a pioneering woman of science, Oxford University named one of its first women's colleges—Somerville College—after her in 1879.

Writes popular books

Somerville's true fame, however, came from the series of books in which she summarized the major scientific developments of her day. At the urging of a friend, in the 1820s she took on the project of translating a work by French mathematician and astronomer Pierre Laplace (1749-1827). The book described the movement of the planets, moons, and other bodies of our solar system. Somerville hoped that by providing an English version of the book, she could increase appreciation of Laplace's theories. Published in 1831 as *The Mechanism of the Heavens,* Somerville's book included complete explanations and diagrams of Laplace's ideas. Because of her careful, detailed descriptions, it was easy to read and understand. An immediate bestseller,*The Mechanism of the Heavens* became a textbook for college students that remained in publication for nearly 100 years. Prominent scientists praised Somerville's understanding of complex subject matter, and she became a spokesperson for new scientific developments. In honor of her achievement, the Royal Society hung a portrait of her in their Great Hall in London.

Somerville's next book was an even greater success. *The Connection of the Physical Sciences,* which was first published in 1834, would eventually go through ten editions. In the work Somerville presented a summary of recent research and important discoveries in the physical sciences. By showing the interconnections among various scientific fields, she contributed to greater public understanding and support of the sciences in the 1800s. She also helped inspire further scientific discoveries. For example, English astronomer John Couch Adams (1819-1892) once stated that a sentence in Somerville's book inspired him to look for the planet Neptune, which he discovered in 1846. As a result of her achievement,

Somerville was one of the first two women to be named honorary members of the Royal Astronomical Society in 1835.

Continues scientific writing

In the late 1830s Somerville's husband developed health problems that required the family to move to the milder climate of Italy. Although Somerville was now removed from the intellectual circles of London, she remained informed about new scientific developments through letters, journals, books, and traveling. She began a third book, this time on the subject of geography, which she had been interested in for a long time. In keeping with her earlier works, Somerville presented the newest developments in the field in *Physical Geography* (1848). Her last major work, the book won her many honors. Among them were the Victoria Gold Medal from the Royal Geographic Society in 1870 and membership in the American Geographical and Statistical Society and the Italian Geographical Society.

After the death of her only surviving son in 1860 and the death of her husband in 1865, Somerville became lonely and depressed. At the urging of her daughter she took on new writing projects to fill her time. By then she was in her eighties and she had begun to lose touch with the latest science innovations. Although her work was still well-received, it was considered unimportant because of her "old-fashioned" approach. During this time Somerville also completed an autobiography. Selections were published after her death as *Personal Recollections from Early Life to Old Age of Mary Somerville* in 1873.

Further Reading

Dictionary of Scientific Biography, Volume XII, Scribner's, 1972, pp. 521-25.

Ogilvie, Marilyn Bailey, *Women in Science: Antiquity through the Nineteenth Century,* MIT Press, 1986, pp. 161-66.

Osen, Lynn M., *Women in Mathematics,* MIT Press, 1974, pp. 95-116.

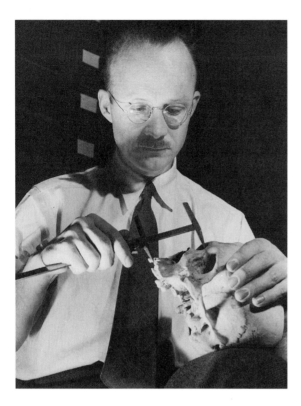

Thomas Dale Stewart

Born June 10, 1901
Delta, Pennsylvania

Thomas Dale Stewart has used his expertise in analyzing human bones to make contributions to the study of early humans as well as the field of forensic anthropology.

Thomas Dale Stewart is a renowned physical anthropologist (a scientist who studies the human body) whose work with the National Museum of Natural History at the Smithsonian Institution has stretched over 70 years. He is an international authority in comparative human osteology (the sciences of bones), human identification, and forensic anthropology (the use of anthropological science in legal issues, such as solving a crime). Among his achievements are studies of pre-Columbian and early post-Columbian man in the Americas. (The pre-Columbian period came before the arrival of Italian explorer Christopher Columbus in the Americas in the late 1400s. The post-Columbian period followed the arrival of Columbus.) Stewart examined the skeletal remains of Tepexpan man in Mexico and Midland man in Texas, which are among the oldest human remains found in North America. Stewart has also reconstructed Neanderthal (an early relative of humans) skeletons from Shanidar in Iraq. In the process he provided new ideas about the physical structure of early humans.

Stewart's expertise as a forensic anthropologist led him into working for the Federal Bureau of Investigation (FBI) and the U.S. Army. He examined human skeletal remains in numerous murder cases for the FBI and worked with the army in the identification of soldiers killed during the Korean War (1950–1953).

Begins Museum of Natural History career

Thomas Dale Stewart was born in Delta, Pennsylvania, on June 10, 1901, the son of Thomas Dale Stewart and Susan Price Stewart. After graduating from the local high school, he entered George Washington University in Washington, D.C., in 1924. Stewart began his long association with the National Museum of Natural History by working as an aide to the famous Czechoslovakian-born American anthropologist Ales Hrdlicka (1869–1943).

Stewart earned a bachelor's degree from George Washington University, then went on to study medicine at Johns Hopkins University in Baltimore, Maryland. Upon completing his medical degree in 1931, Stewart returned to the Museum of Natural History and took a position as an assistant curator (superintendent) of physical anthropology. Appointed curator of the museum in 1942, he became head curator of the department of anthropology in 1961. The following year he was appointed director of the museum, a position he held until 1965. In 1966 the Smithsonian Institution honored Stewart with the rare title of senior scientist. He was given the status of emeritus (honorary) physical anthropologist when he retired in 1971. During his long career Stewart also found time to teach, serving as a visiting professor of anatomy (study of the human body) at Washington Uni-

≡IMPACT≡

Physical anthropologist Thomas Dale Stewart has applied his interest in human bones to a number of projects during his long career with the Smithsonian Institution's National Museum of Natural History. He studied early human fossils, including Neanderthal specimens in Iraq and two of the oldest human fossils found in North America—Tepexpan man and Midland man. Stewart also used his skills to identify soldiers killed in the Korean War and to examine murder victims for the Federal Bureau of Investigation (FBI). A pioneer in forensic anthropology, he has helped to establish the practice as a legitimate scientific field since it was introduced in the 1920s.

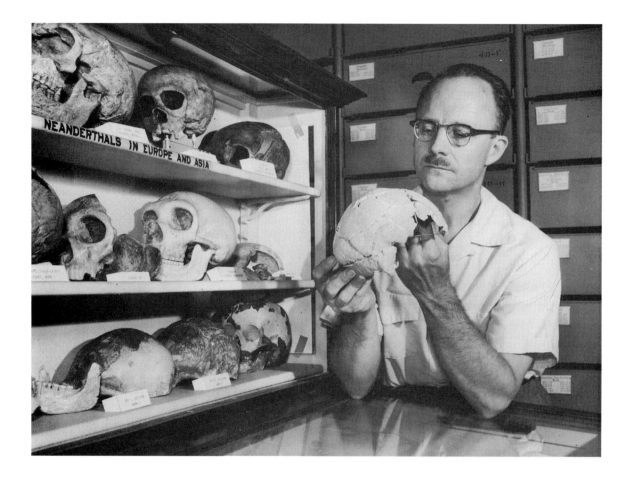

Dr. T. D. Stewart, pictured here in July 1954, assembled bone fragments found by an amateur archeologist to form the "Midland Man."

versity School of Medicine in St. Louis, Missouri. Later he was a visitor professor of anthropology at the Escuela Nacional de Anthropología in Mexico.

Studies remains of early humans

The wide range of Stewart's research was apparent from the outset of his career, and his professional interests led him in several directions. In his first published work (he eventually wrote over 200 papers and books) he covered such topics as monkey muscle systems, tooth decay in Peruvians, and differences in aging among Eskimos and other Native Americans. Stewart's expertise in analyzing human remains has provided a clearer picture of early humans in the Americas and in other parts of the world. In the 1940s his reexamination of a Florida artifact called the Melbourne Skull led him to contradict Hrdlicka's earlier claim that the specimen is similar to the characteristics of Native Americans who had lived in the area. Stewart went on to study human remains in Mexico and Texas, observing the so-called Tepexpan man and Midland man. In papers published in 1949 and 1955, he argued that these specimens were the oldest known humans in North America.

Stewart searched even further back into the human family tree when he was invited to Iraq in 1957 to help restore two Neanderthal skeletons discovered by Ralph Solecki, a Columbia University anthropologist. He returned to Iraq in 1960 and 1962 to recover, restore, and study four other skeletons found by Solecki in caves at Shanidar. Stewart's careful reconstructions of the Shanidar fossils provided new anatomical data about the skull, pelvis, and shoulder blades of Neanderthals.

Pioneers forensic anthropology

While he was a curator at the National Museum of Natural History, Stewart often worked as a forensic anthropologist for the FBI. The museum is located near the FBI offices, so in the 1920s FBI agents started bringing skeletal remains of suspected murder victims to Stewart for analysis. The remains ranged from single bones or a tooth to one or more entire skeletons of unknown age. Stewart not only handled these cases, but began to take on requests from state medical examiners as well. In the beginning, these calls for expert assistance were infrequent, but by the time Stewart retired he was regularly handling at least six cases each month. When the FBI first requested help, forensic anthropology was a poorly developed field. Stewart found that standards for estimating such basic data as the age, sex, and stature from human remains were primitive. By promoting rigorous scientific study to correct these shortcomings, he made forensic anthropology a more accurate and reliable practice.

Learns how bones mature

Stewart also contributed to the field of osteology when he worked with the U.S. Army to help identify the bodies of

American soldiers killed in the Korean War. He recorded detailed observations of growth change in 450 skeletons. Working with fully identified remains, Stewart then determined how bones in the human body matured (reached their final natural shape). In his research he discovered higher variations in the rates of bone maturation than had previously been reported. He also developed a method for estimating the age of a skeleton by studying pubic bones. While working with Eskimo skeletons, Stewart determined that pits and depressions in the cartilage (a somewhat elastic tissue) of the joint between the pubic bones are tell-tale signs of childbirth. These details can be used to identify female remains.

Honored for important work

In recognition of his achievements, Stewart was elected to the National Academy of Sciences in 1962. He was awarded the Viking Medal in Physical Anthropology in 1953 and the Smithsonian's Joseph Henry Medal in 1976. He married Julia Wright in 1932, and they had a daughter. After his first wife died, Stewart was remarried in 1952 to Rita Frame Dewey, a former newspaper reporter and editor.

Further Reading

Angel, Lawrence J., "T. Dale Stewart," *Physical Anthropology,* November 1976, pp. 521–30.

Modern Men of Science, McGraw-Hill, 1968.

Modern Scientists and Engineers, McGraw-Hill, 1980.

Stewart, Thomas Dale, *The People of America,* Scribner, 1973.

George T. Tsao

Born December 4, 1931
Nanking, China

George T. Tsao has been a leader in research on biomass conversion, the process of extracting new energy sources from organic (carbon-based substances, usually from plants or animals) waste materials. As director of the Laboratory of Renewable Resources Engineering at Purdue University in Indiana, he has advanced the development of alcohol fuels such as ethanol from cellulose materials, including urban organic garbage and agricultural waste. Tsao has been instrumental in creating practical alternatives to the burning of petroleum products in order to meet rising world energy demands. His work has earned him the respect of scientists as well as business and government leaders from around the world.

George T. Tsao discovered a way to turn urban garbage and farm waste products into an inexpensive, useable fuel.

Has varied career

George T. Tsao was born on December 4, 1931, in Nanking, China. He received his early education in Taiwan. After earning a bachelor's degree at National Taiwan Univer-

Chemical engineer George T. Tsao has devoted his career to finding alternative fuel sources that can be produced from ordinary organic waste. Working at the Laboratory of Renewable Resources Engineering at Purdue University, Tsao developed a process that could take urban garbage and farm waste, such as cornstalks, and create ethanol, an alcohol-based fuel. Tsao's method not only created a useable fuel, but it actually produced enough valuable by-products to pay for the energy used in the process. The scientist has been instrumental in showing that non-petroleum fuel sources can be produced practically and cheaply.

sity in 1953, he moved to the United States for graduate studies. Tsao received a master's degree from the University of Florida in 1956 and completed his Ph.D. in chemical engineering (the industrial application of chemistry) at the University of Michigan in 1960. His career alternated between industry and academic work for several years. After earning his doctorate, he held a one-year assistant professorship in physics at Olivet College in Michigan.

Tsao then worked as a chemical engineer for Merck & Company for a year before becoming a research chemist for the Tennessee Valley Authority. From 1962 to 1965, he was a researcher for Miles Laboratories, specializing in hydrolysis (breaking down a chemical compound using water) and fermentation (changes in an organic compound through the use of enzymes). In 1966 he took a position as an associate professor of chemical engineering at Iowa State University. After achieving the rank of full professor at Iowa, he moved to Purdue University as professor of chemical engineering and agricultural engineering in 1977. He eventually became the director of Purdue's Laboratory of Renewable Resources Engineering (LORRE).

Produces fuel out of garbage

At Purdue, Tsao set an ambitious goal for himself: to convert cellulose (the primary carbohydrate substance in plants) into glucose, a type of sugar. After converting cellulose waste materials such as garbage and grain stalks into glucose, Tsao could then ferment the sugar into ethanol, a burnable fuel alcohol. Scientists had previously tackled this problem, but with little success. Not only does cellulose have

a strong structure, it is also protected by a layer of lignin (a substance that binds the cellulose fiber together). As Tsao commented in *Pioneers of Alcohol Fuels,* "The structure of a piece of cellulosic material resembles that of a reinforced concrete pillar with cellulose fibers being the metal rods, and lignin the natural cement." The problem, then, was not only to break down the structure of cellulose, but also to somehow tear apart the lignin shield.

Tsao's solution was to use sulfuric acid (a heavy acid that oxidizes and dehydrates) in a multi-step process to convert crop waste into three usable by-products: glucose, lignin, and hemicellulose. (Hemicellulose is a carbohydrate containing several sugars that occurs in plants and that is more easily broken down than cellulose.) In this new process, glucose, which is the primary by-product, is fermented into ethanol. Lignin is dried and then processed into a coal-like substance for fuel. Finally, sugars are extracted from hemicellulose and made into plastic.

New process pays for itself

Tsao had made a major breakthrough in fuel technology. His biomass conversion process not only produced ethanol at approximately 80 per gallon, its by-products also paid for the energy used to create the fuel. Yet Tsao's work had only begun. During the next several years he spent endless hours testifying before Congress and campaigning to obtain government money so he could continue his research.

In addition to his work in biomass conversion, Tsao has also studied industrial carbohydrates, enzyme engineering, and the practical uses of agricultural and natural products as well as waste disposal. He is a member of the American Chemical Society, the American Institute of Chemical Engineers, and the American Society of Engineering Educators.

Further Reading

Burns, Paul, and others, *Pioneers of Alcohol Fuels,* Volume 1, Citizens' Energy Project, 1981, pp. 29–32.

Tsao, George T., *Conversion of Biomass from Agriculture into Useful Products,* U.S. Department of Energy, 1978.

Alessandro Volta

Born February 18, 1745
Como, Lombardy, Italy
Died March 5, 1827
Como, Lombardy, Italy

Alessandro Giuseppi Volta became one of the most famous scientists of his day as a result of his work with electrical currents. He is best known for discovering that electricity can be generated from metals. Before Volta's revolutionary breakthrough, friction (static electricity) was thought to be the only method of producing electricity. Also a gifted inventor, Volta produced the voltaic pile, a device that utilized his concept of metal-generated electricity. The volt (the unit of force in electrical current) was named in his honor.

Alessandro Volta invented the voltaic pile, the first electric battery.

Decides on a career in physics

Allesandro Giuseppe Volta was born on February 18, 1745, in Como, Lombardy, Italy. He was one of the seven children who survived to adulthood of Filippo and Maddelena de' conti Inzaghi Volta. Filippo, like his three brothers, had entered a religious order of the Catholic church. To ensure that the family line did not die out, however, Filippo left the Church to

Physicist Alessandro Volta was the first person to demonstrate that electricity travels in a current. He used this knowledge to invent the voltaic pile, the first electric battery. Volta's device provided other scientists with a steady source of electricity with which to conduct other experiments. Using the voltaic pile, English scientist William Nicholson (1753-1815) discovered electrolysis. In turn, Humphry Davy used electrolysis to break down a number of substances and discovered several new elements. The unit of force in electrical current, the volt, was named in Volta's honor.

marry and have children. His intense religious devotion was carried on by some of those children, who entered religious orders.

After Volta's father died around 1752, the boy's education was handled by his father's brothers. They enrolled him in a Jesuit school, where he was encouraged by his teachers to enter the priesthood. Volta's uncles, who wanted him to become an attorney, removed him from the Jesuits' influence and sent him to the Seminario Benzi when he was 16. But Volta soon developed his own ideas about the profession he would follow. After reading a history of electricity written by English chemist **Joseph Priestley** (1733-1804; for more information, see entry in volume 3, pp. 772-775), Volta became interested in the subject. He then announced his intention of becoming a physicist.

Begins experiments with electricity

During the 1760s Volta devoted himself to the study of electricity. With a friend, Giulio Cesare Gattoni, he carried out several early experiments. One of their projects involved studying the electricity conducted by a lightning rod. Volta also began corresponding with the two leading experts on electricity, French physicist Jean Antoine Nollet (1700-1770) and Italian physicist Giovanni Batista Beccaria (1716-1781). Volta would write to the scientists when he thought of questions or suggestions that related to their work. Somewhat annoyed by the young man's comments, Beccaria suggested that Volta read his (Beccaria's) writings on electricity and begin his own experimentation. Volta eagerly followed the older scientist's advice, but he did not have access to the necessary equipment. Therefore he was forced to invent his own. This talent for creating inexpensive but useful instruments would play an important role in his career.

Invents the electrophorous

In 1774 Volta was appointed professor of physics at the high school in Como. That year he also created one of his most significant inventions, the electrophorous, a device that could store significant electrical charges. The electrophrous replaced the Leyden jar, which until that time had been used for storing smaller charges. Volta's invention expanded on the work of French physicist Charles-Augustine Coulomb (1736-1806). Prior to the late 1700s, scientists were mainly concerned with the type of electrical charge produced by friction (rubbing objects together), also known as static electricity. Coulomb had discovered that electrical charges were located on the surface of a charged body, not inside of it.

Using Coulomb's discovery, Volta made the electrophorou, which was composed of two metal discs. He rubbed one disc to produce a negative electrical charge (a charge that has more electrons, or negative electricity, than protons, or positive electricity). Then he brought the second disc close enough to the first to establish a positive charge on one side, leaving a negative charge on the other. The electrophorous provided scientists with a source of electric charge that could be used to charge other objects without losing its power. Many scientists argued that Volta should not be given credit for the new invention because it was based on ideas developed by others. Most recognized, however, that Volta had made a great contribution by taking these ideas and turning them into a useful instrument.

Becomes popular teacher and scientist

As his scientific reputation grew, Volta also experimented with chemistry. In his most famous chemistry experiment, he found that when he exploded hydrogen gas in a closed container of air, he could measure the amount of oxygen that the hydrogen released from the air. In this way, he was able to make the first accurate measurement of the proportion of oxygen in the air. In 1776 he began applying the same technique to the study of marsh gas (the gas released by decomposing matter in a marsh or swamp). When he exploded hydrogen in the marsh gas, he discovered a new gas, methane.

By 1779 Volta had earned a reputation as an important scientist in the field of electricity, mainly due to his invention of the electrophorous. Because of his place in the scientific world, he was appointed professor of experimental physics at the University of Pavia. He would hold the position for nearly 40 years. Volta was such a popular teacher that the university eventually built a new lecture hall to hold all the students who came to hear him. The hall also accommodated the equipment he had purchased during his travels to scientific centers in Europe. After he had been at Pavia for a few years he announced another invention. This time he had improved upon the electrometers that were used by scientists to measure electrical charges. His new device, which he called the condensing electroscope, was a much more sensitive instrument that allowed for the detection of very small charges. Although Volta's greatest achievement was still to come, he received many honors for his scientific work. In 1791 he was named a fellow of the Royal Society of London, and three years later the society awarded him the prestigious Copley Medal.

Scientific split over "animal electricity"

In 1791 Volta was drawn into a controversy that divided scientific thought about the nature of electricity. An Italian anatomist, Luigi Galvani (1737-1798), announced that he had discovered the existence of "animal electricity." Galvani had noticed that when he touched the muscles in a frog's legs with probes made of two different metals, the legs would twitch. He concluded that frog tissue was the source of an "electrical fluid." This fluid released a charge in the presence of the metal probes, Galvani asserted, causing the contraction in the frog muscles. The concept that there was a kind of electricity other than static electricity was completely new to scientists.

Skeptical of the "animal electricity" described by Galvani, Volta began a series of experiments on the phenomenon. He conducted tests on numerous animals, including himself, and ultimately discovered there was no such thing as "animal electricity." Instead, he found that the two different types of metal probes used in Galvani's experiments were actually the source of the current, not the frog tissue. Volta had come up with a different, but equally new idea—that placing different metals near each other could produce electricity.

Creates first electric battery

The animal electricity controversy raged on until 1800. In that year Volta built an instrument that produced a large flow of electricity. He filled bowls with a saline (containing salt) solution and "connected" them with strips composed of different metals. One end of the strip was copper; the other end was tin or zinc. By bending the strips from one bowl into another, Volta was able to create a constant flow of electrical current. The world's first electric battery had been invented. Volta had also proven that metal was the source of the electricity and that animal electricity did not exist.

Later, in order to make his battery smaller, Volta used round discs of copper, zinc, and cardboard that had been soaked in a saline solution. He stacked the discs one on top of the other. By attaching a wire to the top and bottom of the pile of discs, Volta allowed the electric current to flow. This invention, known as the voltaic pile, was the greatest achievement of Volta's career.

Voltaic pile revolutionizes science

While Volta himself did not fully see the potential uses of his invention, the value of the voltaic pile was quickly recognized by other scientists. It provided, for the first time, a continuous source of electricity, thus allowing for many new directions in research. One of the first scientists to make use of the voltaic pile was the English chemist William Nicholson (1753-1815), who built his own pile when he heard about Volta's invention in 1800. Nicholson placed the ends of his wires in water and discovered the flowing current "electrolyzed" the water (broke it up into hydrogen and oxygen). Earlier, English physicist and chemist Henry Cavendish (1731-1810) had shown that the two elements could be combined to form water. Nicholson had simply reversed the procedure. His discoveries would lead to the work of English chemist **Humphry Davy** (1778-1829; for more information, see entry in volume 1, pp. 211-216), who used electrolysis to identify a number of new elements, including potassium, sodium, calcium, and magnesium.

Honored by Napoléon

Volta was highly celebrated for his last and greatest scientific contribution. The French leader Napoléon Bonaparte (1769-1821) was particularly impressed with the scientist's achievement. He brought Volta to Paris in 1801 to give a special series of lectures on electricity at the National Institute of France (later known as the Academy of Sciences). In honor of the occasion Volta was awarded a special gold medal. Napoléon also granted him a pension, gave him the title of count, and made him a senator of the kingdom of Lombardy. Volta continued to hold his post at the University of Pavia, eventually becoming the director of the philosophy department. In 1819 he retired to his family home in Como, where he died on March 5, 1827, at the age of 82. One the greatest recognitions of Volta's work later came from the world scientific community: In his honor, the unit of force that moves electric current was named the "volt."

Further Reading

Asimov, Isaac, *Asimov's Biographical Encyclopedia of Science and Technology,* new revised ed., Doubleday, 1972, pp. 204-6.

Dictionary of Scientific Biography, Volume XIV, Scribners, 1970, pp. 69-82.

McGraw-Hill Encyclopedia of World Biography, Volume 11, McGraw-Hill, 1973, pp. 170-81.

Franz Weidenreich

Born June 7, 1873
Edenkoben, Germany
Died July 11, 1948

Franz Weidenreich (pronounced "vie-den-rike") is most closely associated with the study of Peking Man (the name given to early human remains found in Asia). He earned a reputation as a cataloger of human fossils and the writer of important evolutionary studies. His research helped to develop some of the fundamental ideas of how human beings may have evolved. According to Weidenreich, the history of human evolution (gradual change over a long period of time) began with a common ancestor. Because of the influence of environment and other factors, he proposed, the original ancestor eventually branched into different groups. In turn each of these groups developed into the distinct racial types found today in *Homo sapiens* (the scientific name for modern humans).

Begins as anatomist

Franz Weidenreich was born on June 7, 1873, in Edenkoben, Palatinate, Germany, the youngest of four children of

Franz Weidenreich formulated a theory of human racial types.

Paleoanthropologist Franz Weidenreich made major contributions to the study of human evolution. His analysis of fossils of *Sinanthropus pekinensis,* or "Peking Man," led him to believe that Peking Man was not a separate species. Weidenreich argued that the fossils instead came from a group of human ancestors already known to have existed in Java. These findings led him to develop a crucial theory of human evolution. Weidenreich concluded that, at some point in time, the descendants of a common ancestor became separated and formed several different groups. These groups then evolved into the various races that exist today.

Carl Weidenreich and Frederike Esesheimer. He received his early education at the Landau Humanist Gymnasium (college preparatory school) and later attended the universities of Munich, Kiel, and Berlin. In 1899 he earned a medical degree at the University of Strassburg, where he taught anatomy (the science of body structures) from 1899 until 1918. He was appointed professor in 1904. At Strassburg, Weidenreich studied with Gustav Schwalbe, a prominent specialist in the study of Neanderthals, an early relative of humans. He also served as president of the democratic party of the French region of Alsace-Lorraine during World War I (1914–1918). In 1918 Weidenreich was forced to leave France because he was a native of Germany (France and Germany were enemies during the war).

Pursues anthropology career

As an anatomist Weidenreich specialized in the study of blood cells, the lymphatic system (the part of the circulatory system that carries fluid for blood cells), and the central nervous system. His work in skeletal anatomy, however, drew him into the field of paleoanthropology (the study of the ancestors of modern humans). He recognized that a skeleton can give clues to the posture, bone structure, and movement of a being when it was alive. Weidenreich then realized that this kind of information could be used to study human evolution. Pursuing a new career as a paleoanthropologist, he went on to apply his theory in several ground-breaking studies.

In 1921 Weidenreich was appointed professor of anthropology at the University of Heidelberg, a post he held until 1924. Moving to the University of Frankfurt in 1928, he remained as a professor of anthropology until 1933. At that

time he was removed from his position by the Nazi government because he was Jewish. (The Nazi government enforced political and economic doctrines based on totalitarian rule, state control of all industry, and the exercise of power by groups considered to be racially superior.) After leaving Germany, Weidenreich briefly worked at the University of Chicago in Chicago, Illinois. He then took a position at Peking Union Medical College in China. He replaced the Canadian paleoanthropologist Davidson Black (1884–1934), who had died suddenly. At Peking Union, Weidenreich began a study of early human remains found in China, concentrating on tooth structure, jaw bones, and skull. During this period he also published a report on three *Homo sapiens* skulls from sites at Zhoukoudien (then called Choukoutien), southwest of Beijing (also known as Peking).

Franz Weidenreich (right) confers with another scientist. Weidenreich's research helped to develop some of the fundamental ideas of how human beings may have evolved.

Neanderthal "bridge" in evolution

When Weidenreich embarked on his new career, pale-oanthropologists were concentrating on finding links between the earliest human forms and modern man. They had located fossil remains of Neanderthals, whom they had identified as human-like species that lived from about 300,000 years ago to 35,000 years ago. A series of studies had determined that the Neanderthals had a large brain, made stone tools, and knew how to make fire. Yet scientists had come upon an even more interesting discovery: The Neanderthal arrived after an earlier species called *Homo erectus,* which had lived one million to 700,000 years ago. As a result of this finding, several theorists proposed that the Neanderthals had acted as a "bridge" between *Homo erectus* and modern *Homo sapiens.* Weidenreich used this concept to formulate his theory of human evolution into different racial types.

Suggests origins of racial differences

When Weidenreich went to Peking Union, the majority of known human fossils consisted of remains found on Java (an island in Indonesia). Scientists called these remains *Pithecanthropus erectus,* which became popularly known as Java Man. In the late 1920s, however, Black had also discovered a fossilized tooth in Zhoukoudien. The fossil came from approximately the same era as Java Man, and Black had given it the name *Sinanthropus pekinensis,* or Peking Man. In the 1930s Dutch anatomist Ralph von Koenigswald found additional *Pithecanthropus* fossils. These discoveries led Weidenreich to compare the two types of early humans, concentrating on Peking Man.

Introduces theory of racial types

Weidenreich presented his findings in a series of papers from 1936 to 1943 and in his best-known book, *Ape, Giants, and Man,* which was published in 1946. In these studies he theorized that Java Man and Peking Man were not separate species, but instead they had a common human ancestor. This creature was massive in size, he wrote, having a large skull and jaw. He further suggested that Java Man and Peking Man had continued to develop as distinct but related types throughout the later stages of evolution. Fortunately, Weidenreich had documented his research in publications. In the mid-1940s, after the fossils had been packed for shipment to the United States, they were reportedly destroyed during the Japanese invasion of China.

Defines phases of human development

By the end of his career, Weidenreich had built upon his earlier findings to formulate a complete theory of the development of racial types. As human-like beings continued to develop along several parallel lines, he hypothesized, they formed distinct groups with specific characteristics. He identified four major racial groups: Australian, Mongolian, African, and Eurasian. According to Weidenreich, these groups went through identical evolutionary phases—all the while keeping their unique racial features—to become modern humans. He identified three phases of development: Archanthropine, Paleoanthropine, and Neoanthropine. The Archanthropine phase, which took place approximately one million years ago, represented the period of Java Man and Peking Man. The Paleoanthropine phase encompassed the era of the Neanderthals, and the Neoanthropine phase includes all evolutions up to modern man. Among the changes that occurred during these stages were a gradual increase in the size of the cranium (the part of the skull that holds the brain) and the development of a more erect posture.

Wins Viking medal

Weidenreich spent the last years of his career in the United States. From 1941 until his death on July 11, 1948, he was associated with the American Museum of Natural History in New York, New York. In 1947 he was awarded the Viking Fund Medal for his work in physical anthropology. At the time of his death, he was married to Matilda Neuberger; they had three daughters.

Further Reading

Bowler, Peter J., *Theories of Human Evolution: A Century of Debate, 1844–1944,* Johns Hopkins University Press, 1986.

Gregory, W. K., "Franz Weidenreich, 1873–1948," *Anthropological Papers of Franz Weidenreich 1939–1948,* edited by S. L. Washburn and Davida Wolffson, Viking Fund, 1949, pp. 251–56.

Howells, W. W., "Franz Weidenreich, 1873–1948," *American Journal of Physical Anthropology,* Volume 56, 1981, pp. 407–10.

Smith, Fred H., and Frank Spencer, *The Origins of Modern Humans: A World Survey of the Fossil Evidence,* Alan R. Liss, 1984.

Weidenreich, Franz, *Apes, Giants, and Man,* University of Chicago Press, 1946.

Anna W. Williams

Born March 17, 1863
Hackensack, New Jersey
Died November 20, 1954
New Jersey

During her long career at the research laboratory of the New York City Department of Health, Anna W. Williams became one of America's pioneering bacteriologists (scientists who study bacteria). Her discovery of the *Corynebacterium diphtheriae* bacillus, the bacterium that causes the dreaded childhood disease diphtheria, led to the development of a diphtheria antitoxin (a substance used to fight or prevent disease). Subsequent immunization programs were highly successful, and the disease is no longer common in many countries. Williams's wide-ranging research also resulted in the development of a rabies vaccine and an improved method for diagnosing rabies in animals. (Rabies is a disease of the nervous system of warm-blooded animals.)

Anna Wessels Williams was born in Hackensack, New Jersey, on March 17, 1863, to William and Jane (Van Saun) Williams. Although her English-born father was a private school teacher, the family—which included her five siblings

Anna W. Williams was instrumental in developing vaccines for both diphtheria and rabies.

191

Bacteriologist Anna W. Williams made several important discoveries that led to improved health conditions in the United States and around the world. One of her earliest, and most influential, contributions to science was isolating the *Corynebacterium diphtheriae* bacillus. This bacterium causes diphtheria, a serious childhood disease that was once very common. Williams's discovery was used to create a vaccine that helped to nearly eliminate the disease in the United States and other countries. Later, Williams made advances in rabies treatment by developing a rabies vaccine and an improved method of identifying rabies infection.

and several half-siblings—could not afford private school tuition. Williams was schooled at home until she was 12. She then entered the State Street Public School, where her father was a trustee. In 1883 she attended college at the New Jersey State Normal School in Trenton, New Jersey. She was a school teacher for two years.

Decides on medical career after family crisis

In 1887 one of Williams's sisters nearly died from complications during childbirth. Disturbed by the fact that the attending doctor seemed unable to help her sister, Williams decided to enter the medical profession herself. In 1891 she obtained her degree from the Women's Medical College of the New York Infirmary, where she remained as an instructor of pathology (the study of the causes and characteristics of disease) and hygiene until 1893. For the next two years she was a department assistant. Williams also served as consulting pathologist at the college from 1902 to 1905.

Discovers diphtheria bacterium

In 1894 Williams volunteered to serve in the bacteriology laboratory at the New York City Department of Health. The nation's first city-operated diagnostic laboratory, it was directed by William H. Park. Williams's work at the Department of Health began with a search for an antitoxin for diphtheria, at that time a leading cause of death among children. Her discovery, in 1894, of the *Corynebacterium diphtheria* bacillus led to the development of a diphtheria antitoxin. The antitoxin was soon used in immunizations throughout North

America and Great Britain. The isolation of this bacillus strain became known as Park-Williams #8. Park was generally credited with the discovery because he was head of the laboratory, even though he was not involved in the initial research. Williams was recognized by many for her work, however, and in 1895 she was officially hired onto the laboratory staff as assistant bacteriologist.

Develops rabies vaccine

Williams also researched infections caused by the streptococcal bacterium, commonly known as strep throat, and pneumococcal bacterium infections (pneumonia). In addition, she conducted studies of chronic eye infections commonly found among New York City's underprivileged children. In 1896 she traveled to the Pasteur Institute in Paris in the hope of developing an antitoxin for scarlet fever (an infection of the none, throat, and mouth caused by streptococcal bacteria). Although Williams was not successful in this effort, her experiments with a rabies virus culture (sample) she obtained at the Pasteur Institute resulted in the mass production of a rabies vaccine by 1898. In 1905 Williams was named assistant director of the laboratory at the Department of Health.

In 1915 Williams became president of the Women's Medical Association, and during World War I (1914–1918) she served on the U.S. government influenza commission. As part of the war effort she also trained medical laboratory workers and participated in a military program for detection of the meningococcal bacterium (the cause of meningitis, or inflammation of the tissues around the brain and spinal chord). In 1931, she was elected vice chair of the laboratory section of the American Public Health Association.

Cuts Time for Rabies Diagnosis

In 1905 Anna Williams published an improved method for diagnosing (identifying the presence of) rabies in animals based on a technique of analyzing brain tissue samples. This method stemmed from her own research and from similar studies conducted by Adelchi Negri, an Italian physician. Before Williams published a report on her method, a diagnosis of rabies took ten days. Williams's technique took only minutes, and was not improved upon for more than 30 years. In recognition of this scientific breakthrough, the American Public Health Association in 1907 appointed Williams as chair of its newly formed committee on the diagnosis of rabies.

Louis Pasteur, creator of the first vaccine against rabies, founded the Pasteur Institute in 1888 to promote research on rabies.

Forced to retire from laboratory

Williams was forced into retirement in 1934 because New York mayor Fiorello La Guardia had mandated retirement for all city employees over the age of 70. Despite the urging of Williams's colleagues and other scientists that she be allowed to continue her important research, La Guardia refused to make an exception. Williams left New York City to reside in Woodcliff Lake, New Jersey. She later moved to Westwood, New Jersey, where she lived with her sister, Amelia Wilson. Williams died from heart failure on November 20, 1954, at the age of 91.

Further Reading

Notable American Women: The Modern Period, Belknap, 1980, pp. 737–39.

Williams, Anna W., with William H. Park, *Pathogenic Microorganisms Including Bacteria and Protozoa: A Practical Manual for Students, Physicians and Health Officers,* Lea Brothers, 1905.

Williams, Anna W., *Streptococci in Relation to Man in Health and Disease,* Williams & Williams, 1932.

Williams, Anna W., with William H. Park, *Who's Who among the Microbes,* Century, 1929.

Picture Credits

Christine Darden

The photographs appearing in *Scientists: Their Lives and Works* were received from the following sources:

On the cover (clockwise from top right): Luis Alvarez, Robert H. Goddard (**AP/Wide World Photos. Reproduced by permission.**); Margaret Mead (**The Bettmann Archive. Reproduced by permission.**). On the back cover (top to bottom): Edwin H. Land (**AP/Wide World Photos. Reproduced by permission.**); George Washington Carver (**The Bettmenn Archive. Reproduced by permission.**).

The Granger Collection, Ltd. Reproduced by permission: v, 43, 82, 108; **Library of Congress. Reproduced by permission:** ix, 7, 57, 77, 194, 197; **Photograph by Stringer/Andre de Wet. Corbis-Bettmann. Reproduced by permission:** xxv, 101; **Corbis-Bettmann. Reproduced by permission:** xxvii, xxxi, 1, 164, 170, 172; **Netscape Communications. Reproduced by permission:** 14; **Photograph by Jean Libby. Reproduced by permission of David Black-**

195

Cumulative Index to Volumes 1-5

Italic type indicates volume numbers; **boldface** type indicates entries and their page numbers; (ill.) indicates illustrations.

Jean Baptiste Lamark

American Ephemeris and Nautical Almanac *4:* 172

American Red Cross *1:* 233, 235–36

American Revolution *3:* 772, 774

Ames, Bruce N. *1:* **19–23,** 19 (ill.)

Ames test *1:* 19–21

Amino acids *4:* 137, 201

Analytical engine *1:* 37, 40–42

Analytical Institutions 5: 4–5

Analytical psychology *2:* 541

Andersen, Dorothy *5:* **7–13,** 7 (ill.)

And Keep Your Powder Dry: An Anthropologist Looks at America 2: 636–37

Andreessen, Marc *5:* **14–20,** 14 (ill.)

Andrews, Thomas *2:* 655

Angus 1: 50

Animal conservation *4:* 92, 94, 96, 98

The Animal Kingdom, Distributed According to Its Organization 1: 206; *4:* 161

Animal psychology *4:* 3

Animals, ethical treatment of *2:* 411, 413

An Anthropologist on Mars 3: 830

Anthropology *4:* 66; *5:* 170, 173–74

Anthropology, forensic *5:* 171, 173

Antimatter *4:* 188

Antinuclear movement *1:* 124–26, 128

Antiproton *4:* 188

Apollo 11 *4:* 29

Apollo *4:* 14, 29

Apollo space program *4:* 24, 29, 30; *5:* 151, 153

Apple Computer Inc. *2:* 508, 510–11

Apple I *2:* 510

Apple II *2:* 510–11

Appleton, Edward *3:* 941–42

Archimedes *4:* 101, 106; *5:* 44

ArgoJason system *1:* 49–50

Argonne National Laboratories *1:* 290

Aristarchus of Samos *4:* 50

Aristotle *1:* 206; *4:* 101–03, 106, 160, 178

Arkwright, Richard *1:* **24–29,** 24 (ill.)

Army Ballistic Missile Agency (ABMA) *4:* 26, 28

Arp, Halton *1:* 121

Arrhenius, Svante *1:* **30–36,** 30 (ill.)

Arrhythmias *3:* 929–31

Arrow (race car) *4:* 84

Arsenic *4:* 112, 114

Articulata 4: 161

Artificial heart *2:* 502–05

Artificial intelligence *2:* 665–69; *4:* 229, 230, 233

Artificial radioactivity *4:* 117, 119, 122

Artificial satellites *3:* 920

Asilomer Conference *3:* 872

Assembly line *4:* 80, 82, 85

Astatine *4:* 188

Aston, Francis *4:* 226

Astronomical unit *4:* 132

Astronomy *4:* 23, 48–50, 53, 56, 100, 103, 126–28, 131, 170–73, 199–202, 206–207; *5:* 82, 83, 115–18

Astrophysical Journal 1: 154

Astrophysics *5:*101

Atanasoff, John Vincent *2:* 367

Atanasoff–Berry Computer *2:* 367

Atmosphere *4:* 16, 17, 19; *5:* 163

Atmospheric motion *4:* 17, 20

ATOC (Acoustic Thermometry of Ocean Climate) *5:* 130

Atomic bomb *1:* 10, 127 (ill.), 268; *2:* 402, 680, 683, 687–88, 689 (ill.)

Atomic number *2:* 657–58

Atomic structure *1:* 98–100; *3:* 805–06, 811; *4:* 222, 224

Atomic theory *1:* 197, 199–201; *4:* 7, 11

Atomic weight *1:* 197, 199, 202; *2:* 656–57; *4:* 7, 9, 11

Bueker, Elmer *4:* 153
Bunsen, Robert *2:* 655
Burbank, Luther *1:* **112–16,**
112 (ill.), 115 (ill.)
Burbidge, E. Margaret
1: **117–23,** 117 (ill.)
Burbidge, Geoffrey *1:* **117–23**

C

Cairns, John, Jr. *3:* 735, 735 (ill.)
Calculus *4:* 176–177, 180, 229;
5: 3–4
Caldicott, Helen *1:* **124–30,**
124 (ill.)
Calypso 1: 170
Campbell–Swinton, A. A. *3:* 1021
Camp Leakey *4:* 97
Cancer *4:* 36
Cancer research *1:* 20;
3: 776, 778
Cannon, Annie Jump *1:* **131–36,**
131 (ill.), 134 (ill.)
Cantor, Georg *3:* 799, 803,
803 (ill.)
Carbohydrate metabolism
1: 163–64, 166
Carcinogens *1:* 20–22
Carnot, Nicholas *1:* 225
Carson, Benjamin *4:* **33–38,**
33 (ill.), 36 (ill.)
Carson, Rachel *1:* **137–43,** 137
(ill.), 141 (ill.); *2:* 597; *3:* 970
Carver, George Washington
1: **144–49,** 144 (ill.), 149 (ill.);
2: 535
Cassini, Giovanni Domenico
4: 132
Cassini's Division *4:* 132
Catalysts *4:* 7, 11
Cathode rays *3:* 789–90;
4: 223–25
Cathode–ray tubes *3:* 943,
1018–21; *4:* 225; *5:* 41
Caton–Thompson, Gertrude
2: 577
CAT scan (computer axial
tomography) *2:* 483–85

Cavendish Laboratory *1:* 176,
179; *2:* 618; *3:* 806, 812, 935;
4: 223, 227
CDC 1604 *4:* 62
CDC 6600 *4:* 59, 62
CDC 8600 *4:* 62
CD–ROMs *2:* 369
Cech, Thomas R. *1:* 91
Celsius scale *3:* 909
Cells *4:* 181
Center for the Biology of Natural
Systems *3:* 743
Center for the Study of Multiple
Birth *2:* 549–50
Centigrade scale *3:* 909
Cepheid *2:* 491; *5:* 84–85
Ceres *2:* 371–72
Cerium *4:* 11, 12
CF (Cystic fibrosis) *5:* 1, 9–12
Chadwick, James *2:* 642,
642 (ill.); *3:* 812
Challenger space shuttle *4:* 218
Chamberlain, Owen *4:* 188
Chandrasekhar, Subrahmanyan
1: **150–57,** 150 (ill.), 155 (ill.)
Chang, Min-Chueh *5:* **28–32,**
28 (ill.)
Channel rays *4:* 226
Chanute, Octave *3:* 989
Character displacement *3:* 970
Charcot, Jean–Martin *1:* 311
Chargaff, Erwin *1:* 177; *3:* 935
Charles, Jacques *3:* 907
Cheetahs *4:* 5
Chemical symbols *4:* 13
Child development *4:* 142, 143
Chimpanzees *2:* 405–10, 517;
4: 93, 97
Chladni figures *5:* 48
Chlorine *1:* 215
Chlorofluorocarbons (CFCs)
2: 597; *5:* 161, 162
Chromosomes *2:* 623–26
Chronometer *4:* 181
Clark, Barney *2:* 502, 504–05
Clark, Kenneth B. *4:* **40–47,** 40,
(ill.), 45 (ill.)
Classification system, Lamark
5: 79

Classification system, Linnaean
4: 157–61, 163; 5: 78, 79
Clausius, Rudolf 3: 761, 906,
908, 908 (ill.)
Cloning 1: 78
Coalition for Responsible Genetic
Research 3: 873
COBOL (COmmon Business
Oriented Language) 5: 60,
63–64
Codons 4: 137
Cohen, Stanley 1: 78; 4: 150,
154 (ill.), 155
Coke, Thomas 3: 915
Colby, Kenneth 2: 566
Cold front 4: 19, 20
Cold Spring Harbor, New York
3: 934, 936
Color blindness 1: 200
Colossus 4: 230–32
Comets, origin of 4: 174
Coming of Age in Samoa
2: 633, 635
Commodore computer 2: 366
Commoner, Barry 3: 743,
743 (ill.)
Communication with
Extra–Terrestrial Intelligence
(CETI) 4: 202
Complimentarity, theory of 1: 98,
101; 3: 742
Computer chips 1: 158–59
Computer memory 3: 924
Computers 4: 59–64, 228–34
Computer simulation
2: 563–64, 566
"Computing Machinery and
Intelligence" 4: 233
Congenital heart disease 4: 210
*Congenital Malformations of the
Heart* 4: 212
Congestive heart failure 3: 929
Conic sections 5: 3
*The Connection of the Physical
Sciences* 5: 168
Conservation 5: 89–92
Conservation in Action 1: 139
Conservation International
3: 766, 768

Conservation of energy
2: 526–27
Conservation of mass 2: 571–72
Conservation of parity 3: 1012,
1014–15
Conshelf Saturation Dive program
1: 171–72
Contact 2: 418
Contergan 4: 212, 214
Continental drift 3: 784, 951,
953, 955–56, 957 (ill.), 958
Contributions to Embryology 5: 8
Control Data Corporation (CDC)
4: 61, 62
Conway, Lynn 1: **158–60**
Cooper, Leon 3: 866
Copernican theory 4: 102,
107, 108
Copernicus, Nicolaus 2: 443–44,
444 (ill.), 446–47, 490; 4:
48–54, 48 (ill.) 102, 107, 127,
128, 131, 178, 183
Corbino, Orso Mario 1: 287
Cori, Carl Ferdinand 1:
161–67, 161 (ill.), 165 (ill.)
Cori, Gerty T. 1: **161–67,**
161 (ill.), 165 (ill.)
Cormack, Allan M. 2: 485
Corpus Hippocraticum 5: 58–59
Coronal streamer 5: 116–17
Correlation of parts theory 4: 161
Correspondence, principle of
1: 98, 101
Cosmic Background Explorer
(COBE) 2: 438
The Cosmic Connection 2: 418
Cosmos 2: 418; 4: 198, 200, 204
Cotton 1: 298–301
Coulomb, Augustin 1: 214
Courtois, Bernard 1: 215
Cousteau, Jacques 1: **168–73,**
168 (ill.), 171 (ill.), 241; 5: 161
Cousteau Society 1: 172
Covalent bond 5: 98
Cowings, Patricia S. 4: **55–58,**
55 (ill.)
Cow milk 4: 76, 77
CRAY 1 4: 62, 63
CRAY 2 4: 63
CRAY 3 4: 63

CRAY 4 *4:* 64

Cray Computers Corporation *4:* 63, 64

Cray Research Corporation *4:* 62

Cray, Seymour *2:* 512, 512 (ill.); *4:* **59–65,** 59 (ill.)

Creation science *2:* 419

Cretaceous catastrophe *1:* 9

Crick, Francis *1:* **174–80,** 174 (ill.), 302, 304–06; *2:* 385, 469; *3:* 933, 935–37, 936 (ill.)

Critical Exposition of the Philosophy of Leibniz 3: 799

Crookes, William *3:* 790, 1020; *4:* 223, 225

Crop rotation *3:* 911–12, 915–16

Crossbreeding *2:* 623, 649–50

Cry of the Kalahari 2: 410

Cryptology *4:* 230, 231

Curie, Jacques *1:* 181–83

Curie, Marie *1:* **181–91,** 181 (ill.), 184 (ill.); *4:* 117–19, 121, 122

Curie, Pierre *1:* **181–91,** 181 (ill.), 185 (ill.); *4:* 117–19, 121

Cuvier, Georges *1:* 206, 206 (ill.); *4:* 161

Cyanotic heart disease *3:* 897–98, 901–02; *4:* 208, 210–13

Cybernetics *3:* 959–61

Cybernetics 3: 961

Cyclones *4:* 19

Cytology *2:* 623

D

Daimler, Gottlieb *1:* 227; *4:* 83, 87 (ill.)

Daimler Motor Company *4:* 87

Dallmeier, Francisco *1:* **192–96,** 192 (ill.)

Dalton, John *1:* 98, **197–202,** 197 (ill.); *4:* 7, 9, 11

Darden, Christine *5:* **33–36,** 33 (ill.)

Dark matter *1:* 270, 272, 274; *2:* 382

Dart, Raymond A. *2:* 518, 518 (ill.); *4:* **66–73,** 66 (ill.)

Darwin, Charles *1:* **203–10,** 203 (ill.), 322; *2:* 518; *4:* 66, 68, 70, 161, 162, 184; *5:* 81, 120, 121–22

Davies, J. A. V. *2:* 465

Davies–Hinton test *2:* 463, 465

Davis, Noel *3:* 914

Davy, Humphry *1:* **211–16,** 211 (ill.), 276–78; *3:* 773; *4:* 9; *5:* 184

Dawson, Charles *2:* 521

DDT (Dichlorodiphenyl-trichloroethane) *1:* 106, 137–38, 140, 142

Dearborn Independent 4: 89

Decimal system *4:* 106

Deep Rover 1: 240–41

Deep–sea exploration *3:* 754, 756

Deforestation *4:* 166, 167

De Forest, Lee *1:* **217–23,** 217 (ill.)

Degenerative diseases *4:* 155

Delbrück, Max *3:* 934, 936

Democritus *1:* 200, 200 (ill.)

The DemonHaunted World: Science as a Candle in the Dark 4: 205

De Niro, Robert *3:* 828

Deoxyribonucleic acid (DNA) *1:* 75–79, 81, 88–89, 174, 176–79, 178 (ill.), 302–06; *2:* 384, 386, 389, 469, 471; *3:* 870, 933–36; *4:* 135, 137, 138

De revolutionibus orbium coelestium 4: 50, 53

The Descent of Man 1: 209

Desertification *4:* 167

Detroit Automobile Company *4:* 83

Deuterons *2:* 682–83

Devik, Olav M. *4:* 18

De Vries, Hugo *2:* 652, 652 (ill.)

DeVries, William C. *2:* 504

Dialogue Concerning the Two Chief World Systems–Ptolemaic and Copernican 2: 446; *4:* 108

Dian Fossey Gorilla Fund *4:* 98

Dickinson, Richard *3:* 891

Didymium *4:* 12

Die Mutationstheorie ("The Mutation Theory") *2:* 652

Diesel engine *1:* 224–28, 226 (ill.)

Diesel, Rudolf *1:* **224–28,** 224 (ill.)

Difference engine *1:* 37, 39, 41 (ill.), 42

Difference method *2:* 552

Differentiation of cells *4:* 152

Digestion *3:* 746–48

Diggs, Irene *1:* **229–32**

Digit Fund *4:* 96, 98

Dinosaurs *1:* 9, 12, 14

Diptheria *5:* 191, 192–93

Dirac, Paul *1:* 153, 286; *4:* 188

Displacement *4:* 106

The Diversity of Life *3:* 969, 977

DNA (deoxyribonucleic acid) *1:* 75–79, 81, 88–89, 174, 176–79, 178 (ill.), 302–06; *2:* 384, 386, 389, 469, 471; *3:* 870, 933–36; *4:* 135, 137, 138

DNA technology, recombinant *1:* 75, 77, 79, 81; *3:* 871–74

Doppler, Christian Johann *1:* 122

Doppler effect *1:* 120–22

The Double Helix *1:* 305, 307

Downbursts *1:* 329–30

The Dragons of Eden: Speculations on the Evolution of Human *2:* 418; *4:* 205

Drake, Frank *1:* 72

Dreams, interpretation of *1:* 313; *2:* 538

Drew, Charles Richard *1:* **233–38,** 233 (ill.)

Drosophila *2:* 623–24

Du Bois, W. E. B. *1:* 230

Duryea brothers *4:* 83

Dymaxion automobile *1:* 333, 335

Dymaxion Deployment Unit *1:* 336

Dymaxion house *1:* 333, 335

Dynamic Meteorology and Hydrography *4:* 18

Dynamite *2:* 670, 672

E

Earle, Sylvia A. *1:* **239–43,** 239 (ill.), 242 (ill.)

Earthquakes *1:* 1–4, 3 (ill.), 328; *3:* 780–85

Easter Island *2:* 451

Eastman, George *4:* 82

Eastman Kodak *2:* 558

Eckert, J. Presper *2:* 367, (ill.)

E. coli (*Escherichia coli*) *1:* 77, 79; *2:* 386

Ecology *1:* 192, 194; *3:* 977

Ecosystems *1:* 193; *2:* 598; *5:* 91

Ectotoxicology *3:* 735

Eddington, Arthur Stanley *1:* 150, 152–53, 266–68

The Edge of the Sea *1:* 140

Edgerton, Harold *1:* 172

Edison, Thomas Alva *1:* 66, **244–53,** 244 (ill.), 249 (ill.); *2:* 557, 614; *3:* 891–92, 894–95, 983, 985; *4:* 82, 145–49

Edwards, Robert G. *3:* 883–87

E=mc^2 *1:* 260, 265, 269

Ego *1:* 314

The Ego and the Id *1:* 314

Ehrlich, Anne H. *1:* 254 (ill.), 255

Ehrlich, Paul *1:* 296, 296 (ill.)

Ehrlich, Paul R. *1:* **254–59,** 254 (ill.)

Eight Minutes to Midnight *1:* 129

Einstein, Albert *1:* **260–69,** 260 (ill.), 289; *2:* 434; *3:* 764–65, 813; *4:* 184, 221; *5:* 69, 95

Eisenhower, Dwight D. *2:* 690

Elasticity *5:* 43, 47–48

Eldredge, Niles *2:* 417

Electra complex *1:* 312

Electrical discharges in gases *4:* 222, 223

Electricity, alternating–current *1:* 251; *3:* 889, 891–93

Electricity, animal *5:* 182–83

Electricity, direct–current *1:* 251; *3:* 890–92

Electrocardiograph *4:* 210

Electrochemical theory *4:* 10

Electrochemistry *1:* 211–13;
3: 775

Electrodynanics *4:* 16

Electrogasdynamics (EGD)
2: 422, 424

Electrolytes *1:* 30–34

Electromagnetic radiation *1:* 263;
2: 610

Electromagnetic spectrum *2:* 619

Electromagnetic theory *2:* 618;
3: 789; *4:* 221

Electromagnetism *1:* 275–76,
278; *2:* 374; *2:* 610, 619;
3: 806; *4:* 221

Electrons *4:* 121, 220, 222, 224,
226; *5:* 97, 98

Electrophorous *5:* 181

Electroweak force *3:* 832, 834–35

Elementary Seismology 3: 785

*Elementary Theory of Nuclear
Shell Structure 2:* 403

Elementary Treatise on Chemistry
2: 572

The Elements 2: 374

Elion, Gertrude Belle
2: **468–73,** 468 (ill.)

ELIZA *2:* 566

Elliot Smith, Grafton *4:* 67–70

Ellis, G. F. R. *2:* 435

El Niño *4:* 19

*The Emperor's New Mind:
Concerning Computers, Minds,
and the Laws of Physics 2:* 436

Encephalitis lethargica (sleeping
sickness) *3:* 829

Endangered species *4:* 5

Endangered Species Act *5:* 91

Enders, John F. *3:* 818, 840, 843

Endocrine system *3:* 847–48,
1009

Endocrinology *5:* 9

Engineering Research Associates
4: 60

ENIAC (electronic numerical
integrator and computer)
2: 367, 676; *4:* 232

Enigma machine *4:* 230; *5:* 157

Environmental activism *4:* 2, 6,
164–69, 190–93

Environmental Protection Agency
1: 138

Eötvös force *3:* 955–56

Epidermal growth factor (EGF)
4: 154

Epps, Maeve *2:* 584

Erbium *4:* 12

Erosion *4:* 167

Estés, Clarissa Pinkola *2:* 540

Ethanol *5:* 176–178

Ethology *1:* 320–21; *2:* 405–06,
588, 590

Euclid *2:* 373–74, 374 (ill.), 456

Euclidean geometry *2:* 374;
3: 795

Euler, Leonhard *5:* 45, 46

European Center for Nuclear
Research (CERN) *3:* 835

Evans, Alice *3:* 731; *4:* **74–79**

Evans, David *2:* 563

*Ever Since Darwin: Reflections in
Natural History 2:* 418

Evolution, theory of *1:* 203–04,
207, 209; *2:* 415–16, 419–20;
3: 747, 907; *4:* 66, 68, 71, 161,
162; *5:* 80–81, 121–23

Exner, Sigmund *1:* 321

Exobiology *4:* 199

*Experimental Researches in
Electricity 1:* 279

Experiments With Plant Hybrids
2: 653

Explorer I *3:* 920; *4:* 28

Explorer III *3:* 920

Explorer space program *4:* 28

Exploring the Dangerous Trades
4: 116

Exploring the Deep Frontier
1: 243

ExProdigy 3: 963

Extraterrestrial intelligence *1:* 72

Extraterrestrial life *4:* 198, 199, 202

F

Faber, Sandra M. *1:* **270–74**

Faber–Jackson relation *1:* 270–72

Faraday, Michael *1:* 31, 216,
246, **275–79,** 275 (ill.);
2: 557, 618

Farnsworth, Philo T. *3:* 1021; *5:* **37–42,** 39 (ill.)

Farnsworth Radio and Television Corporation *5:* 41

Fauci, Anthony S. *1:* **280–84,** 280 (ill.)

Fermat, Pierre de *2:* 460; *5:* 5, 47

Fermentation *3:* 723, 726–27, 729

Fermi, Enrico *1:* **285–91,** 285 (ill.); *2:* 399, 401–02, 644, 683, 688; *3:* 1013; *4:* 185–88

Fermi–Dirac statistical mechanics *1:* 285–86

Fertilization *2:* 545–47

Fessenden, Reginald *1:* 219

Fitzgerald, George Francis *1:* 263

The Flamingo's Smile *2:* 420–21

Flamsteed, John *2:* 447

Fleas *5:* 156, 157–58

Fleming, Alexander *1:* **292–97,** 292 (ill.)

Fleming, John Ambrose *1:* 220

Fleming, Williamina P. *1:* 133

Florey, Howard W. *1:* 295, 297

Fluoroscope *4:* 210

FNRS 2 *3:* 756

FNRS 3 *3:* 756

Folklore *3:* 718–19

Food preservation *2:* 427, 429–30

Ford Foundation *4:* 90

Ford, Henry *1:* 28, 28 (ill.); *4:* **80–91,** 80 (ill.), 84 (ill.)

Ford Motor Company *4:* 84–86, 89, 90

Ford Quadricycle *4:* 83

Forever Free *4:* 5

Formalism *2:* 461

Fossey, Dian *2:* 408, 408 (ill.); *4:* **92–99,** 92 (ill.), 98 (ill.)

Foucault, Jean–Bernard–Léon *4:* 52

Foucault's pendulum *4* 52

Foundational analysis *2:* 459

The Foundations of Ethology *2:* 592

Fowler, Ralph H. *1:* 153

Fowler, William A. *1:* 119

Fox, Sally *1:* **298–301**

FoxFibre *1:* 298–301

Francis, Thomas, Jr. *3:* 839

Franklin, Rosalind *1:* 176–77, **302–07;** *3:* 935

Fraunhofer, Joseph *4:* 179

Freedom 7 *4:* 29

Free energy *5:* 97

Freemartin *2:* 547

French Revolution *2:* 574; *3:* 772, 775; *5:* 44

Freon *4:* 62

Freud, Anna *1:* 314

Freud, Sigmund *1:* **308–15,** 308 (ill.), 313 (ill.); *2:* 536, 538–41; *3:* 750

Frey, Gerhard *2:* 460

Friction *5:* 179

Friend, Charlotte *1:* **316–19,** 316 (ill.)

Frisch, Karl von *1:* **320–25,** 320 (ill.)

Frisch, Otto *1:* 288; *2:* 639, 644–46

Frost, Edwin B. *2:* 489

FTP (File Transfer Program) *5:* 16

Fujita, Tetsuya Theodore *1:* **326–32,** 326 (ill.)

Fuller, R. Buckminster *1:* **333–37,** 333 (ill.), 335 (ill.)

G

Gadolin, Johan *4:* 12

Gagarin, Yury *4:* 216

Gaia: A New Look at Life on Earth *2:* 599

Gaia hypothesis *2:* 596, 598–99

Galápagos Islands *2:* 450

Galaxies *1:* 119, 270–74, 273 (ill.); *2:* 380–82, 487–88, 491–92

Galdikas, Biruté *4:* 97 (ill.)

Galileo Galilei *1:* 267; *2:* 444–46, 490; *3:* 789; *4:* **100–09,** 100 (ill.), 104 (ill.), 128, 178, 182

Gallagher, John *1:* 272

Galle, Johann Gottfried *2:* 373

Gallium arsenide circuits *4:* 63

Game Management *5:* 87, 91

Game theory *3:* 962; *4:* 197; *5:* 21–22, 24–26

Game theory proof *5:* 26
Gasoline engine *4:* 87
Gates, Bill *2:* **363–70,** 363 (ill.)
Gauss, Karl Friedrich *2:* **371–75,** 371 (ill.); *5:* 47
Gayle, Helene D. *2:* **376–79,** 376 (ill.)
Gay–Lussac, Joseph *1:* 215
Geiger counter *3:* 808; *3:* 920
Geiger, Hans *3:* 808–11, 810 (ill.)
Geissler, Heinrich *3:* 1020
Gelfond, A. O. *2:* 458
Geller, Margaret *2:* **380–83,** 380 (ill.)
Gene, artificial *4:* 133, 139
Gene, recessive *5:* 10
General Motors *4:* 90
Genes and Genomes: A Changing Perspective *3:* 874
Genes, Mind and Culture *3:* 977
Genes *4:* 135
Genetic code *1:* 78, 179, 209
Genetic engineering *1:* 76–78, 80; *3:* 870, 873–74
Genetic transposition *2:* 622, 624–25, 627
Geodesic dome *1:* 333–34, 336–37
Geophysics *4:* 18; *5:* 129
George C. Marshall Space Flight Center *4:* 28
George III (of England) *2:* 443–47
Germain, Sophie *5:* **43–49,** 43 (ill.)
German Society for Space Travel *4:* 23
Germ theory *3:* 726
Gifted Hands: The Ben Carson Story *4:* 38
Gilbert, Walter *1:* 81; *2:* **384–91,** 384 (ill.)
Gilbreth, Frank *5:* 51–53, 54
Gilbreth, Lillian *5:* **50–56,** 50 (ill.)
Glaser, Donald *1:* 11
Glashow, Sheldon L. *3:* 832, 835, 836 (ill.)
Glass, nonreflecting *1:* 92, 94
Glaucoma *2:* 531
Gliders *3:* 989–93

Global warming *2:* 597; *5:* 130
Goddard, Robert H. *2:* **392–98,** 392 (ill.), 397 (ill.)
Gödel, Kurt *2:* 372, 461
Goeppert-Mayer, Maria *2:* **399–404,** 399 (ill.)
Gold, Lois Swirsky *1:* 21–22
Gold, Thomas *1:* 71
Golka, Robert *3:* 891
Gombe Stream Reserve, Tanzania *2:* 405, 407, 409
Gondwanaland *3:* 956
Goodall, Jane *2:* **405–14,** 405 (ill.), 412 (ill.); *4:* 93, 94, 97
Gopher (search engine) *5:* 16
Gorillas in the Mist *2:* 408; *4:* 93, 94, 96
Gosling, Raymond *1:* 304–06
Gough, John *1:* 198
Gould, Gordon *2:* 601, 604, 604 (ill.)
Gould, Stephen Jay *2:* **415–21,** 415 (ill.); *3:* 976
Gourdine, Meredith *2:* **422–26,** 422 (ill.), 425 (ill.)
Graphophone *1:* 62, 67
Gray, Elisha *1:* 64, 66, 66 (ill.)
The Great Train Robbery *1:* 250
Green Belt Movement *4:* 164, 166–68
Greenhouse effect *1:* 30, 33–35
The Greenhouse Effect, Climate Change, and Ecosystems *1:* 34
Green Revolution *1:* 105, 107–09
Greylag geese *2:* 589
Grissom, Virgil I. "Gus" *4:* 26
Growing Up in New Guinea *2:* 636
Growth factors *4:* 154
Guillemin, Roger *3:* 1009, 1010 (ill.)
Gutenberg, Beno *3:* 781, 784
GUTs (grand unification theories) *2:* 435; *5:* 135–136
Guyots *3:* 954
Gypsum *2:* 569
Gyroscope *4:* 52

H

Hadar, Ethiopia *2:* 519–20, 523

Hadrons *2:* 500

Hahn, Otto *1:* 289; *2:* 401, 641–42, 644–45, 647

Hale, George E. *2:* 489

Half–life, radioactive *3:* 807, 809

Halley, Edmond *4:* 180

Hall, Lloyd A. *2:* **427–31,** 427 (ill.)

Hamburger, Viktor *4:* 152, 153

Hamilton, Alice *4:* **110–16**

Hardy, G. H. *3:* 960

Hardy–Weinberg law *2:* 552

Hargreaves, James *1:* 24–25

Harrar, George *1:* 107

Harris, Geoffrey W. *3:* 1009

Harvard University *4:* 110, 115

Hawkes, Graham *1:* 239–41

Hawking, Stephen *2:* **432–40,** 432 (ill.)

Hazardous waste *4:* 190–92

Head Start *4:* 143

Heavy water *5:* 98–99

Hektoen, Ludwig *4:* 112

Heliocentric theory *4:* 48, 50, 51, 53, 102, 107

Helmholtz, Hermann von *1:* 63; *2:* 527–28, 527 (ill.); *3:* 760

Hemispherectomy *4:* 36

Henry Ford Company *4:* 84

Henry, Joseph *1:* 64; *2:* 374; *3:* 984

Henslow, John *1:* 204

Heredity *2:* 625–26, 648, 650–52; *4:* 135

Herschel, Caroline *2:* 442, 447

Herschel, John *2:* 447

Herschel, William *2:* **441–47,** 441 (ill.)

Hertz, Heinrich *1:* 262; *2:* 610; *4:* 16

Herzfeld, Karl *2:* 401

Hesselberg, Theodor *4:* 18

Hess, Harry Hammond *3:* 954, 958

Hevesy, Georg von *4:* 123

Hewish, Antony *1:* 69–71

Hewlett–Packard *2:* 509

Heyerdahl, Thor *2:* **448–53,** 448 (ill.)

Hidden hunger *4:* 142

High–energy physics *3:* 805

High–speed flash photography *1:* 172

Hilbert, David *2:* **454–62,** 454 (ill.); *3:* 803; *4:* 196–97, 229; *5:* 139

Hilbert's tenth problem *4:* 194, 196

Hinton test *2:* 463, 465

Hinton, William Augustus *2:* **463–67,** 463 (ill.)

Hipparchus *2:* 443

Hippocrates of Cos *5:* **57–59,** 57 (ill.)

Hippocratic Oath *5:* 57

Hiroshima, Japan *2:* 688

Hisinger, Wilhelm *4:* 9, 10, 12

The History of the Corruption of Christianity 3: 775

History of Western Philosophy 3: 802

Hitchcock, Dian *2:* 598

Hitchings, George H. *2:* **468–73,** 468 (ill.)

Hitler, Adolf *1:* 268; *2:* 461; *3:* 765, 849

Hittorf, Johann *3:* 1020

HIV (human immunodeficiency virus) *1:* 81, 280, 283–84; *2:* 376, 378, 378 (ill.)

Hodgkin, Dorothy *2:* **474–79,** 474 (ill.)

Høiland, Einar *4:* 21

Holldobler, Bert *3:* 977

Holley, Robert W. *4:* 137, 138

Home economics *4:* 142

Hominids *2:* 516–17, 519–20, 522

Homo erectus 2: 583

Homo habilis 2: 516, 520, 522, 580, 583, 586

Homo sapiens 2: 580

Homosexuality *3:* 973

Hooke, Robert *4:* 179–81, 183

Hooke's law *4:* 181

Hopper, Grace *5:* **60–64,** 60 (ill.)

Hormones *3:* 848, 853

Horowitz, Paul *1:* 72, 72 (ill.)

Horseless carriage *4:* 82, 83, 85
Hounsfield, Godfrey *2:* **483–86,**
  480 (ill.)
Houssay, Bernardo A. *1:* 161
How to Know the Butterflies
  1: 255
Hoyle, Fred *1:* 119, 121;
  5: **65–72,** 65 (ill.)
Hubbard, Gardiner *1:* 63–64
Hubble, Edwin *2:* **487–97,**
  487 (ill.), 495 (ill.)
Hubble Space Telescope *1:* 117,
  122, 274; *2:* 493, 493 (ill.)
Huchra, John P. *2:* 381–82
Hull House *4:* 112–14
Human ecology *4:* 141
Human evolution *4:* 66, 68, 71
Human genome project *2:* 384,
  387–88; *3:* 933, 937
The Human Mind *2:* 663
Human rights *5:* 101, 103–106
Human Use of Human Beings
  3: 963
Huntsman, Benjamin *1:* 84
Hutton, James *2:* 599, 599 (ill.)
Huxley, Aldous *3:* 885
Huygens, Christiaan *4:* 101,
  132, 181
Hybridization, plant
  1: 112–14, 116
Hydraulics *4:* 106
hydrodynamics *4:* 15, 16
Hydrogen bomb *2:* 686, 690
Hydroponics *3:* 914
Hhydrostatic balance *4:* 101
Hydrostatics *4:* 101, 106
Hydrothermal vents *1:* 51

I

I Am a Mathematician *3:* 963
IBM *2:* 368, 511, 514
Iconoscope *3:* 1019
Id *1:* 314
Idealism *3:* 796, 798
*If You Love This Planet: A Plan to
  Heal the Earth* *1:* 129
Illinois Commission on
  Occupational Diseases *4:* 113

Iindustrial disease *4:* 113, 114
Industrial hygiene *4:* 112, 114, 115
Industrial medicine *4:* 113–15
Industrial poisons *4:* 110, 113, 115
*Industrial Poisons in the United
  States* *4:* 115
Industrial Revolution *1:* 82, 84;
  3: 946, 949, 983
Infectious diseases *3:* 723, 728,
  855, 858
Information superhighway *2:* 370
Ingram, Vernon *1:* 178
Inheritance, patterns of
  2: 651 (ill.)
Inquisition *4:* 108
Instant camera *2:* 556, 559–60
Institute of Cell Biology of the
  Italian National Research
  Council *4:* 155
Institute for Theoretical Physics
  1: 98, 100–01
Institute of Food Technologists
  2: 427
Institute of Nautical Archaeology
  1: 57
Insulin *2:* 479; *3:* 1008
Integrated circuit *2:* 674, 676–77
Intel Corporation *2:* 674, 677
Internal–combustion engine
  1: 224–25; *4:* 81, 82
International Center for Maize and
  Wheat Improvement *1:* 110
International Geophysical Year
  3: 920
International Gravity Foundation
  Prize *5:* 105
International Rice Research
  Institute *1:* 108–10
Internet *5:* 14, 16–19
The Interpretation of Dreams
  1: 313–14
In the Shadow of Man *2:* 405, 410
*Introduction to Mathematical
  Philosophy* *3:* 802
*An Introduction to the Study of
  Stellar Structure* *1:* 153
Invariant theory *2:* 454, 456
Inverse square law *4:* 177
Invertebrates *5:* 78, 79

In vitro fertilization *3:* 882, 884, 887; *5:* 31–32
Ionosphere *3:* 941–42
Iron lungs *3:* 819 (ill.)
Iroquois Confederacy *3:* 718
Isomers *4:* 7, 11
Isotopes *4:* 226
Is Peace Possible? 2: 478

J

Jackson, Robert *1:* 272
Jackson, Shirley Ann *2:* **498–501,** 498 (ill.)
Jacob, Francois *2:* 386
Janzen, Daniel H. *3:* 769, 769 (ill.)
Jarvik, Robert K. *2:* **503–07,** 502 (ill.)
Jarvik–7 *2:* 502, 504–05
Java Man *5:* 189
Jefferson, Thomas *3:* 775
Jensen, J. Hans D. *2:* 399, 403
Jobs, Steven *2:* 508–14, 508 (ill.)
Johanson, Donald *2:* **515–23,** 515 (ill.), 584; *4:* 68
Johns Hopkins University *3:* 823, 898, 900, 903
Joliot-Curie, Frédéric *1:* 288; *2:* 642; *4:* **117–25,** 117 (ill.)
Joliot-Curie, Irène *1:* 166, 185, 288; *2:* 642, 644–45; *4:* **117–25,** 117 (ill.), 120 (ill.)
Juno I *4:* 28
Juno II *4:* 28
Juno launch vehicle *4:* 22, 28
Joule, James Prescott *2:* **524–28,** 524 (ill.); *3:* 907
Joule–Thomson effect *2:* 528; *3:* 907
Julian, Percy L. *2:* 529–35, 529 (ill.), 533 (ill.)
Jung, C. G. *1:* 314; *2:* **536–42,** 536 (ill.)
Jupiter *4:* 173
Jupiter C launch vehicle *4:* 22, 28
Jupiter missile *4:* 22, 26
Jupiter, moons of *4:* 105
Just, Ernest Everett *2:* **543–48,** 543 (ill.)

K

Kahn, Reuben Leon *2:* 465
Kapitsa, Pyotr *3:* 891
Karisoke Research Center *2:* 408; *4:* 94, 96, 98
Karl Menninger School of Psychiatry *2:* 662
Karroo deposits *4:* 71
Keith, Arthur *2:* 521; *4:* 70
Keith, Louis *2:* **549–55,** 549 (ill.)
Kekulé, Friedrich *3:* 741
K–electron capture *1:* 9
Kelley, William *1:* 84
Kelsey, Frances Oldham *4:* 214
Kelvin, Lord. *See* **Thomson, William, Lord Kelvin**
Kelvin scale *3:* 905–06, 909
Kenya Department of Wildlife Services *2:* 584
Kenyapithecus 2: 580
Kepler, Johannes *1:* 156, 267; *2:* 490, 490 (ill.); *4:* 51, 53, 105, **126–32, 126 (ill.), 130 (ill.),** 178, 183
Khorana, Har Gobind *4:* **133–40,** 133 (ill.), 136 (ill.)
Khush, Gurdev S. *1:* 108
Kieselguhr *2:* 671–72
Kimeu, Kamoya *2:* 585 (ill.)
A Kind of Alaska 3: 828
Kinescope *3:* 1019, 1021
King Solomon's Ring 2: 592
Kipfer, Paul *3:* 755
Kirchhoff, Gustav *3:* 760–61; *4:* 179
Kittrell, Flemmie Pansy *4:* **141–44**
Kitty Hawk, North Carolina *3:* 991–93
Klaproth, Martin *4:* 11, 12
Kleew 2: 591
K–meson *3:* 1002, 1012, 1014–15
Knorr 1: 48, 50
Koch, Robert *3:* 858–60, 858 (ill.)
Kolff, William *2:* 503, 505
Konishi, Masakazu *5:* **73–76**
KonTiki 2: 448, 450, 451 (ill.)
KonTiki: Across the Pacific by Raft 2: 450

Lilienthal, Otto *3:* 989–90, 990 (ill.)

Lillie, Frank Rattray *2:* 545, 547

Lindbergh, Charles *2:* 396

Link, Edwin A. *2:* 563

Linnaeus, Carl *1:* 206, 206 (ill.), 208; *4:* **157–63,** 157 (ill.); *5:* 77

Lions *4:* 1, 3, 4

Lippershey, Hans *4:* 103

Lister, Joseph *3:* 726, 726 (ill.)

Lithium *4:* 10

Living Free 4: 5

Lizhi, Fang *5:* **101–107,** 101 (ill.)

Loeb, Jacques *2:* 545–46

Logic gates *4:* 230

Long, Esmond R. *3:* 857

Lonsdale, Kathleen *2:* 478, 478 (ill.)

Lorentz, Hendrik *1:* 263

Lorenz, Konrad *1:* 325; *2:* **588–95,** 588 (ill.), 593 (ill.)

Los Alamos National Laboratory *1:* 58–59; *2:* 680, 684–85, 688

Lovelace, Ada *1:* 40, 42, 42 (ill.)

Lovelock, James E. *2:* **596–600,** 596 (ill.)

Lubricating cup *2:* 629–30, 632

Lucy *2:* 515, 520, 522, 584, 586

Lumsden, Charles *3:* 977

Luria, Salvador *3:* 934

Lusitania 1: 50

Lymphatic system *3:* 822–24

Lysozyme *1:* 294

M

Maathai, Wangari *4:* **164–69,** 164 (ill.)

MacArthur, Robert H. *3:* 971

Mach 1 *5:* 34

Macrophage *1:* 284

Magic numbers *2:* 403

Magnetic core memory *3:* 923, 925

Magnetohydrodynamics *2:* 424

Maiman, Theodore *2:* **601–06,** 601 (ill.)

Mall, Franklin P. *3:* 823

Malnutrition *4:* 166, 167

Malta fever *4:* 77, 78

Mammals, origin of *4:* 71

Manhattan Project *1:* 7, 10, 103, 268–69, 285, 289–91; *2:* 399, 402; *2:* 680, 683–85; *3:* 779, 1002

Manus (people) *2:* 635, 635 (ill.)

The Man Who Mistook His Wife for a Hat 3: 827, 830

Marconi, Guglielmo *1:* 218–19; *2:* **607–15,** 607 (ill.), 609 (ill.); *3:* 806, 896

Mariner 9 4: 200, 201

Mark I *3:* 924, 926; *5:* 62–63

Mark II *5:* 63

Marriage and Morals 3: 802

Mars *4:* 129, 132, 200, 201, 204

Marsden, Ernest *3:* 809, 811

Martin, Pierre–Emile *1:* 86

Marx, Karl *3:* 797

Maser *2:* 602

Mass production *4:* 80, 82, 86, 90

Mass spectrometer *4:* 226

Mass–energy equivalence *4:* 221

A Matter of Consequences 3: 880

Matzeliger, Jan Ernst *5:* **108–14,** 108 (ill.)

Mauchly, John William *2:* 367, 367 (ill.)

Maunder, Annie Russell *5:* **115–18**

Maury, Antonia *1:* 133

Maxam, Allan *2:* 387

Max Planck Society *3:* 765

Maxwell, James Clerk *2:* 610, **616–21,** 616 (ill.); *3:* 789, 906, 908; *4:* 221, 225

Maybach, Wilhelm *1:* 227; *4:* 87

Mayer, Joseph E. *2:* 400–01

Mayer, Julius *2:* 527

Mayr, Ernst *5:* **119–25,** 119 (ill.)

McCarthy, Senator Joseph *2:* 690

McClintock, Barbara *2:* **622–27,** 622 (ill.)

McCormick, Cyrus *4:* 82

McCoy, Elijah *2:* **628–32,** 628 (ill.)

Mead, Margaret *2:* **633–38,** 633 (ill.), 635 (ill.)

Meaning of Evolution 2: 416

MS–DOS (Microsoft Disk
Operating System) *2:* 368
Muller, Hermann *3:* 934; *4:* 199
Multiple births *2:* 549–54
Munk, Walter *5:* **126–31**
Myers–Briggs personality
assessment *2:* 538
Mysterium Coniunctionis *2:* 542
Mysterium Cosmographicum
4: 127

N

Nagama *4:* 78
Nagasaki, Japan *2:* 688
Nambu, Yoichiro *5:* **132–37**
National Aeronautics and Space
Administration (NASA) *1:* 59;
2: 598; *4:* 28–31, 55–58, 198,
200–02, 205, 218; *5:* 33, 34
National Earthquake Information
Center *1:* 4
National Foundation for Infantile
Paralysis *3:* 841
National Labor Relations Act *4:* 90
National Oceanic and
Atmospheric Administration
1: 239
National Recovery Act *4:* 90
National Space Institute *4:* 31
Natural History *2:* 417
Natural History of Invertebrates
1: 208
Natural philosophy *1:* 245
Natural selection, theory of
1: 203–04, 207; *2:* 589–90,
653; *3:* 747; *4:* 162; *5:* 121–22;
5: 122–23
*The Nature of the Chemical Bond
and the Structure of Molecules
and Crystals* *3:* 740
Navajo (people) *1:* 58, 60
Nazi *5:* 142, 186–87
Nazism (National Socialism)
1: 268; *2:* 461, 593
Nebulae *2:* 441–42, 444, 446
Neddermeyer, Seth *2:* 685, 687
Neon *4:* 226
Neptune *2:* 373

Nereis *2:* 545
Nerve growth factor (NGF) *4:* 150,
152, 154–56
Nervous system *3:* 847–48;
4: 151, 152
Netscape *5:* 14, 18–19
Netscape Navigator *5:* 14
Neurobiology *5:* 73
Neuroendocrinology *3:* 847–48,
851–52, 1009
Neuroendocrinology *3:* 852
Neurohormones *3:* 849
Neurons *3:* 848, 852; *5:* 75
Neurosecretion *3:* 847–50, 853
Neurosurgery *4:* 33, 35
Neutrino *1:* 285, 287
Neutron stars *1:* 71, 153
New Guinea *2:* 635
The New Science *3:* 764
*A New System of Chemical
Philosophy* *1:* 202
New York State Archeological
Association *3:* 721
Newcomen, Thomas *3:* 947
Newlands, J. A. R. *2:* 656
Newton, Isaac *1:* 38, 41, 246,
266, 267, 267 (ill.); *2:* 435; *3:*
764; *4:* 102, 103, 128, **176–84,**
176 (ill.); *5:* 45, 166
NeXT Company *2:* 513–14
Nez Percé (people) *3:* 721
Night vision *3:* 1022
999 (race car) *4:* 84
Nipkow, Paul *3:* 1018
Nirenberg, Marshall Warren
4: 137
Nitroglycerin *2:* 671
Nitrous oxide *1:* 211, 213; *3:* 773
Nobel, Alfred *2:* **670–73,**
670 (ill.)
Nobel Foundation *2:* 672–73
Nobel Peace Prize *1:* 105, 109,
129; *2:* 684, 686; *3:* 738,
740, 744
Nobel Prize for chemistry *1:* 30,
33, 75, 81, 91, 96, 189, 251;
2: 389, 474, 477, 639, 647,
654; *3:* 738, 740, 805–06,
809, 895–96
Nobel Prize for literature *3:* 802

P

Paleoanthropology *4:* 66, 68, 69; *5:* 186

Paleontology *4:* 161

Palermo, Gianpiero *3:* 887

The Panda's Thumb *2:* 419

Pangaea *3:* 953, 956

Parallel processing *4:* 64

Parc National des Virungas, Zaire *4:* 94

Parity, principle of *3:* 999, 1002–03

Parker, Arthur C. *3:* **717–22**

Parker, John P. *5:* **145–50**

Parthenogenesis *2:* 543, 545

Particle accelerator *1:* 10; *2:* 499; *3:* 812

Particle physics *2:* 682; *3:* 805

Particulars of My Life *3:* 880

Passages from the Life of a Philosopher *1:* 43

Pasteur Institute *3:* 724, 732; *5:* 193

Pasteur, Louis *2:* 468; *3:* **723–32,** 723 (ill.)

Pasteurization *3:* 730–31; *4:* 74, 76--79

Patent system *1:* 244, 247–48; *3:* 982; *4:* 146–49, 201

Pathology *4:* 111, 112; *5:* 9

Patrick, Ruth *3:* **733–37,** 733 (ill.), 737 (ill.)

Pauli, Wolfgang *1:* 153, 286–87; *2:* 403

Pauli's Exclusion Principle *1:* 286

Pauling, Linus *1:* 176, 305; *3:* **738–45,** 738 (ill.), 935

Pavlov, Ivan *3:* **746–52,** 746 (ill.), 750 (ill.)

Peano, Guiseppe *3:* 798–99

Pediatrics *5:* 11

Peking Man *5:* 186, 188–89

Pendulum *4:* 101

Penicillin *1:* 292, 294–97; *2:* 474, 477

Penrose, Roger *2:* 434, 436

Pergament, Eugene *3:* 887

Period luminosity relation *5:* 84–85

Periodic law *2:* 655–56, 658

Periodic table of the elements *2:* 654, 656–59, 658 (ill.): *4:* 185, 186; *5:* 97–98

Perrin, Jean Baptiste *1:* 262

Pershing missile *4:* 22, 28

Person, Waverly *1:* 4

Personal computers *2:* 363–64, 368–69, 508, 510–11, 513

Pesticides *1:* 106, 137–38, 140

Petty, William, Earl of Shelburne *3:* 774

Phages *3:* 934

Pheromones *3:* 969, 971

Philosophia botanica *4:* 162

Philosophiae naturalis principia mathematica *1:* 267; *4:* 176, 182, 183

Philosphical Propositions *5:* 2–3

Philosophical Society of Albany *3:* 721

Phinney, Archie *3:* 721

Phlogiston *2:* 570; *3:* 774

Phocomelia *4:* 212

Phoenix Foundry *5:* 149–50

Photoelectric effect *1:* 260, 262–63; *3:* 764

Photography *1:* 251; *2:* 556

Phylon: A Review of Race and Culture *1:* 230

Physical Foundations of Radiology *3:* 779

Physical hydrodynamics, theory of *1:* 330; *4:* 17

Physicians for Social Responsibility *1:* 124, 127, 129

Physostigmine *2:* 529, 531

PhytoFarm *3:* 914

Piazzi, Guiseppe *2:* 372

Piccard, Auguste *3:* **753–58,** 753 (ill.), 755 (ill.)

Piccard, Jacques *3:* **753–58,** 753 (ill.)

Piccard, Jean *3:* 753

Pickering, Edward *1:* 132

Piezoelectricity *1:* 181, 183

Piltdown Man *2:* 521

The Piltdown Men *2:* 521

Pincus, Gregory Godwin *5:* 30

Pio Instituto Trivulzio *5:* 5–6

Pioneer IV *4:* 28

Pioneer space program *4:* 28,
201, 202
Pippa's Challenge 4: 5
Pixar Animation Studios
2: 513–14
Planck, Max *1:* 99–100, 262;
2: 640–41, 643; *3:* **759–65,**
759 (ill.), 813
Planck's constant *3:* 759–60, 763
Planetary motion *4:* 129
Planetology *4:* 199
Plant sexuality *4:* 158
Plasma *1:* 234–35
Plasma physics *1:* 59; *2:* 424;
3: 891
Plate tectonics *1:* 51; *3:* 784,
951, 957
Plato *5:* 58
Plotkin, Mark *3:* **766–71,**
767 (ill.)
Plucker, Julius *3:* 1020
"Plum pudding" atomic structure
4: 224
Plutonium *4:* 188
Pohlflucht 3: 955–56
Poincare, Jules Henri *1:* 263;
4: 16
Polaris 5: 151, 152
Polonium *4:* 119, 121
Polarized glass *2:* 558–59
Polarized light *2:* 557; *3:* 725
Polaroid Corporation *2:* 556,
558–59
Polio (poliomyelitis) *2:* 480–82;
3: 815–17, 820, 838, 840–44
Polio vaccine *3:* 814, 816–18,
820, 838, 840, 842
Polonium *1:* 181, 186, 189
Polynesia, settlement of
2: 448–50, 452
Positive reinforcement *3:* 877
PowerGlove *2:* 564
Powless, David *4:* **190–93**
PPD (purified protein derivative)
3: 856, 860–61
Pregnancy, high–risk *2:* 552
Priestley, Joseph *2:* 571; *3:*
772–75, 772 (ill.); *5:* 180
Primate behavior *2:* 406–07, 409
Primatology *4:* 92, 94, 97

Principia Mathematica 3: 797,
800–01
"The Principles of Arithmetic,
Presented by a New Method"
3: 798
The Principles of Mathematics
3: 799, 801
Principles of Social
Reconstruction 3: 800
Prison system *2:* 663
The Problems of Philosophy
3: 800
Proconsul africanus 2: 579
Progesterone *2:* 530, 532;
5: 29–31
Project Paperclip *4:* 26
Project Phoenix *1:* 72
Prokhorov, Aleksandr *2:* 602–03
Promethean Fire 3: 977
Propositiones philosophicae
5: 2–3
Proteins *4:* 138
Protons *4:* 121; *5:* 103
Protoplasm *2:* 546–47
Psychoanalysis *1:* 308, 310,
312–14; *2:* 536, 538
Psychological Types 2: 541
Psychology *5:*50, 52–54
Psychology of Management 5: 53
The Psychology of the
Unconscious 2: 540
Psycho–neuroimmunology *3:* 853
Pterodactyl *4:* 161
Ptolemaic system *2:* 443–44, 446;
4: 108
Ptolemy *2:* 443; *4:* 50, 51, 54,
102, 107
Public health *4:* 112, 114
Pugwash Conferences on Science
and World Affairs *2:* 684
Pulsars *1:* 69, 71, 73
Punctuated equilibrium *2:* 417
Putnam, Frederick Ward *3:* 719
Pyramids *1:* 13
Pyroelectricity *1:* 183
Pythagoras *2:* 458, 458 (ill.), 460
Pythagorean theorem *2:* 460

Q

Quantum mechanics *1:* 101, 262;
    2: 680–82; *3:* 739–40; *4:* 222
Quantum theory *1:* 99–100;
    3: 759–60, 763–64
Quarks *3:* 835; *5:* 136
Quarterman, Lloyd Albert *1:* 290
Quasars *1:* 70, 117, 119–22, 121
    (ill.); *5:* 70, 105
QuasiStellar Objects *1:* 120
Queen of Shaba 4: 5
Quimby, Edith H. *3:* **776–79,**
    776 (ill.)

R

Ra 2: 452
Ra II 2: 452
Rabies *3:* 731; *5:* 193
Radar *1:* 7, 9; *3:* 939–41, 943
Radiata 4: 161
Radiation *1:* 125–26; *3:* 776–79,
    790, 807–09
Radiation sickness *1:* 187; *2:* 688
Radio *1:* 217, 222; *2:* 614
Radioactive elements *4:* 121
Radioactive fallout *2:* 688
Radioactive tracer analysis
    4: 122, 123
Radioactive isotopes *3:* 776;
    4: 121
Radioactivity *1:* 181, 186–88;
    3: 789, 805, 807–09;
    4: 119, 121
Radioimmunoassay (RIA)
    3: 1004, 1006–09, 1011
Radiological Research Laboratory
    3: 778
Radiometer *4:* 225
Radio waves *2:* 607–08, 610–12;
    3: 893–94
Radium *1:* 181, 186, 189; *4:* 112,
    114, 118, 119
Radium Institute *4:* 118, 120, 124
Radium–D *4:* 123
Rain forests *1:* 257; *3:* 766,
    768–70
Raman, Chandrasekhar V. *1:* 151
Ramart–Lucas, Pauline *2:* 643

RAND Corporation *5:* 24–25
Randall, John T. *1:* 303
Rare earth elements *4:* 10, 12
Rayleigh, John *3:* 763
RCA (Radio Corporation of
    America) *5:* 38, 40
The Realm of the Nebulae 2: 496
Recycling *4:* 192
Redshifting *1:* 120–21, 266, 268;
    2: 381, 492
Redstone missile *4:* 22, 26, 28
Reflecting telescope *4:* 176, 179
*Reflections on the Decline of
    Science in England and on
    Some of Its Causes 1:* 43
Reflex, conditioned *3:* 746,
    749–50, 752
Reflex, unconditioned *3:* 749
Reifenstein, Edward *1:* 73
Relativity, theory of *1:* 260,
    263–67, 269; *3:* 764; *5:* 140
Repression *1:* 310, 312
Reuleaux, Franz *1:* 227
Revelle, Roger *1:* 17
*Revolution of the Heavenly
    Spheres 2:* 444
Rhenium *4:* 185-87
Rheticus, Georg *4:* 51
Rheumatic fever *4:* 210, 212
Rheumatoid arthritis *2:* 530
Ribet, Kenneth *2:* 460
Ribosomes *4:* 137
Rice *1:* 108–10
Richer, Jean *4:* 132
Richter, Charles F. *1:* 1, 4, 328;
    3: **780–86,** 780 (ill.), 783 (ill.)
Richter scale *1:* 1, 4, 328; *3:* 780,
    782
Ride, Sally *4:* 218
RNA (ribonucleic acid) *1:* 76,
    90–91, 304, 306
The Road Ahead 2: 370
*Roads to Freedom: Socialism,
    Anarchism and Syndicalism
    3:* 802
Road to Survival 1: 255
Robbins, Frederick *3:* 818,
    841, 843
Roberts, Ed *2:* 365–66
Robinson, Julia *4:* **194–97**

Rockets *2:* 393–94, 396; *4:* 24

Rockoon *3:* 920

Röntgen, Wilhelm *1:* 132;
   3: **787–93,** 787 (ill.)

Roosevelt, Franklin D. *1:* 268

Rosenwald, Julius *2:* 546

Rosing, Boris *3:* 1018

Ross, Mary *5:* **151–53**

Rotation of Earth *4:* 52

Rotblat, Joseph *2:* 684

Rothschild, Miriam *5:* **154–59**

Royal Society *1:* 39–40

Rudolphine Tables *4:* 129, 131

Russell, Bertrand *3:* **794–804,**
   794 (ill.), 801 (ill.), 960

Russell, Frederick Stratten *1:* 17

Rutherford, Ernest *1:* 99, 102;
   2: 400, 641; *3:* **805–13,**
   805 (ill.), 810 (ill.); *4:* 226

S

Sabin, Albert *3:* **814–21,**
   814 (ill.), 841, 843, 845

Sabin Committee *3:* 826

Sabin, Florence R. *3:* **822–25,**
   822 (ill.), 825 (ill.)

Sacks, Oliver Wolf *3:* **827–31,**
   827 (ill.)

Sagan, Carl *2:* 418, 418 (ill.);
   4: **198–207,** 198 (ill.), 203 (ill.)

Sakharov, Andrei *2:* 686, 686 (ill.)

Salam, Abdus *2:* 385; *3:* **832–37,**
   832 (ill.), 836 (ill.)

Salam–Weinberg theory *3:* 835

Salk Institute for Biological
   Research *1:* 177, 179; *3:* 846

Salk, Jonas *3:* 818, **838–46,**
   838 (ill.), 845 (ill.)

Salts, decomposition of *4:* 9

Salvarsan *1:* 296

Samoa *2:* 634–35, 638

A Sand County Almanac *5:* 87

Sanders, Thomas *1:* 63, 65

Sandström, Johann Wilhelm *4:* 18

Sanger, Frederick *2:* 387, 389,
   389 (ill.)

Santa Rosa National Park, Costa
   Rica *3:* 769

Sarnoff, David *3:* 1021

Saturn *4:* 132, 173, 174

Saturn rockets *4:* 22, 24, 28, 29, 30

Savitch, Pavle *2:* 644

Sayer, Malcolm *3:* 828

The Sceptical Chymist *2:* 573

Schaller, George *4:* 93, 94

Schally, Andrew V. *3:* 1009,
   1010 (ill.)

Scharrer, Berta *3:* **847–54**

Scharrer, Ernst *3:* 847,
   849–50, 852

Schawlow, A. L. *2:* 602–604

Scheele, Carl Wilhelm *3:* 774

Scheutz, Georg *1:* 42

Schrieffer, J. Robert *3:* 866

Schrödinger, Erwin *3:* 739

Science and the Modern World
   3: 797

Scientific method *3:* 789; *4:* 183

Scientific Revolution *4:* 178, 183

Scripps Institute of Oceanography
   1: 17

Scuba (self–contained underwater
   breathing apparatus)
   1: 239, 241

The Sea Around Us *1:* 139

Sea Cliff *1:* 243

Seafloor spreading *3:* 954, 958

Seaman, Gary *2:* 411

*Seeing Voices: A Journey Into the
   World of the Deaf* *3:* 831

Segrè, Emilio *3:* 1001; *4:* 188 (ill.)

Segregation, hereditary law of
   2: 650, 652

Seibert, Florence *3:* **855–61,**
   855 (ill.)

Seismicity of the Earth *3:* 782

Seismic tomography *1:* 5

Seismograph *1:* 4; *3:* 780, 782

Seizures *4:* 37

Selenium *4:* 10

Selfridge, Thomas *3:* 995

Semiconductors *2:* 675; *3:* 862,
   864–65; *4:* 59

Sequential analysis *5:* 24

Serengeti National Park *4:* 5

Serengeti Plain, Tanzania *2:* 584

Set theory *3:* 803

Seven Samurai project *1:* 272

Stellar evolution *5:* 67

Stellar spectroscopy *1:* 132–33

Steptoe, Patrick *3:* **882–88,** 882 (ill.); *5:* 32

Sterols *2:* 534

Stevin, Simon *4:* 102, 106

Stewart, Thomas Dale *5:* **170–74,** 170 (ill.)

Stoney, G. J. *4:* 224

Strassmann, Fritz *1:* 289; *2:* 401, 644–45, 647; *4:* 187

"A Structure for Deoxyribose Nucleic Acid" *1:* 305

Studies in Hysteria 1: 312

Subatomic particles *5:* 132, 135–37

Sun, rotation of *4:* 105

Sunspots *4:* 105, 173; *5:* 115, 117

Supercomputer *2:* 512; *4:* 59, 61, 62, 64

Superconductivity *3:* 866

Superego *1:* 314

Supernova *1:* 69, 71, 73, 119, 156

Sutherland, van *2:* 563

Sverdrup, Harald Ulrik *4:* 18, 21

Svedberg, Theodor *3:* 860

Swaminathan, M. S. *1:* 110

Swan, Joseph Wilson *1:* 248–49, 251, 251 (ill.)

Swedish Academy of Science *4:* 9, 10

Synthesizer, electronic *2:* 668

Syphilis *1:* 296; *2:* 463–65, 466 (ill.)

Syphilis and Its Treatment 2: 465

Systema Naturae 4: 159

Szilard, Leo *1:* 268

T

Taieb, Maurice *2:* 517, 519

The Tale of John Sickle 2: 591

Tales of a Shaman's Apprentice: An Ethnobotanist Searches for New Medicines in the Amazon Rain Forest 3: 768, 770

Taniyama, Yutaka *2:* 460

Tanjung Puting reserve, Indonesia *4:* 97

Taphonomy *4:* 72

Taussig, Helen Brooke *3:* 900–01, 901 (ill.); *4:* **208–14,** 208 (ill.), 211 (ill.)

Technetium *4:* 186, 188

Tektite II project *1:* 241

Telegraph *1:* 246, 248; *3:* 980, 983–85

Telephone *1:* 62, 64, 66; *3:* 982

Telepresence *1:* 49–50

Telescope *4:* 103

Telescope, reflector *2:* 442, 489; *4:* 176, 179

Television *3:* 1017, 1019, 1021; *5:* 37, 38–41

Telkes, Maria *3:* 967

Teller, Edward *2:* 399, 401–02

Telomerase *1:* 90

Template theory *5:* 73, 74–75

Tensegrity dome *1:* 336

Terbium *4:* 12

Tereshkova, Valentina *4:* **215–19,** 215 (ill.)

Tesla coil *3:* 894

Tesla, Nikola *1:* 251; *3:* **889–96,** 889 (ill.), 893 (ill.)

Testosterone *2:* 530, 532

Test tube babies *3:* 882, 884–85

Thalidomide *4:* 208, 210, 214

Thallium *4:* 225

Thenard, Louis *1:* 215

Thermodynamics *4:* 15; *5:* 97

Thermodynamics and the Free Energy of Chemical Substances 5: 96

Thermometer *4:* 102

The Starry Messenger 4: 105

The Theory of Games and Economic Behavior 3: 962

The Theory of Games and Statistical Decisions 5: 25–26

Theory of the Earth 2: 599

This Is Biology: The Science of the Living World 5: 124

Thomas, Vivien *3:* **897–904,** 897 (ill.); *4:* 212

Thomson, J. J. *1:* 99, 102, 102 (ill.); *3:* 806, 1021; *4:* **220–27,** 220 (ill.)

Thomson, William, Lord Kelvin
   2: 526, 611; *3:* **905–10,**
   905 (ill.)
Thorium *3:* 807–08; *4:* 10
Thorium–X *3:* 808
Three Mile Island nuclear reactor
   1: 127
Throckmorton, Peter *1:* 54–55
Through a Window *2:* 411
Tides *5:* 129–30
Tiling *2:* 436
Tinbergen, Nikolaas *1:* 325;
   2: 590–91, 591 (ill.)
Tirio (people) *3:* 769
Titanic *1:* 48, 50
Tobacco mosaic virus (TMV)
   1: 306
Todd, Alexander *4:* 134
Topeka Institute for
   Psychoanalysis *2:* 662
Tornadoes *1:* 328–31, 329 (ill.)
Townes, Charles H. *2:* 602–04,
   603 (ill.)
Townshend, Charles *3:* **911–16,**
   911 (ill.)
Toy Story *2:* 513–14
Transfer ribonucleic acid (tRNA)
   4: 137, 138
Transistor *2:* 675–76; *3:* 862,
   864–67; *4:* 59, 61
Trefusis–Forbes, Katherine
   3: 944
Treponema pallidum *2:* 466 (ill.)
Trieste *3:* 757, 757 (ill.)
Trounson, Alan *3:* 887
Truman, Harry S *2:* 688
Trypanosome *4:* 78
Tsao, George T. *5:* **175–178**
Tsetse flies *4:* 78
Tuberculosis *3:* 824, 855–56,
   858–61
Tuck, James *2:* 687
Tull, Jethro *3:* 915
Turing, Alan *4:* **228–34,**
   228 (ill.); *5:* 157
Turing machine *4:* 230, 232
The Turing Option *2:* 669
"Turing Test" *4:* 228, 233
Tuskegee Institute *1:* 146–48

Two New Sciences *4:* 108
Tychonic System *4:* 128
Typhoid fever *4:* 113

U

ULTRA project *4:* 228, 231
Underground Railroad *5:* 147–48
*The Undersea Odyssey of the
   "Calypso"* *1:* 173
*The Undersea World of Jacques
   Cousteau* *1:* 168
Under the SeaWind *1:* 139
Underwater archaeology *1:* 53–55
Undulant fever *4:* 74, 76, 77
Unification theory *3:* 834
United Auto Workers (UAW)
   4: 90
United States Coast Survey *4:* 172
UNIVAC (universal automatic
   computer) *2:* 367; *4:* 61; *5:* 63
Uranium *1:* 126, 185–86; *2:* 683,
   687; *3:* 807–08
Uranium–235 (U–235)
   2: 683, 685
Uranus *2:* 441–42
Urban VIII *4:* 108
Urey, Harold *2:* 402; *4:* 199

V

V–2 rocket *4:* 22, 24-26, 28
Vaccine, killed–virus *3:* 818,
   838–39, 841
Vaccine, live–virus *3:* 817,
   840–41, 845
Vacuum tubes *4:* 231
Valadium *4:* 10
*Valence and the Structure of
   Atoms and Molecules* *5:* 99
Van Allen belts *3:* 917–18, 921,
   921 (ill.)
Van Allen, James *3:* **917–22,**
   917 (ill.)
Veblen, Oswald *3:* 960
Venera IV *4:* 201
Venus *4:* 201
Venus, phases of *4:* 105

Vertebrata 4: 161

Viking space missions *4:* 201

Virtual reality *2:* 562–64, 565 (ill.), 566–67

Virus, computer *2:* 365

Viscose rayon industry *4:* 116

The Vitalizer 2: 431

Vitamin B^{12} *2:* 474, 477

Vitamin C *3:* 745

Vitamin C and the Common Cold 3: 745

Vivamos Mejor/USA *1:* 47

Volta, Alessandro *1:* 213–14, 214 (ill.); **179–184**

Voltaic pile *1:* 214; *4:* 9; *5:* 179, 180, 183–84

Von Braun, Wernher *2:* 395, 395 (ill.); *4:* **22–32,** 22 (ill.), 27 (ill.)

Von Neumann, John *3:* 962–63, 962 (ill.); *5:* 23

Vorlesungen über Thermodynamik 3: 761

Vortex rings *4:* 222

Vostok I 4: 216

Vostok 5 4: 217

Vostok 6 4: 217

Voyager space missions *4:* 202

Vries, Hugo de *2:* 626, 653

V–2 rocket *2:* 395; *3:* 919

W

Walden Two 3: 878–79

Wang, An *3:* **923–28,** 923 (ill.)

Wang Laboratories *3:* 923–25, 927

War Crimes Tribunal *3:* 804

Warm front *4:* 19, 20

War of the Worlds 2: 393

Washkansky, Louis *2:* 506

Wassermann, August von *2:* 465

Water frame *1:* 25, 27 (ill.)

Water pollution *3:* 734–36

Watkins, Levi, Jr. *3:* **929–32,** 929 (ill.)

Watson, James D. *1:* 174, 176, 178, 180, 302, 304–06; *2:* 384–85, 469; *3:* **933–38,** 933 (ill.), 936 (ill.)

Watson, Thomas A. *1:* 63–65

Watson-Watt, Robert *3:* **939–44**

Watt, James *3:* **945–50,** 945 (ill.)

Weak force *1:* 287; *3:* 833

Weather forecasting *4:* 15—17, 19, 20

Weber, Wilhelm *2:* 373

Webster, Arthur Gordon *2:* 393

Wegener, Alfred *3:* **951–58,** 951 (ill.)

Wegener's granulomatosis *1:* 281

Wiedenreich, Franz *5:* **185–90,** 187 (ill.)

Weinberg, Steven *3:* 832, 834–35, 836 (ill.)

Weinberg, Wilhelm *2:* 552

Weizenbaum, Joseph *2:* 566

Weller, Thomas *3:* 818, 841, 843

Wells, H. Gideon *3:* 857

Westinghouse, George *3:* 892; *3:* 1020

What Mad Pursuit: A Personal View of Scientific Discovery 1: 179–80

Wheat *1:* 107–09

Wheatstone, Charles *2:* 375

Wheelwright, George *2:* 558

White dwarf star *5:* 67

Whitehead, Alfred North *3:* 796–97, 797 (ill.), 799

Whitehouse, E. O. W. *3:* 909

Whiting, Sarah Frances *1:* 132

Whitney, Eli *4:* 82

Why Men Fight: A Method of Abolishing the International Duel 3: 800

Wien, Wilhelm *3:* 762–63

Wiener, Norbert *3:* **959–63,** 959 (ill.)

Wigner, Eugene Paul *2:* 403

Wildlife conservation *4:* 5

Wildlife management *5:* 92

Wiles, Andrew J. *2:* 460

Wilkins, A. F. *3:* 941

Wilkins, Maurice *1:* 176–77, 302, 304, 306; *3:* 933–36

Williams, Anna W. *5:* **191–94**

Williams, Robin *3:* 828

Williamson, James S. *3:* **964–68**

Wilson cloud chamber *4:* 120

Wilson, Edward O. *3:* **969–79,** 969 (ill.)

Wilson, Woodrow *3:* 801

Wind shear *1:* 326, 330–31

Winton, Alexander *4:* 83

Wireless receiver *2:* 609, 609 (ill.)

"Witch of Agnesi" *5:* 5

Wollaston, William Hyde *4:* 179

Woman's Medical School of Northwestern University *4:* 112

Women Who Run with the Wolves 2: 540

Wonderful Life: The Burgess Shale and the Nature of History 2: 420

Wong–Staal, Flossie *1:* 283, 283 (ill.)

Woods, Granville T. *3:* **980–86,** 980 (ill.)

Woods Hole Oceanographic Institute *1:* 49; *2:* 544, 547

Woodwell, George M. *1:* 142, 142 (ill.)

Worlds in the Making 1: 35

Worldwatch Institute *1:* 258

World Wide Web *5:* 14, 16–19

Wozniak, Stephen *2:* 508–11, 513

Wright, Almroth *1:* 293

Wright Flyer I *3:* 993

Wright Flyer III *3:* 994

Wright, Orville *3:* **987–98,** 987 (ill.), 992 (ill.)

Wright, Wilbur *3:* **987–98,** 987 (ill.), 995 (ill.)

Wu, ChienShiung *3:* **999–1003,** 999 (ill.), 1012, 1015

X

X–ray crystallography *1:* 177; *2:* 474–76, 478

X–ray diffraction *1:* 175–76, 303–04, 306

X–ray imaging *1:* 44–45, 47

X–ray photograph *3:* 791 (ill.)

X rays *2:* 483; *3:* 776–77, 779, 787, 789–93, 807

X–ray spectroscopy *2:* 657

X–ray telescope *1:* 45

Y

Yalow, Rosalyn Sussman *3:* **1004–11,** 1010 (ill.), 1004 (ill.)

Yang, Chen Ning *3:* 999, 1002, **1012–16,** 1012 (ill.)

The Year of the Greylag Goose 2: 592

Yerkes Observatory (University of Chicago) *2:* 489

Young, Thomas *2:* 617

Ytterite *4:* 12

Yttria *4:* 12

Yukuna (people) *3:* 768

Z

Zero Population Growth *1:* 257

Zero–sum game *5:* 24–25

Zinjanthropus 2: 579–80

Zion, Élie de *3:* 747

Zionist movement *1:* 269

Zoological Institute, University of Munich *1:* 321, 324

Zoological Philosophy 1: 208

Zooplankton *1:* 15, 17–18

Zwicky, Fritz *1:* 156

Zworykin, Vladimir *3:* **1017–22,** 1017 (ill.); *5:* 38